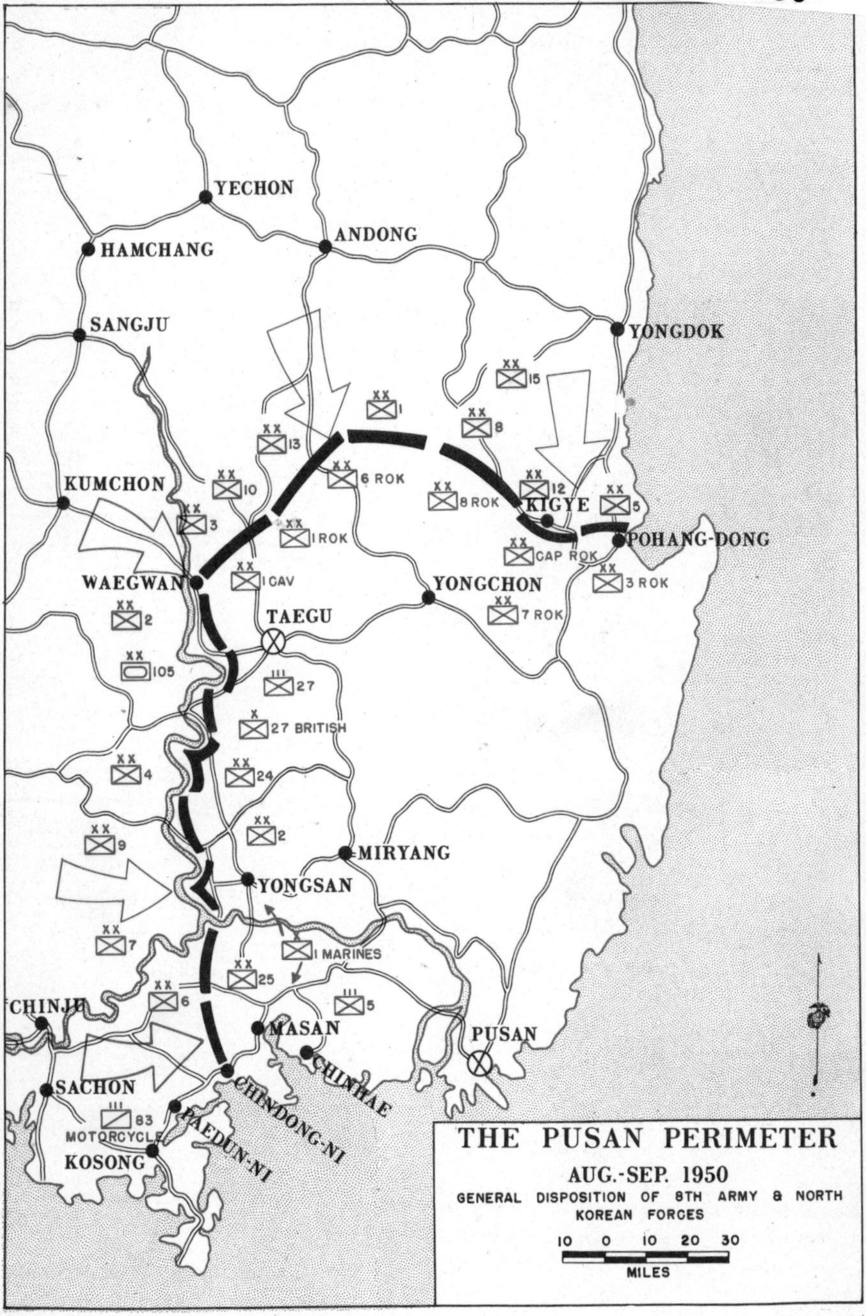

THE PUSAN PERIMETER
AUG.-SEP. 1950
GENERAL DISPOSITION OF 8TH ARMY & NORTH KOREAN FORCES
10 0 10 20 30
MILES

U. S. MARINE OPERATIONS IN KOREA

1950–1953

VOLUME I

The Pusan Perimeter

by

LYNN MONTROSS

and

CAPTAIN NICHOLAS A. CANZONA, USMC

Historical Branch, G–3

Headquarters, U. S. Marine Corps

Washington, D. C., 1954

Foreword

An ability to furnish skilled forces to meet emergency situations on short notice has long been a hallmark of the Marine Corps. When the call came for such a force to be dispatched to Korea on 2 July 1950, the Corps was handicapped by the strictures of a peacetime economy. Nevertheless, a composite brigade consisting of a regiment and an air group was made available within a week's time.

With a reputation built largely on amphibious warfare, Marines of the 1st Brigade were called upon to prove their versatility in sustained ground action. On three separate occasions within the embattled Perimeter—south toward Sachon and twice along the Naktong River—these Marine units hurled the weight of their assault force at the enemy. All three attacks were successful, and at no point did Marines give ground except as ordered. The quality of their performance in the difficult days of the Pusan Perimeter fighting made them a valuable member of the United Nations team and earned new laurels for their Corps.

Lemuel C. Shepherd, Jr.,
General, U. S. Marine Corps,
Commandant of the Marine Corps.

Preface

THIS IS THE first volume of a planned series dealing with United States Marine Operations in Korea during the period 2 August 1950 to 27 July 1953. Volume I is designed to give the military student and the casual reader an accurate and detailed account of the operations in which Marines of the 1st Provisional Brigade and Marine Air Group 33 participated during the fighting in the Pusan Perimeter, from the date of their landing on 2 August until their withdrawal on 13 September 1950, in preparation for the Inchon landing.

Since this is primarily a Marine Corps story, the activities of other services during this period are not described in detail except to present a proper background to the overall account.

Many officers and men who participated in this campaign have contributed to the preparation of the book by answering inquiries, submitting to interviews, and commenting on the preliminary manuscript. Their assistance has been invaluable. Special acknowledgment is also extended to the Office of the Chief of Military History, Department of the Army, Pacific Section, and particularly Lieutenant Colonel Roy E. Appleman, USA, for enemy intelligence material; to the Marine Corps Board Study: *An Evaluation of the Influence of Marine Corps Forces on the Course of the Korean War* for its interpretations and conclusions; and to *Life Magazine* for courtesy shown in permitting use of Korean photographs made by Mr. David D. Duncan. Maps included herein were prepared by the Reproduction Section, Marine Corps Schools, Quantico, Va. United States Army, Navy and Marine Corps photographs have also been used to illustrate this monograph.

T. A. WORNHAM,
Brigadier General, U. S. Marine Corps.
Assistant Chief of Staff, G–3

Contents

Appendixes

Illustrations

Photographs

Sixteen-page sections of photographs follow pages 70 and 156.

Maps and Sketches

CHAPTER I

Korea, Doorstep of Strategy

The Historical Background—The Russo-Japanese War—Korea as a Japanese Colony—The Partition of Korea—Red Victory in China—Civil Strife in Korea

IT MEANT LITTLE to most Americans on 25 June 1950 to read in their Sunday newspapers that civil strife had broken out in Korea. They could hardly have suspected that this remote Asiatic peninsula was to become the scene of the fourth most costly military effort of American history, both in blood and money, before the end of the year. Yet the danger of an explosion had been present ever since the end of World War II, when the United States and the Soviet Union rushed into the political vacuum created in Korea by the defeat of Japan.

The Korean question came up officially for the first time at the Cairo Conference of December 1943. With Soviet Russia not yet being represented as a belligerent in the Far East, the United States, Great Britain and China agreed that "in due course Korea shall become free and independent."[1]

Any discussion of this issue had to take into consideration Korea's status as a Japanese possession since 1910. Government, industry, commerce, agriculture, transportation—every phase of Korean life had been administered by Japanese for the benefit of Japan. As a consequence, the 25,000,000 inhabitants of the peninsula were woefully lacking in experience to fit them for the responsibilities of independence.

Syngman Rhee, the elderly Korean patriot, had long been clamoring for recognition of his Korean government in exile. The United States hung back because of reluctance to offend Joseph Stalin, the Soviet dictator, at a time when Russia was a powerful military ally. Moscow had a strong bargaining point, moreover, in the prospect of giving military

[1] Quoted in James F. Byrnes, *Speaking Frankly* (New York: Harper, 1947), 221.

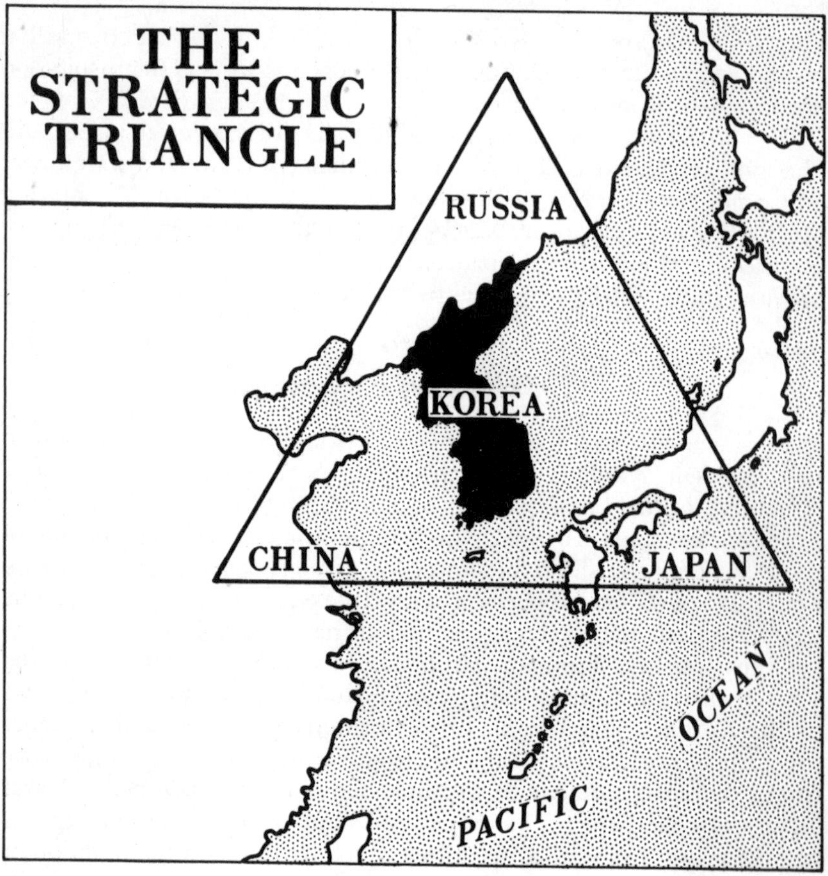

aid to the United States in the fight against Japan. Such an alliance was particularly desirable from the American viewpoint early in 1945 because of the losses resulting from Japanese *kamikaze* tactics. In the belief that active Soviet participation might shorten the war and save thousands of American lives, President Franklin D. Roosevelt was disposed to compromise with Stalin.

The two agreed informally at the Yalta Conference of February 1945 that Korea should be independent ". . . and that if a transition period were necessary, a trusteeship should be established," according to James F. Byrnes, United States Secretary of State. He added in his memoirs that "a desire to help the Koreans develop the skills and experience that would enable them to maintain their independence was the inspiration for President Roosevelt's acquiescence in the trusteeship idea." [2]

The Soviet dictator made a plea at Yalta for historical justice. Although Czar Nicholas II had been execrated as a tyrant and warmonger in Communist doctrine, Stalin demanded that the "wrongs" resulting from the Russo-Japanese War be righted 40 years later. The price of Soviet military aid against Japan, in short, was the restoration of Russian territory in the Far East that had been lost in the defeat of 1905.

The Historical Background

It was inevitable that the fate of Korea would be involved in any such readjustment. Korea is one of those tragic areas of the earth's surface which are destined in all ages to be a doorstep of strategy. As the focal point of the China-Russia-Japan triangle, the peninsula offers each of these powers a threshold for aggression against either of the other two. Possession of Korea has been for centuries an aim of aspiring conquerors in the Far East, and all three rival nations have had a turn.

China was first. From ancient times down to the last quarter of the 19th century, the Chinese Empire held a loose suzerainty acknowledged by the Koreans. Japan won a brief foothold in the 16th century under the great war lord Hideyoshi, only to learn the painful lesson that control of the sea is requisite to a seaborne invasion of a peninsula. Naval victories by the Koreans cut Hideyoshi's line of comunications, and he withdrew after frightful devastations which left an enduring tradition of fear and hate. Both Japan and Korea then entered upon a period of self-imposed isolation lasting until their political hibernation was rudely interrupted by Western nations clamoring for trade.

The United States took the lead in inaugurating a new era in the Far East. Commodore Perry and his American warships opened up Japan to commerce in 1853. Several persuasive bombardments of coastal cities by American, British and French naval guns were required to end Japan's seclusion; and in 1871 an American squadron was sent to Korea after the destruction of an American merchant ship and massacre of its crew. United States Marines and bluejackets stormed Korean river forts defended by cannon. All objectives were taken and heavy casualties

[2] Byrnes, *loc. cit.*

inflicted, but it remained for Japan to open up the "Hermit Kingdom" to trade 4 years later with the threat of war.

Russia had not been a disinterested bystander during this era of cannon-ball diplomacy. Her participation in Far Eastern affairs dated back to the 17th century and had once extended to the North American mainland. The sale of Alaska to the United States in 1867 indicated a renunciation of this phase of expansion, but Russia had no intention of abandoning her ambitions in the Far East. Shortly after Japan compelled Korea to sign a treaty of amity, the Russians offered to train Korean officers and lend military aid to the faction-ridden kingdom.

At this point China took a hand. Suspecting that the two rival nations were dabbling in Korean affairs for purposes of their own, the Celestial Empire attempted to restore her suzerainty.

This policy was bound to lead to a collision. Western nations were not surprised when Japan and China resorted to arms, but few observers expected the supposed dwarf to beat the giant with ease. Japan's well led army, equipped with the best modern weapons, landed at Chemulpo (Inchon) and captured the Chinese fortress at Pyongyang in northwest Korea. Sweeping across the Yalu into Manchuria, the invaders overran the strategic Liaotung Peninsula, taking Port Arthur and Dairen.

It was all over in a few months. When the Empire proper was threatened with invasion, the Chinese government sued for peace in 1895.

The Japanese terms were more than severe, they were humiliating. They included: (1) a large indemnity; (2) the cession "in perpetuity" of the Liaotung Peninsula as well as Formosa and the Pescadores group; and (3) Chinese recognition of what the Japanese were pleased to call "Korean independence."

But the victors had overdone it. Russia, Germany, and France formed the Triple Intervention which compelled Japan to relinquish the Liaotung Peninsula. The three European powers preferred that this strategic bastion remain in the possession of China, which was ripe for despoiling at the convenience of the Western nations.

Russia now assumed the role of a friend binding China's wounds. The secret treaty of alliance signed by the two empires in 1896 was aimed like a pistol at Japan. In return for promises of support in the event of further Japanese aggressions, China gave Russia the right to extend the Trans-Siberian Railroad to Vladivostok across Chinese territory in Manchuria.

The precept was not lost upon other European nations. England, Germany, and France also established spheres of influence in China after

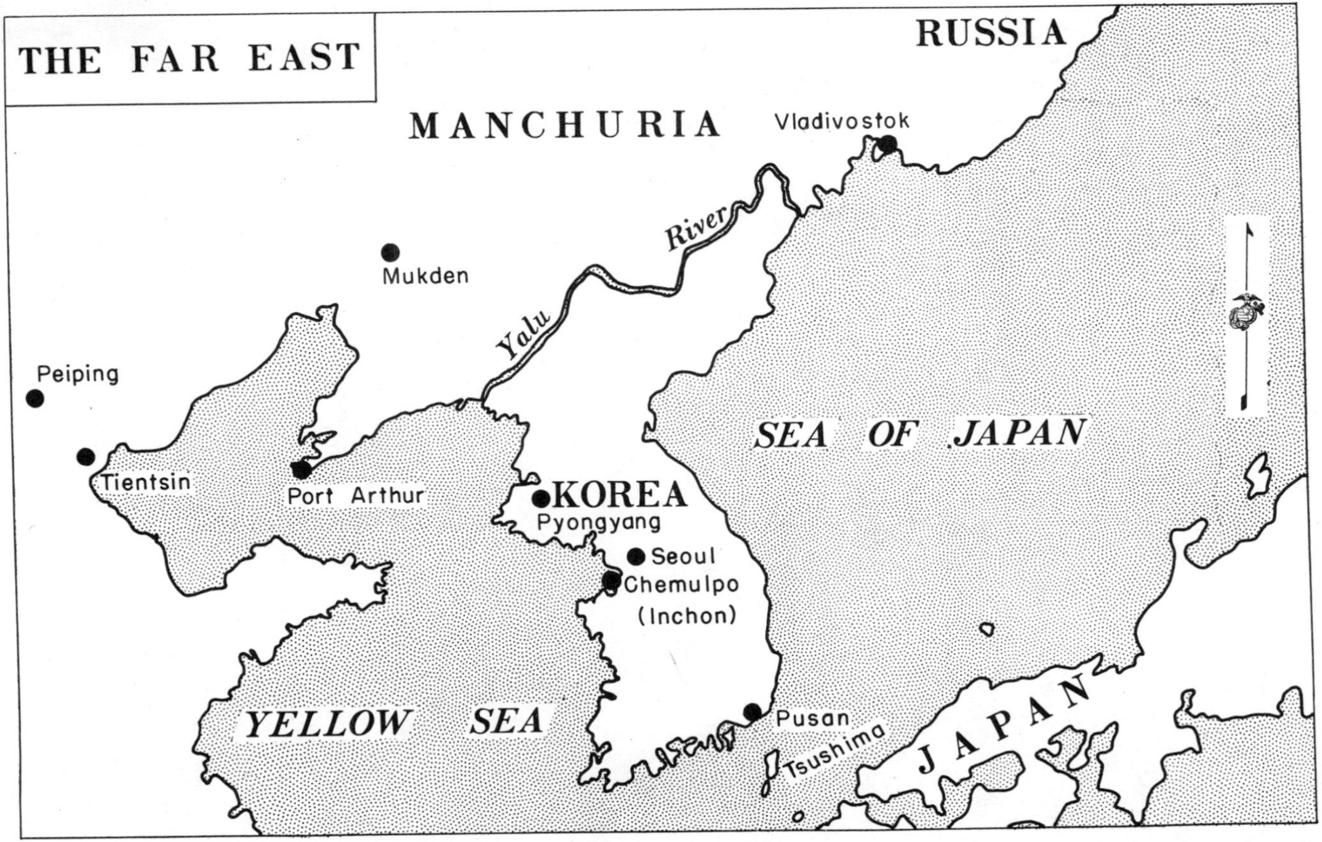
THE FAR EAST
RUSSIA
MANCHURIA
Vladivostok
Mukden
Peiping
Tientsin
Port Arthur
Yalu River
KOREA
Pyongyang
Seoul
Chemulpo
(Inchon)
Pusan
Tsushima
SEA OF JAPAN
YELLOW SEA
JAPAN

305713 O-F-55--2

forcing the government to lease territory or grant special privileges. And Russia added to former gains by a 25-year lease of the Liaotung Peninsula.

China's Boxer Rebellion of 1900 interrupted the march of events, but two treaties in 1902 indicated that Japan and Russia would soon be at each other's throats. Japan acquired an ally in England, as a result of that nation's alarms over Muscovite designs, so that the neutrality of European powers was practically assured. Russia and China drew closer meanwhile with a new treaty of alliance. The stage was set for a fight to the finish in the Far East.

Possession of the Philippine Islands had given the United States a new interest in Far Eastern affairs since the Spanish-American War of 1898. John Hay, Secretary of State, realized that the American "open door" policy was imperiled by the situation in Asia.[3] But he admitted in April 1903 that nothing short of the threat of armed force could have checked Russia's encroachments.

The Russo-Japanese War

A candid comparison would reveal a striking similarity between the aggressions of Czarist Russia in the early 1900's and those of Soviet Russia half a century later. The expression "cold war" was not current in 1903, but the account of Russia's threats, seizures and violated agreements has a dismally familiar aspect to the modern reader. Rudyard Kipling paid a bitter tribute at the turn of the century to these techniques of the Russian Bear in his lines:

> When he stands up like a tired man, tottering near and near;
> When he stands up as pleading, in wavering, man-brute guise,
> When he veils the hate and cunning of his little swinish eyes;
> When he shows as seeking quarter, with paws like hands in prayer,
> That is the time of peril—the time of the Truce of the Bear!

Following the Sino-Japanese War, the truce between Russia and Japan in "independent" Korea was broken by both nations whenever a favorable opportunity arose. Both of them intrigued constantly at Seoul. For a time, indeed, the Korean government was directed from the Russian legation with the backing of Russian troops.

[3] Pauline Tompkins, *American-Russian Relations in the Far East* (New York: Macmillan, 1949), 21.

Twice, in 1896 and 1898, Russia and Japan signed agreements reaffirming Korea's independence and promising anew to withdraw their forces. These pacts were promptly violated by both contestants for power, but Japan prepared more realistically for the forthcoming struggle. On a February night in 1904, without the formality of a declaration of war, a Japanese squadron attacked the Russian warships anchored at Port Arthur. This surprise blow was followed shortly by the landing of Japanese troops at Chemulpo. They advanced to the frontier and defeated the Russians in the battle of the Yalu—a victory that has been compared with the battle of Valmy in the French Revolution as a landmark of history.

Certainly the West was made aware that an Oriental nation had risen to the stature of a world power for the first time in modern history. The value of Korea as a strategic springboard was demonstrated when Japanese land and sea forces isolated the fortresses on the Liaotung Peninsula. Port Arthur fell after a bloody siege of 6 months. Next, the Japanese invaders of Manchuria defeated an army of 350,000 Russians and inflicted 150,000 casualties in the four-week battle of Mukden. This was the decisive clash on land; and in the one-sided naval battle of Tsushima, Admiral Togo annihilated the Baltic fleet which the Czar had ordered on the long voyage to the Pacific.

The end came abruptly in the summer of 1905. In the Treaty of Portsmouth, signed on 5 September, Russia ceded the southern part of Sakhalin Island to the victors while recognizing their "paramount" interests in Korea. All rights in the Liaotung Peninsula went to Japan as well as important concessions in Manchuria. Not much was left to Russia in the Far East except a precarious foothold in northern Manchuria.

Korea as a Japanese Colony

For 5 years Japan kept up a pretense of a protectorate in Korea. Then, in 1910, came outright annexation.

Europe's "balanced antagonisms" soon flared up in World War I, leaving Japan free to exploit Korea as a colony. Western observers might have noted such evidences of modernization as new docks, railroads, factories and highways. But they were administered by Japanese overseers as Koreans sank to the level of coolies without a voice in the government.

Although Japan joined the fight against the Central Powers in World

War I, her military efforts were made against allies as well as enemies. Using Korea as a beachhead, she attempted to enlarge her empire on the Asiatic mainland at the expense of Russia, then in the throes of revolution. Three years after the Armistice, a Japanese army still occupied the Vladivostok area; but the United States took such a firm diplomatic stand that Tokyo backed down.

This retreat was only a postponement. During the next decade Japan set up a strategic shield to the east and south by fortifying the mandated islands of the Pacific, awarded to her after the war. Treaties and agreements were violated whenever convenient, and in 1931 she turned westward again to satisfy her appetite for Russian and Chinese territory.

The time was well chosen. With the Western nations in the depths of an industrial depression, Japan began a series of aggressions against the Chinese in Manchuria. The gains were consolidated in a puppet state known as Manchukuo, comprising a fertile and populous area as large as California. China was unable to offer much resistance, and Soviet Russia could not risk a major war in the Far East. Even so, some of the Soviet border clashes with the Japanese in time of "peace" were actually battles fought with tanks and planes.

In 1937 came the Japanese invasion of China proper. Germany and Italy were launching aggressions of the same stamp in Europe and Africa, and the world was to know little stability until all three totalitarian states had been crushed in World War II.

Soviet Russia had a grim struggle for survival while resisting the full tide of Nazi invasion. But at the time of the Yalta Conference, Stalin was in a position to ask a stiff price for military aid in the Pacific. The United States agreed that the Port Arthur area and southern Sakhalin should be returned to Russia to redress the "wrongs" of 1905. Concessions were also made in Manchuria and outer Mongolia.

Stalin, for his part, consented to sign a treaty of friendship with Nationalist China as an ally of the United States. Later events made it evident that he had no intention of keeping his pledges. On the contrary, Soviet policy already visioned a Communist empire in the Far East which would include China as well as Korea.

The Yalta Agreement was stridently criticized in the United States after Stalin's duplicity became apparent. But the War Department took a realistic view as early as the spring of 1945:

"The concessions to Russia on Far Eastern matters which were made at Yalta are generally matters which are within the military power of Russia to obtain regardless of United States military action short of war. . . . The Russians can, if they choose, await the time when United States efforts will have practically completed the destruction of Japanese military power and can then seize the objectives they desire at a cost to them relatively much less than would be occasioned by their entry into the war at an early date."[4]

This was precisely what happened. Moscow waited to declare war until 8 August 1945—6 days before the imminent collapse of Japan. Soviet forces fought only a few actions in Siberia with a Japanese army stripped of planes for home defense. As a consequence, Russian propagandists found it hard to paint a convincing picture of "the heroic deeds of our brave Far Eastern warriors."[5] Obviously they had met little resistance while overrunning Manchuria and northern Korea to accept the surrender of nearly 600,000 Japanese troops, including 148 generals. These prisoners were sent to Siberia for years of servitude; and the "conquerors" despoiled Manchuria of heavy machinery, turbines, dynamos and rolling stock.[6]

The value of this booty has been estimated at a billion dollars, and the forced labor of Japanese war prisoners during the next 5 years was worth at least another billion. Not satisfied with these spoils, Moscow also demanded a share in the occupation of Japan. This design was balked by General of the Army Douglas MacArthur, supreme Allied commander, who made it plain that he needed no such assistance.[7]

Even after the guns fell silent, there was no peace. One enemy had been exchanged for another, since Soviet Russia took advantage of war-weary allies to follow in the footsteps of Germany and Japan. There was the same familiar pattern of encroachment both in Europe and the Far East. There were the same violations of treaties, the same unfriendly acts falling just short of hostilities. The cold war had begun.

Oppression at home and aggression abroad—this had been the policy of Russia's czars, and it became the policy of Russia's dictators. Despotism had been replaced by Communism, but there was little difference. Communism proved to be an old tyranny presented as a new ideology, and Joseph Stalin succeeded where Nicholas II failed. Circumstances

---

[4] U. S. War Dept memo for Acting Sec of State, 21 May 45, quoted in Joseph C. Grew, *Turbulent Era: A Diplomatic Record of Forty Years* (Boston: Houghton Mifflin, 1952), 2:1457–1458.

[5] David J. Dallin, *Soviet Russia and the Far East* (New Haven: Yale University Press, 1948), 213.

[6] *Ibid.*, 214, 244. Such seizures were in violation of international law, of course, and Soviet Russia had pledged the prompt repatriation of Japanese prisoners at the Potsdam Conference in July 1945.

[7] *Ibid.*, 214, 239.

were kinder to Stalin, and he gobbled up territory in Poland, Estonia, Latvia, Czechoslovakia, Austria, Germany, Hungary, Rumania, Mongolia and Manchuria.

Never before had one man ruled so much of the earth's surface. Yet there was something neurotic and fear-ridden about the Kremlin's outlook which success could not cure. It has long been a historical theory that this psychosis may be traced back to Russia's bondage in the Middle Ages under the Mongols and Tartars. At any rate, victory and enormous spoils did not give Moscow a sense of security in 1945. Buffer state was piled upon buffer state, and thousands of World War II prisoners were enslaved behind the "iron curtain" to build new Soviet military installations.

The Partition of Korea

The importance of Korea in the Soviet scheme of things was indicated by the haste with which Russian troops crossed the frontier on 12 August 1945, three days after the declaration of war. They were the vanguard of an army numbering a quarter of a million men led by General Ivan Chistyakov, a hero of the battle of Stalingrad.

The surrender terms called for a joint American and Soviet occupation, with the 38th parallel serving as a temporary line of demarcation. Not until 8 September, however, did Lieutenant General John R. Hodge reach southern Korea with the first American troops.

By that time the Russians had gone through their usual routine, and the machinery taken from northern Korea was estimated at 30 to 40 percent of the industrial potential. Looting by Soviet troops went unpunished, and regular supplies of food for the huge army were demanded from an impoverished people just freed of the Japanese yoke.[8]

The Russians had a tremendous advantage over United States occupation forces. Since World War I more than a million Koreans had found a refuge from Japanese bondage on Russian or Chinese soil. Thousands of men had been indoctrinated with Communist principles and given military training to aid the Chinese Reds fighting the Japanese invaders of China. Thus in 1945 the Russians could count on the efforts of Korean revolutionists to establish Communist rule in their homeland behind a façade of democracy.

The United States forces, on the contrary, did not even have enough

---

[8] *Ibid.*, 285.

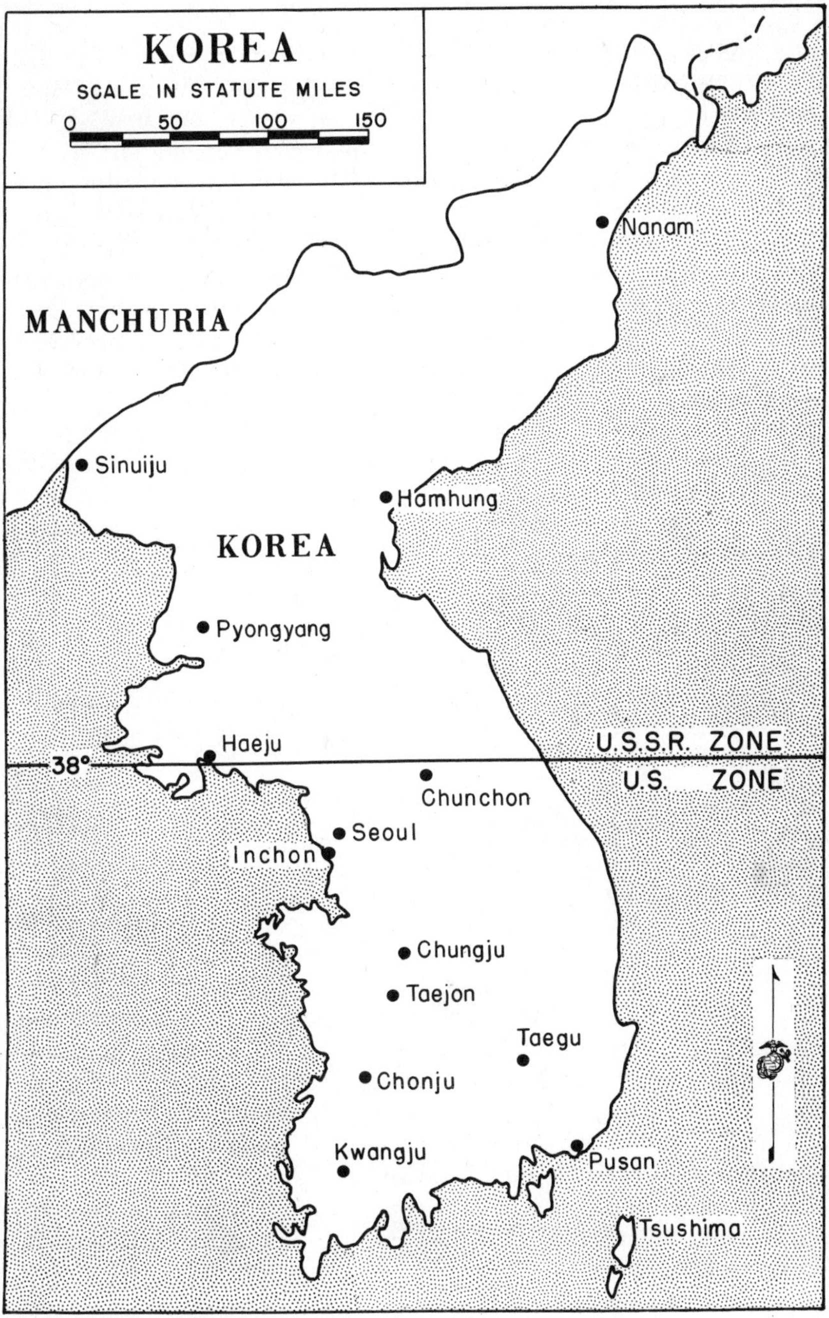
KOREA
SCALE IN STATUTE MILES
0 50 100 150
MANCHURIA
Nanam
Sinuiju
Hamhung
KOREA
Pyongyang
Haeju
38°
U.S.S.R. ZONE
U.S. ZONE
Chunchon
Seoul
Inchon
Chungju
Taejon
Taegu
Chonju
Kwangju
Pusan
Tsushima

interpreters. They impressed the Koreans at first as being alien occupation troops setting up a military government. Meanwhile, the Russians had installed an interim civil government at Pyongyang. Korean Reds filled the key positions, and Stalin's portraits and the hammer and sickle emblem were seen at political rallies.

Koreans of all persuasions opposed the division of their country into two zones on either side of the 38th parallel. The Reds at Pyongyang contrived to lay the blame on the Americans. They made a further appeal to Koreans on both sides of the boundary by announcing a land reform in the northern zone. Ever since 1905 a Japanese landlord had been the hated symbol of oppression. Pyongyang won a great propaganda victory, therefore, by announcing the confiscation of all large estates, Korean as well as Japanese, and the division of the land among the peasantry.

The bait was so tempting that the hook did not become apparent until too late. Then the beneficiaries of the Agrarian Reform discovered that they could neither sell not rent the land, nor could they use it as security for loans. If anyone ceased to work his holding, it reverted to the People's Committee, which allocated it to some other family. The State retained possession, in short, and the peasant remained as much of a serf as ever. Worse yet, the taxes disguised as "production quotas" eventually amounted to 60 percent of the total crop, which was more than the Japanese had extorted.[9]

This is a sample of the methods used to reduce North Korea to a police state, just as similar states were being organized in occupied lands of Europe by local Reds doing the bidding of Moscow. In the Soviet zone of Korea all banks, factories and industries of any consequence were nationalized by the so-called People's Committee.[10] Military training for offensive warfare was given to men armed with captured Japanese weapons. Pressure was put upon these recruits to "volunteer" for combat service with the Chinese Reds waging a civil war against the Nationalists.[11]

Red Victory in China

Moscow was secretly backing the Communists led by Mao Tse-tung in their efforts to wrest China from the Nationalist government of Chiang

[9] Robert T. Oliver, *Why War Came to Korea* (New York: Fordham University Press, 1950), 149.

[10] Dallin, *op. cit.,* 291.

[11] Oliver, *op. cit.,* 5.

Kai-shek. Such activities, of course, were in violation of the treaty of friendship and alliance with Nationalist China which Stalin had signed on 14 August 1945. But agreements were never allowed to interfere with Soviet ambitions, and Moscow aimed to create in Asia a bulwark of Communist puppet states extending from the Arctic to the tropics.

Asiatic soil was peculiarly suited to the growth of such institutions. Although Communism derived originally from the theories of a German revolutionist, Karl Marx, it was adapted by Lenin and Stalin to the political climate of Asia. Human lives and liberties have always been held cheaply in the East, and absolutism has been the rule in government. Communism, as it developed in Russia after the revolution of 1917, would probably have been better understood by Genghis Khan than Marx. For it is significant that no Western nation has ever embraced this political faith voluntarily, even though it has attracted a minority of radicals and malcontents in nearly every country.

Asia was ripe for change after World War II. In spite of Japan's defeat, that nation had made a good deal of progress with its "Asia for the Asiatics" propaganda. The Far East seethed with unrest in 1946, and Communism spread ominously through a China weakened by three decades of invasion, revolution and civil war.

While Nationalists and Communist armies contended for the ancient empire, an undeclared war went on in the background. This was the cold war between the United States and Soviet Russia as they supplied arms and munitions to the opposing forces. Russia also supplied troops and laborers. For it has been estimated that no less than 250,000 North Korean Reds were induced to serve in various capacities with the Chinese Communists in Manchuria.[12] There the soldiers completed their military training in actual combat, with veteran Chinese officers as instructors.

By 1948 there was no longer much doubt about the outcome in China. In the battles of Tsinan, Changchun and Mukden, the Nationalists lost 33 divisions, totaling more than 320,000 men, in killed, wounded and missing. Losses of equipment included 250,000 rifles and vast quantities of other arms and equipment. During the four and a half months following the fall of Tsinan in September 1948, the Nationalist losses were estimated at a million men and 400,000 rifles. Even planes of United States manufacture were captured by the Reds, who also acquired a

[12] GHQ, FECOM, MilIntelSec, GS, Allied Translator and Interpreter Sec (FECOM, ATIS), *Enemy Forces* (Interrogation Reports [InterRpt], Sup No. 4), 16.

cruiser that the British had transferred to the Nationalists.[13]

"The unfortunate but inescapable fact," concluded the United States State Department in 1949, "is that the ominous result of the civil war in China was beyond the control of the Government of the United States. Nothing that this country did or could have done within the reasonable limits of those capabilities could have changed that result; nothing that was left undone by this country could have contributed to it. It was the product of internal Chinese forces, forces which this country tried to influence but could not. A decision was arrived at within China, if only a decision by default."[14]

As a result, Mao Tse-tung's forces could claim a sweeping victory by the end of 1949. Only the island of Formosa was left to Chiang Kai-shek and his battered remnants. Meanwhile, it grew increasingly plain that Korea was destined to be the scene of the next great tug-of-war between Communism and the free nations.

Civil Strife in Korea

Not only had the Russians made the 38th Parallel a political boundary in Korea; they had also resisted all American attempts at unification. This meant that economic recovery was badly handicapped. For the mines, heavy industries and hydroelectric plants were located in the north, while the south had most of the agriculture. Products once exchanged with mutual benefit now had to be imported from abroad.

Trusteeship was hotly resented by all Koreans, even though few of them had gained administrative or technical experience under the Japanese. This prejudice was exploited by Soviet propagandists who denounced the "undemocratic" American policy of bringing in administrators, technicians and educators. As a consequence, the United States military government made a poor showing at first in comparison to the puppet government of Communist-trained Koreans installed at Pyongyang by Russians pulling the strings behind the scenes. Anti-American propaganda won converts to the south as well as north of the 38th Parallel, with General Hodge being accused of maintaining a harsh military rule.

At the Moscow Conference of 1945 the Soviet Union had agreed with

[13] U. S. Dept of State, *United States Relations With China* (Washington, U. S. Government Printing Office [GPO], 1949), 357.

[14] *Ibid.*, xvi.

the United States that the whole of Korea was to be given a democratic government after passing through the trusteeship phase. A Soviet-American Joint Commission was to meet and make recommendations for this purpose; but as early as 1946 it became evident that the Soviet representatives had been instructed to sabotage any attempt to create a united Korea with its own government.

After the failure of the first year's efforts, Hodge ordered the establishment of an Interim Legislature at Seoul as the counterpart of the People's Assembly at Pyongyang. Of the 90 seats, half were to be filled by popular vote and the remaining 45 by Korean appointees of the Military Government. The election was a triumph for the American-educated Dr. Syngman Rhee and the rightists. Hodge tried to give the other South Korean factions a voice by appointing moderates and liberals, but the Interim Legislature had no solution for the discontent in Korea as the economic situation went from bad to worse in spite of American aid.

Although the Americans on the Joint Commission did their best, they were blocked by all manner of Soviet-contrived delays and obstacles. Finally, in 1947, the United States submitted the question to the United Nations. After long discussion, the General Assembly resolved that all the people of Korea be given an opportunity in the spring of 1948 to elect a national assembly for the entire country.

A commission representing nine member nations was appointed to visit Korea and supervise the voting. But the Russians not only refused to participate in the election; they went so far as to bar the commissioners from entering North Korea.

The new National Assembly elected in May 1948 by South Korea had the task of forming a government. On 17 July the first constitution in 40 years of Korean history was approved by the deputies, who elected Syngman Rhee to a 4-year term as president.

It was an eventful summer south of the 38th Parallel. The Republic of Korea came into being on 15 August, and on that day the American military government ended. John J. Muccio was appointed by President Truman to represent the United States in Korea with the rank of ambassador. Plans were made to withdraw the 50,000 United States occupation troops during the next 8 months, leaving only 500 officers and men as military instructors for the training of a Republic of Korea security force.

In the northern zone the Communists organized demonstrations against the United Nations Commission. Strikes and disorders were fomented south of the 38th Parallel, and 200,000 North Koreans marched in protest at Pyongyang.

There was an air of urgency about such attempts to prevent the election in South Korea. The exposure of the Agrarian Reform as a fraud had hurt the Communists, and the disinterested spirit of the United States occupation was gaining recognition throughout Korea in spite of initial blunders. Pyongyang could not afford to let South Korea take the lead in forming a government, and July 1948 dated the creation of a Communist state known as the People's Democratic Republic of Korea. After adopting a constitution modeled after that of Communist Bulgaria, the Supreme People's Council claimed to represent all Korea. In justification it was charged that "American imperialists carried out a ruinous separate election and organized a so-called National Assembly with the support of a traitor minority and with the savage oppression of the majority of the Korean people."[15]

The Russians announced in December 1948 that they were withdrawing all occupation troops. It was no secret, however, that they would leave behind them an NK army that far surpassed the ROK military establishment.[16] Kim Il Sung, the Red Korean prime minister, referred to it pointedly as a "superior army" in an address at Pyongyang.

"We must strengthen and improve it," he declared. "Officers and men must establish iron discipline and must be proficient in the military and in combat techniques."[17]

Numbers at the end of 1948 were estimated at 60,000 regulars in addition to constabulary, railroad guards, and trainees. These troops were equipped by the Russians with captured Japanese weapons, and Russian arms were shipped into northern Korea to meet the needs of an expanding army.[18]

It was a military force of an entirely different character that American officers organized on the other side of the 38th Parallel. The new ROK army was strictly a defensive force, trained and equipped to maintain internal security and guard the border and seacoast. Neither tanks nor military planes were provided by the Americans, who leaned backward to avoid any suspicion of creating an instrument for offensive internecine warfare.

---

[15] *New York Times,* 12 Jul 48, quoted in Redvers Opie *et al., The Search for Peace Settlements* (Washington: Brookings Institution, 1951), 311.

[16] ROK, of course, denotes the Republic of Korea, and NK (North Korea) is the abbreviation usually applied to the self-styled People's Democratic Republic of Korea at Pyongyang. Both sets of initials are used more often as adjectives than nouns. See the Glossary in Appendix A for definitions of other symbols and military terms found in text.

[17] FECOM, ATIS, *History of the North Korean Army,* 23.

[18] *Ibid.*

Raids by Red Korean troops across the border became a frequent occurrence throughout 1949. One of these forays, supported by artillery, was a large-scale NK thrust into the Ongjin Peninsula. Heavy fighting resulted before the invaders were driven back into their own territory.

Having failed to prevent the formation of a democratic Korean government—the only government in Korea recognized by the United Nations—the Reds at Pyongyang were making every effort to wreck it. Since 80 percent of the ROK electric power originated north of the frontier, they were able to retard economic recovery by cutting off the current at intervals. There was no other unfriendly act in the Communist bagful of tricks that Pyongyang neglected to employ while its radio stations blared forth a propaganda of hatred.

Early in 1950 the situation grew more tense daily as thousands of veterans returned to North Korea after serving in the Communist armies which overran China. When Radio Pyongyang began making appeals for peace that spring, it should have become obvious to practiced observers of Communist techniques that preparations were afoot for war. On 10 June 1950 the Pyongyang government announced a new plan for unification and peace after branding the top ROK officials as "traitors." The motive behind this proposal was apparently the usual Communist attempt to divide an enemy on the eve of an aggression. For the long-planned blow fell at 0400 (Korean time) on Sunday morning, 25 June 1950. Russian-made tanks spearheaded the advance of the NK ground forces across the 38th Parallel, and Russian-made planes strafed Seoul and other strategic centers.

Captured NK documents offer proof that the invaders had already set the machinery of aggression in motion while making their plea for peace. This evidence included the written report of instructions given by one Lieutenant Han to a group of picked men on an intelligence mission. On 1 June 1950 they were to proceed by power boat to an island off Inchon, where confederates would help them make their way to the mainland. "Our mission," explained Han, "is to gather intelligence information concerning South Korean forces and routes of advance ahead of our troops. We will perform this task by contacting our comrades who are scattered throughout the length and breadth of South Korea."[19]

The lieutenant explained that the forthcoming attack on South Korea was to be the first step toward the "liberation" of the people of Asia.

---

[19] FECOM, ATIS, *Documentary Evidence of North Korean Aggression* (InterRpt, Sup No. 2), 65.

And his concluding remarks leave no doubt as to the complete confidence with which the Korean Communists began the venture:

"Within 2 months from the date of attack, Pusan should have fallen and South Korea will be again united with the North. The timetable for this operation of 2 months' duration was determined by the possibility of United States forces intervening in the conflict. If this were not so, it would take our forces only 10 days to overrun South Korea." [20]

---

[20] *Ibid*

CHAPTER II

Red Aggression in Korea

Units of North Korean Army—NKPA Command and Leadership—The NKPA Infantry Division—NKPA Air and Armor—NKPA Officer Procurement and Conscription—The NKPA Order of Battle

IT WAS AN army of veterans that broke the world's peace in Korea. There were thousands of veterans of the Chinese civil war and Manchurian guerrilla operations. There were even a few scarred warriors who had served with the Soviet forces in such World War II operations as the defense of Stalingrad.

Practically all the commissioned and noncommissioned officers were battle-hardened, and a majority of the rank and file had seen action. The origins of this army were deeply rooted in Asiatic soil. During World War II an endless stream of Koreans escaped from Japanese bondage and found a refuge in Soviet or Chinese territory. Some of them took to banditry, others were absorbed into the Soviet or Red Chinese armed forces. These refugees dreamed of a united and independent homeland; and at Yenan, China, the Chinese Communists encouraged this movement as early as 1939 by supplying arms to a force known as the Korean Volunteer Army. During the first month alone the KVA attracted 3,000 recruits, and at the end of the war an advance column marched back to Korea under a leader named Kim Mu Chong.[1]

Although the heads of the KVA had been thoroughly impregnated with Communist doctrine at Yenan, they were coldly received by General Chistyakov and the Russian occupation forces. It was a Soviet puppet state that the Kremlin wished to see established in Korea, not a Red-tinted independent Korean government. Communist right-thinking did not save Kim Mu Chong and his KVA troops from the humiliation of

[1] FECOM, ATIS, *History of the North Korean Army, op. cit.,* 17–28.

being stopped at the frontier in September 1945 and disarmed.

The Russian commander piously justified his decision on grounds of upholding international law. But he offered to return the confiscated arms if the Korean Reds would retrace their steps and join the CCF fight against the Nationalists. He promised that after the struggle had been won, the KVA would be welcomed back to Korea.[2]

Accepting these terms, Kim Mu Chong marched into Manchuria to aid the Chinese Reds. His force numbered nearly 20,000 the following spring, but the KVA lost its identity when the men were mingled with Chinese and Mongolians in the CCF Northeast Democratic United Army. Most of the officers and NCO's of the former KVA were organized into teams to recruit and train Korean volunteers both in Manchuria and Korea. As combined military instructors and political commissars, they created an integrated Communist force out of such oddly assorted material as peasants, guerrillas and bandits. Used first as security troops and later welded into a regular army structure, these thousands of Korean Reds undoubtedly had the principal part in "liberating" Manchuria from the Chinese Nationalists.

Meanwhile, the Russian occupation forces did not neglect the conversion of North Korea into a satellite state. One of the first steps was the establishment of a military academy at Pyongyang in the autumn of 1945. Founded ostensibly for the training of police, it had as its primary purpose the instruction of army officers. Graduates of the first and second classes became teachers when branches of the academy were set up at Nanam, Sinuiju and Hamhung. These offshoots, known as the Peace Preservation Officers' Schools, turned out the cadres which were later activated as the 1st, 2d and 3d Divisions of the new North Korean army. For more than 2 years, however, the fiction was maintained that graduates were to patrol rural areas, protect railroads and guard the frontier.

Units of North Korean Army

Not until 8 February 1948 did the "North Korean People's Army" come into official being with the activation of the 1st, 2d and 3d Infantry Divisions. At that time there were some 30,000 troops and 170,000 trainees in North Korea, according to later United States Army intelligence estimates.[3]

[2] *Ibid.*
[3] *Ibid.*, 23–24.

The 4th Infantry Division was formed in 1948 from trainees plus a veteran regiment transferred from the 2d Division. Two new infantry divisions, the 5th and 6th, were organized the following year when Korean veterans of the 164th and 166th CCF Divisions returned as units with their arms and equipment.[4]

It is probable that the leaders of the North Korean state were committed early in 1950 to the invasion of the Republic of Korea. At any rate, the training and organization of new units was accelerated during the spring months. From February to June nine new divisions were activated—the 7th, 8th, 9th, 12th, 13th, 14th, and 15th Infantry Divisions, 10th Mechanized Infantry Division and 105th Armored Division.[5]

Two factors combined to hasten the NKPA aggression. It had undoubtedly become evident to the Kremlin in 1949 that the Republic of Korea could never be brought into the Communist fold by propaganda, subversion, incitation of disorders or any other means short of a victorious civil war. Moreover, a successful war of invasion was equally desirable as a cure for political discontent at home. Not only was the Agrarian Reform resented everywhere in North Korea, but taxes had gone up as high as 60 percent of the crops to maintain the top-heavy military structure and pay for tanks, planes, howitzers and other arms supplied by the Soviet Union.

Although most of the heavy industries of Korea were located north of the 38th Parallel, they included no arms plants with the exception of a small factory capable of turning out submachineguns and ammunition. North Korea was also able to produce 80 percent of its own POL products for military purposes and some of the army uniforms. Other supplies, all the way from the Tokarev semiautomatic pistol (adapted from the U. S. .45 Colt) to the T-34 tank, were imported from the U. S. S. R.[6]

Most of the weapons were old models of recent manufacture. The heaviest load came by rail from Siberia through Manchuria via Antung and crossed the Yalu into Korea at Sinuiju. As many as three freight trains a day rumbled over the bridge between those cities and continued along the west coast to Pyongyang. Supplies were also received from Vladivostok by water to Chongjin or by the east coast rail line to Wonsan.[7]

---

4 *Ibid.*, 52–75.

5 *Ibid.*

6 FECOM, ATIS, *North Korean Forces* (InterRpt, Sup No. 1), 17–23.

7 *Ibid.*

305713 O-F-55—3

It must also be remembered that thousands of Korean veterans of the Chinese civil war returned with their arms and equipment, including American-manufactured weapons surrendered by the Nationalists. The NKPA was second only to the Soviet Army itself in the spring of 1950 as the best armed and equipped military force of its size in the Far East.

The U. S. S. R. did not limit its aid to arms. Lieutenant General Vasilev and a group of Soviet military instructors arrived at Pyongyang in 1949 to train NKPA staff and line officers for offensive warfare. About 3,000 promising NKPA candidates were sent to Soviet schools that year for courses in such specialties as artillery, air and tank tactics.

Of the original 14 NKPA divisions, the first 6 were composed largely of well trained troops. The 12th Division, like the 5th and 6th, consisted of Korean veterans of the Chinese civil war. Constabulary troops made up the 8th and 9th, while the 7th, 13th, 14th, and 15th Infantry Divisions and the 10th Mechanized Infantry Division were formed of conscripted trainees for the most part.[8]

The picture grows confused in the spring of 1950, with 8 new divisions being organized in 5 months. Many of the recently drafted men received only the most sketchy training; and some of the older units were weakened by drawing off well trained men to stiffen the new outfits. All accounts agree, however, that the NKPA leaders anticipated an effort of only a few days, ending with the destruction of the ROK army. This was not an unreasonable assumption, since a swarm of NKPA spies had brought back accurate reports of unpreparedness. Not only was the Republic of Korea weak militarily, but a bad economic situation had been made worse by increased population due to immigration.

Altogether, Pyongyang could put nearly 100,000 fairly well-trained and armed troops in the field, with about half of that number in reserve as replacements, occupation troops or constabulary. But the problem of man power did not worry Communists who were not squeamish about violations of international law. For the aggressors planned to make war nourish war by conscripting both soldiers and laborers in invaded regions of the Republic of Korea. It was an old Asiatic custom.

NKPA Command and Leadership

With few exceptions, the North Korean war leaders proved to be willing and able instruments of policies formulated in Moscow. Kim Il

[8] FECOM, ATIS, *History of the North Korean Army, op. cit.,* 52–75.

Sung, the prime minister and commander in chief, was an imposter named Kim Sung Chu who made a bid for popular support by taking the name of a dead Korean resistance hero. As a youth he had fled from Korea and joined the Communist party in Manchuria. There he distinguished himself in guerrilla operations against the Japanese. In 1938, after rising to the stature of a corps commander, he met military reverses and found a refuge in Soviet territory. Legend has it that he attended a Soviet military academy and took part in the battle of Stalingrad. However this may be, he returned to Korea in August 1945 as a 35-year-old captain in the Soviet army of occupation.[9]

South Korean descriptions of Kim Il Sung as an uneducated ruffian were doubtless prejudiced, but certainly he was a ruthless guerrilla leader who showed an uncommon aptitude for politics. His rise in the new North Korean state was spectacular, for in September 1948 he became the first prime minister. The following year he went to Moscow for conferences at the Kremlin, and nine days after the outbreak of civil war in Korea he was appointed commander in chief of the invading army while retaining his position as prime minister.

In contrast to this rough diamond, Marshal Choe Yong Gun cut a reserved and dignified figure as deputy commander in chief and minister of national defense. Born in Hongchon, Korea, at the turn of the century, he had the equivalent of a high school education. In 1925 he went to China and is believed to have attended the Whampoa Military Academy at Nanking and the Yenan Military School. At Yenan, after being converted to communism, he became a political instructor and later served in the 8th Route Army. Choe was commander of the Korean Volunteer Army in 1941 and fought against the Japanese in Manchuria. Returning to Korea in 1945, he commanded the Cadre Training Center until 1948, when he was named the first commander in chief.

Even Choe's enemies in South Korea credited him with a high order of intellectual capacity and moral courage. Despite his Communist party membership, he opposed the invasion of the Republic of Korea. He was cool, moreover, toward Lieutenant General Vasilev and the other Soviet advisers who reached Pyongyang in 1949 to prepare the Korean armed

---

[9] *Ibid.*, 90–99. Communist chiefs preferred to work behind a screen of secrecy and deception, so that it was difficult to obtain accurate personal data. Not only did some of the NKPA war leaders have obscure origins, but they added to the difficulties of biographers by deliberately falsifying the record for propaganda purposes. It is to the credit of U.S. Army intelligence officers that they have managed to piece out this material from prisoner interrogations and captured enemy documents.

forces for an offensive war. This attitude probably explains why he was sidetracked in March 1950, when Vasilev took charge of the combat training and re-equipment program. Although Choe was not on good terms with Kim Il Sung at this time, he was regarded as a superior strategist and administrator. And after being bypassed temporarily, he continued to be respected as a leader by the North Korean army and peasantry.

Nam Il stood out as the most cosmopolitan and polished of the North Korean war leaders. Born in 1911, he was Kim Il Sung's schoolmate in Manchuria and the two remained lifelong friends. As a young man, Nam Il made his way across the U. S. S. R. to Smolensk and attended college and a military academy. He entered the Soviet army at the outbreak of World War II and is said to have participated along with Kim Il Sung in the Stalingrad defense.

Both of them returned to Korea with the rank of captain in the Soviet army of occupation, and both entered upon successful Communist political careers. In 1948 Nam Il was elected to the Supreme People's Council and became vice-minister of education in charge of military instruction. The most Russianized of the North Korean leaders, he took pains to cultivate the good will of the Soviet advisers. Speaking English, Russian, and Chinese as well as Korean, he held an advantage over his North Korean rivals in such contacts. He also made a better appearance, being tall for an Oriental and always well turned out in a meticulously pressed uniform and gleaming boots.

A major general without an active fiield comand at the outbreak of war, he was rapidly advanced to the rank of lieutenant general and chief of staff. His stern demeanor, while seated stiffly in his black Chrysler driven by a uniformed chauffeur, soon became one of the most impressive sights of Pyongyang. But his talents remained more political than military, and he never won the respect which the army accorded to Choe Yong Gun.

Among the corps commanders, there was none more able than Lieutenant General Kim Ung. About 40 years old at the outbreak of war, he had graduated from the Kumchon Commercial School in Korea and the Whampoa Military Academy in China. As an officer of the 8th Route Army, he won a reputation for daring in 1939 by tossing hand grenades into a conference of Japanese generals at Peiping and escaping after inflicting numerous casualties. Returning to Korea in 1946, he started as a regimental commander and made a relatively slow rise because of his CCF background. But after lining up with the Soviet faction in the army, he was promoted to the command of the 1st Division in 1948 and of I Corps during the invasion.

The rapid ascent of Lieutenant General Yu Kyong Su to the command of III Corps would indicate that promotion was sometimes due to political influence. A graduate of a Red Army tank school in 1938 at the age of 33, Yu served throughout World War II as a company grade officer in a Soviet tank unit. After his return to Korea, he married Kim Il Sung's sister and shot up from the command of an NK tank regiment in 1948 to the rank of corps commander late in 1950. During the first few weeks of the invasion, he was awarded the highest NKPA decoration, the "Hero of the Korean Democratic People's Republic," with a concurrent award, the "Order of the National Flag, 1st Class."

On the other hand, the career of former Lieutenant General Kim Mu Chong, ex-commander of II Corps and ex-chief of artillery, was blasted by the opposition of Kim Il Sung and Nam Il. A CCF veteran, Mu had served under Mao Tse-tung on the "Long March" as one of 30 Koreans to survive the ordeal. He commanded a Chinese artillery brigade and was rated the best CCF artilleryman. In 1945 he came back to Korea and conducted a speaking tour stressing the desirability of cooperating with Red China and omitting any reference to the Soviet Union. This lapse explains his failure in North Korean politics, but in deference to his high military reputation he was given command of II Corps in June 1950. The poor showing made by his units on the central front was ascribed by Mu to the fact that Kim Il Sung picked him for missions which could not succeed. Although he did not lack for support in the army, Mu was relieved of his command and other positions in the late summer of 1950. Expulsion from the North Korean Labor Party followed after Kim Il Sung denounced him in a speech for disobedience of orders.

Mu's downfall was only one chapter in the bitter struggle for power waged by two opposing tactical schools in the North Korean army from 1948 to 1950. Veterans of CCF campaigns against the Japanese and Chinese Nationalists upheld a system of large-scale guerrilla warfare refined into a military science. Approach marches under cover of darkness, infiltrations, probing night attacks—these were the basic tactics employed by Mao Tse Tung's forces for the conquest of China. Although mobility was the keynote, a rigid tactical system allowed little latitude of decision to officers below the regimental level. School solutions were provided for every military problem that could be foreseen, and many of the North Korean officers had graduated from the CCF military academy at Yenan.

Another group of officers advocated the tactics learned at Soviet military schools and in Soviet campaigns of World War II. This system, of course, made the CCF tactics seem primitive in comparison. For the Russians placed much more dependence in armor and artillery as preparation for infantry envelopments. Such tactics called for more supplies and ammunition than could have been provided by the elementary CCF logistics.

The CCF veterans seemed to have the upper hand in the North Korean army early in 1948. But a survey of NKPA officers' careers during the next 2 years indicates that their opponents triumphed. Thus, at the onset of civil war, most of the key positions in the army were filled by men who had hitched their wagons to the red star of Moscow, both militarily and politically.

This does not mean that CCF tactics had been put aside entirely. On the contrary, these methods had evolved out of military poverty and were admirably adapted to an Asiatic peasant army. The North Korean forces, being compelled to import arms, were never able to afford enough planes, tanks, and artillery to make the best of the Soviet system. And it was inevitable that heavy losses of such equipment in combat would cause a reversion to CCF tactics.

The NKPA Infantry Division

No child ever bore a more striking likeness to its parent than did the NKPA to the Soviet organization of World War II.

The army as a whole came under the overall control of General Headquarters at Pyongyang, which planned and directed the invasion of ROK territory. As the troops advanced, a Front Headquarters was set up to control corps operations. This organization of Soviet origin was the highest tactical echelon of command. Normally including three or four corps of several divisions each, it resembled an army group in military establishments of other nations. Front Headquarters had only a wartime mission and could be disbanded in time of peace.[10]

Next to the corps in the chain of command was the infantry division, the basic tactical formation, modeled after that of the Red Army in World War II. Of triangular design, numbering some 11,000 men, it was reported by POW's to consist of a headquarters, three rifle regi-

[10] FECOM, ATIS, *North Korean Forces, op. cit.,* 3–13.

ments, an artillery regiment, a signal battalion, an antitank battalion, a training battalion, a reconnaissance troop, and such division rear services as medical, veterinary, transport, and supply units.[11]

Division Headquarters, with about 120 men, included the commander, a major general, and officers of the division and special staff. Closely associated with the CG, and possessing almost as much power and responsibility, was the division political deputy, usually a senior colonel, who supervised politico-military activities and reported any deviations from doctrine. This was a peculiarly Communistic institution, of course, and it was the duty of the deputy to see that officers and men of the division remained well indoctrinated.

The NKPA rifle regiment, with a T/O strength of about 2,500 men, consisted of 3 rifle battalions and supporting artillery. Each of these battalions, numbering some 650 officers and men, included 3 rifle companies, a heavy machinegun company, a mortar company, an antitank gun platoon and an antitank rifle platoon in addition to signal, medical, and supply platoons.

An NKPA rifle company, which had a T/O strength of about 150 men, was made up of a headquarters, 3 rifle platoons and a heavy machinegun section. The rifle platoon had 4 squads and a T/O strength of 45 men. Squad weapons were said to include a light machinegun, a submachinegun and Soviet M1891/30 rifles. Two hand grenades were carried by each rifleman.

An army patterned after the Soviet system was certain to emphasize artillery, and the NKPA artillery reserve at the outset of the invasion consisted of 3 regiments—1 attached to GHQ, and 1 to each of the 2 corps operating at that time. But shortages of equipment and logistical problems made it necessary in actual combat for the NKPA to concentrate most of its artillery potential within the rifle division.

The organic artillery support of each division included a regiment with a T/O total of approximately 1,000 men. Two 76-mm. gun battalions, a 122-mm. howitzer battalion and a headquarters company numbered some 250 men each. A battalion consisted of 3 firing batteries with 12 artillery pieces each, and personnel carried M1938 carbines.

There was also a self-propelled artillery battalion made up of 3 gun companies, a signal platoon and a rear services section with a total of 16 SU-76 pieces. A lieutenant colonel commanded this unit, which had a T/O strength of 110 officers and men.

---

[11] *Ibid.*

The other major components of the NKPA infantry division were as follows:

SIGNAL BATTALION.—a wire company, radio company and headquarters company, making a total of 260 officers and men.

ANTITANK BATTALION.—about 190 officers and men in three 45-mm. antitank companies and an antitank rifle company.

ENGINEER BATTALION.—T/O of 250 officers and men carrying M1944 rifles and equipped with picks, shovels, axes, saws and mine detectors.

TRAINING BATTALION.—About 500 officers and men charged with the responsibility of training NCO's for the division.

RECONNAISSANCE COMPANY.—an estimated strength of 4 officers and 90 enlisted men equipped with 80 submachineguns, 20 Tokarev pistols, 4 telescopes and 5 pairs of binoculars.

REAR SERVICES.—a medical battalion, a transport company, a veterinary unit and a supply section. Of the 200 personnel in the medical battalion, about 60 were women, according to POW testimony. The transport company, with some 70 men, was composed of 50 2½-ton trucks, 6 or 7 motorcycles and 10 horse-drawn wagons.[12]

The NKPA infantry division, in short, was a faithful copy of the World War II Soviet model. But it must be remembered that the foregoing T/O and T/E statistics represented the ideal more often than the reality. Owing to the speeding up of preparations in anticipation of an easy victory, many NKPA units lacked their full quotas of men and equipment at the outset of the invasion.

NKPA Air and Armor

POW interrogations revealed that NKPA military aviation evolved from the North Korean Aviation Society, founded in 1945 at the Sinuiju Airfield by Colonel Lee Hwal, a Korean who had served in the Japanese air force. The organization consisted at first of about 70 students and 17 pilots who were veterans of Japanese air operations. Equipment included a few aircraft of Japanese manufacture and several gliders.[13]

In 1946 the Society was required to transfer its aircraft and trained personnel to the Aviation Section of the Pyongyang Military Academy. Soviet-trained Korean officers were placed in positions of responsibility

[12] *Ibid.*

[13] FECOM, ATIS, *North Korean Air Force* (InterRpt, Sup No. 100), 2–15.

under the command of Colonel Wang Yun, a former captain in the Soviet air force who replaced Lee Hwal.

The Aviation Section numbered about 100 officers, 250 enlisted men and 500 students by November 1948. Estimates of aircraft are contradictory, but one source reported 7 Japanese trainers, 6 Japanese fighters and a Japanese twin-engine transport. Shortly afterwards the first Soviet aircraft were received, and the NKPA Air Force was created from the Aviation Section and moved to the Pyongyang air base.

The final phase of development came in January 1950 with the expansion of the air regiment into a division under the command of Wang Yun, promoted to major general. Strength of the unit in April 1950 was estimated at about 1,675 officers and men, including 364 officers, 76 pilots, 875 enlisted men, and 360 cadets. The receipt of more Soviet planes at this time brought the number of aircraft up to 178, including 78 YAK-7B fighters, 30 PO-2 primary and YAK-18 advanced trainers, and 70 Il-10 ground attack bombers.

Captured documents indicate that the aviation training program was speeded up along with other NKPA activities during the last few months before the invasion. In June 1950 each pilot was required to fly 40 training missions and attend 40 hours of lectures. As preparations for the invasion neared completion, a forward displacement of tactical aircraft was put into effect.[14]

The North Korean armored division, a copy of its Soviet counterpart, had only about half of the overall strength. Thus the NKPA 105th Armored Division, comprising some 6,000 officers and men, included 3 medium tank regiments, the 107th, 109th, and 203d, with 40 tanks each. Organic supporting units were the 206th Mechanized Infantry Regiment and the 308th Armored Battalion equipped with self-propelled 76-mm. guns. POW reports also mentioned reconnaissance, engineer, signal, ordnance and medical battalions and a mixed unit identified as the 849th Antitank Regiment, attached to the division after the invasion started.[15]

All reports indicate that the division was split in combat, with each tank regiment being assigned to an infantry division. Even the training of the regiments had been conducted separately, and there is no evidence of prewar maneuvers on the division level.

Each tank regiment had an estimated T/O strength of about 600 officers and men. The three medium tank battalions were supported by

---

[14] *Ibid.*

[15] FECOM, ATIS, *Enemy Forces, op. cit.,* 27–32.

a regimental submachinegun company, a supply and maintenance company and a headquarters section in addition to engineer, signal, reconnaissance, and medical platoons. Forty T–34/85 medium tanks were divided into 13 for each battalion and 1 for the headquarters section, which also rated a CAZ/67 jeep.

Responsibility for the indoctrination of the regiment rested with a political section headed by a lieutenant colonel. As assistants he had 2 officers and 3 sergeants.

An NKPA tank battalion included a headquarters section and three 25-man companies. A company contained three platoons, each of which was assigned a medium tank. The standard crew consisted of the commander, usually a senior lieutenant, the driver and assistant driver, the gunner in charge of the 85-mm. rifle, and the assistant gunner operating the 7.62-mm. machinegun. The usual ammunition load was 55 85-mm. shells and 2,000 rounds of machinegun ammunition.

Not much was known about the 206th Mechanized Infantry Regiment, but it was believed to consist of three motorized infantry battalions, a 76-mm. howitzer battalion, a 45-mm. antitank battalion, a 120-mm. mortar battalion, a signal company, and an NCO training company.[16]

NKPA Officer Procurement and Conscription

Officer procurement problems were solved in large part by the fact that thousands of North Koreans had seen combat service with the CCF forces. Many of these veterans were qualified as junior officers or NCO's without further training. Remaining vacancies for company-grade officers were filled by officer candidate schools or the commissioning of qualified NCO's.

The West Point of the NKPA, located at Pyongyang, turned out an estimated 4,000 junior officers from the time of its activation in 1946 to the beginning of the invasion. Courses normally ranged in length from 6 to 10 months, but were abbreviated to 3 months during the autumn of 1949 in anticipation of the invasion. After hostilities began, the need for replacement officers became so urgent that one entire class at the Pyongyang academy was commissioned wholesale on 10 July 1950 and sent to the front after 20 days of instruction.[17]

---

[16] *Ibid.*

[17] FECOM, ATIS, *North Korean Forces, op. cit.*, 35–42.

Three Soviet officers, a colonel and two lieutenant colonels, reportedly acted as advisers to a faculty composed of NKPA majors. The five departments of the Academy were devoted to infantry, artillery, engineering, signaling, and quartermasters' duties.

A second military academy at Pyongyang specialized in subjects which Communists termed "cultural." So much importance was attached to political indoctrination that graduates of this school were commissioned as senior lieutenants and given unusual authority in their units. Although a 2-year Russian language course was offered, most of the candidates took the standard 9-month term.

Branches of the Pyongyang military academy were established as officer candidate schools in Hamhung, Chinnampo, Chorwon, Mesanjin, Kaechon and Kanggye. Applicants were required to have an acceptable political background and a 6-year minimum of schooling, though the last was sometimes waived.

A command and staff school at Pyongyang offered advanced tactical and administrative courses at the battalion and regimental level to selected officers. At the other extreme, NCO schools were located at Sadong, Sinuiju, Sinchon and Nanam. Tactical instruction was given at the platoon and squad level with emphasis on weapons courses. NCO training was accelerated in preparation for hostilities, and 4,000 veterans of CCF service in Manchuria completed 2-month courses at the Sadong school alone in the spring of 1950.

Technical training in aircraft, artillery, tank and engineering specialties was offered in schools for junior officers as well as enlisted men. But it appears that most of the officers above the company level received their instruction in Soviet schools.[18]

Conscription, according to POW accounts, was introduced as early as 1948. In the rural districts each *myon* (a political subdivision smaller than a county but comprising several villages) was given its quota of recruits to be furnished between the ages of 18 and 35. The village chiefs then assembled all the men in this age group and made their decisions on an arbitrary basis. Selectees had little or no hope of appeal, but were assured that provision would be made for their families during the 3-year term of service.[19]

The system was much the same in North Korean cities, which were divided into sections for conscription purposes. Sometimes the leaders in

---

[18] *Ibid.*

[19] *Ibid.*, 29–31.

urban areas called for volunteers. If the response was lacking in enthusiasm, men were singled out and requested to "volunteer." This method was invariably successful, since a man who refused could be deprived of employment.

The conscription program was speeded up along with other preparations as invasion plans neared completion. About 12,000 men were inducted from March through May 1950 and given 6 weeks of basic training at such camps as the No. 2 People's Training Center at Sinuiju.

In some communities the men eligible for military service were requested to attend a meeting. Upon arrival, they were taken in trucks to a training center and compelled to enlist.

Harsh as such methods might seem, they were gentle as compared to the forced conscription of ROK civilians after the invasion got underway. Both men and women in captured cities were crowded into school buildings, given political indoctrination and forced to learn Communist songs. After a week of this curriculum, the men were inducted both as combat recruits and laborers. And though the women were told that their service would be limited to duty as nurses or clerks, some of them were coerced into carrying out reconnaissance or espionage missions.[20]

The NKPA Order of Battle

The transition from a cold war to a shooting war in Korea should not have surprised anyone familiar with the events of the past 2 years. For several hours, indeed, there was a reasonable doubt on the historic morning of 25 June 1950 whether an undeclared war had begun or merely another large-scale NKPA raid across the frontier.

But this time it was the real thing. Commencing at 0400, 7 infantry divisions and an armored division swept across the 38th Parallel, with 2 infantry divisions in reserve. From right to left, the NKPA order of battle was as follows:

The 6th Infantry Division along the west coast, sealing off the Ongjin Peninsula and moving on Kaesong; the 1st Infantry Division advancing on Kaesong and Seoul; the 4th and 3d Infantry Divisions and 105th Armored Division attacking in west-central Korea and converging on Seoul; the 2d and 15th Infantry Divisions driving toward the Hwachon-Chunchon axis in east-central Korea; and the 5th Infantry Division tak-

---

[20] *Ibid.*

ing the route along the east coast. Following close behind were the two reserve infantry divisions, the 13th and 15th.[21]

There was no question as to the outcome in the minds of observers who knew the composition of the ROK army. The very name was misleading, for it might more accurately have been described as a large constabulary in process of being converted into an army. Given another year of training and added arms and equipment, the Republic of Korea would perhaps have built up an adequate defense establishment. But the enemy took good care to strike while this development was still at the blueprint stage.

In June 1949, at the conclusion of the occupation, the United States forces turned over arms and equipment to the value of about $110,000,000. These supplies included 100,000 small arms (rifles, pistols and machineguns) and 50,000,000 rounds of ammunition; more than 4,900 vehicles of all types; about 2,000 2.36″ rocket launchers and 40,000 rounds of ammunition; and a large number of 105-mm. howitzers, 37-mm. and 57-mm. antitank guns, and 60-mm. and 81-mm. mortars, together with 700,000 rounds of ammunition for those weapons. Twenty training planes (L4 and L5 types) were transferred as well as 79 light naval craft suitable for patrolling the coast.[22]

It is noteworthy that this list was limited to light arms for a constabulary of about 50,000 men. Tanks, military aircraft and medium or heavy artillery were significantly lacking.

At the request of the ROK government, a Korean Military Advisory Group remained in South Korea after the conclusion of the American occupation. Composed of 500 United States Army officers and enlisted men, the KMAG took on the task of directing the training of a ROK constabulary. The group was under the control of Ambassador Muccio, since General MacArthur's responsibility for the defense had ended along with the occupation.[23]

After the NKPA invasion, the United States was severely criticized in some quarters for failing to provide the Republic of Korea with arms and training equal to those of the enemy. American reluctance was due in some measure to indiscreet declarations by that fiery old Korean patriot, Syngman Rhee. The ROK president, 74 years old at the outbreak of civil war, did not shrink from advocating the unification of Korea by

[21] FECOM, ATIS, *History of the North Korean Army,* 25–27.

[22] U. S. Military Academy, Dept of Mil Art and Eng (U. S. MilAcad), *Operations in Korea* (West Point, 1953), 4–5.

[23] *Ibid.*

armed force. On 20 February 1949 he predicted that his troops "could defeat North Korea within 2 weeks" if the U. S. S. R. did not interfere. Eight months later, on 7 October, his confidence had increased to the point where he was "sure that we could take Pyongyang in 3 days."[24]

Such remarks placed the United States in an uncomfortable position. If aid to the Republic of Korea were to include tanks, military aircraft and training for offensive warfare, Americans would be open to the charge of inciting civil strife. Communist propagandists would scream that accusation in any event, of course, but there would be grounds for the suspicion of other members of the United Nations. Ambassador Muccio made sure, therefore, that United States assistance did not extend beyond the legitimate needs of ROK frontier defense and internal security.

The triangular ROK infantry division was modeled after the United States unit but numbered about 9,500 troops. Eight divisions and a regiment had been organized and partially trained by June 1950. They were the 1st, 2d, 3d, 5th, 6th, 7th, 8th, and Capital Divisions and the 17th Regiment.[25] Only 4 of these divisions, the 1st, 2d, 6th, and 7th, had their full complement of 3 regiments. All the others had 2 except the 5th, which had 2 and a battalion.[26]

ROK military strength was estimated at 98,808 troops by the KMAG in June 1950. About 65,000 of them had been given unit training for combat. They were fairly proficient in the employment of small arms and mortars, but their instruction had not included defense against tanks. Command and staff work were still at a rudimentary stage, and both officers and NCO's needed seasoning.

The ROK Army of June 1950 had made good progress, in short, when it is considered that most of its components had been activated within the past year. But it was no match for the Red Korean columns which attacked at dawn on 25 June 1950. The ROK order of battle, if such it could be called, consisted of a regiment and four infantry divisions ranged from left to right across the peninsula—the 17th Regiment and the 1st, 7th, 6th, and 8th Divisions. The remaining divisions were dispersed for purposes of internal security: the Capital at Seoul; the 2d

---

[24] A. Wigfall Green, *Epic of Korea* (Washington: Public Affairs Press, 1950), 125–26.

[25] The absence of a 4th Division is explained by an old Korean superstition. Because the symbol for that number resembled the ancient symbol for death, it was regarded as unlucky. Apparently the North Koreans managed to overcome this superstition, however, in numbering their units.

[26] LtCol Roy E. Appleman, USA, ms. history of UN operations in Korea, Jul–Nov 50.

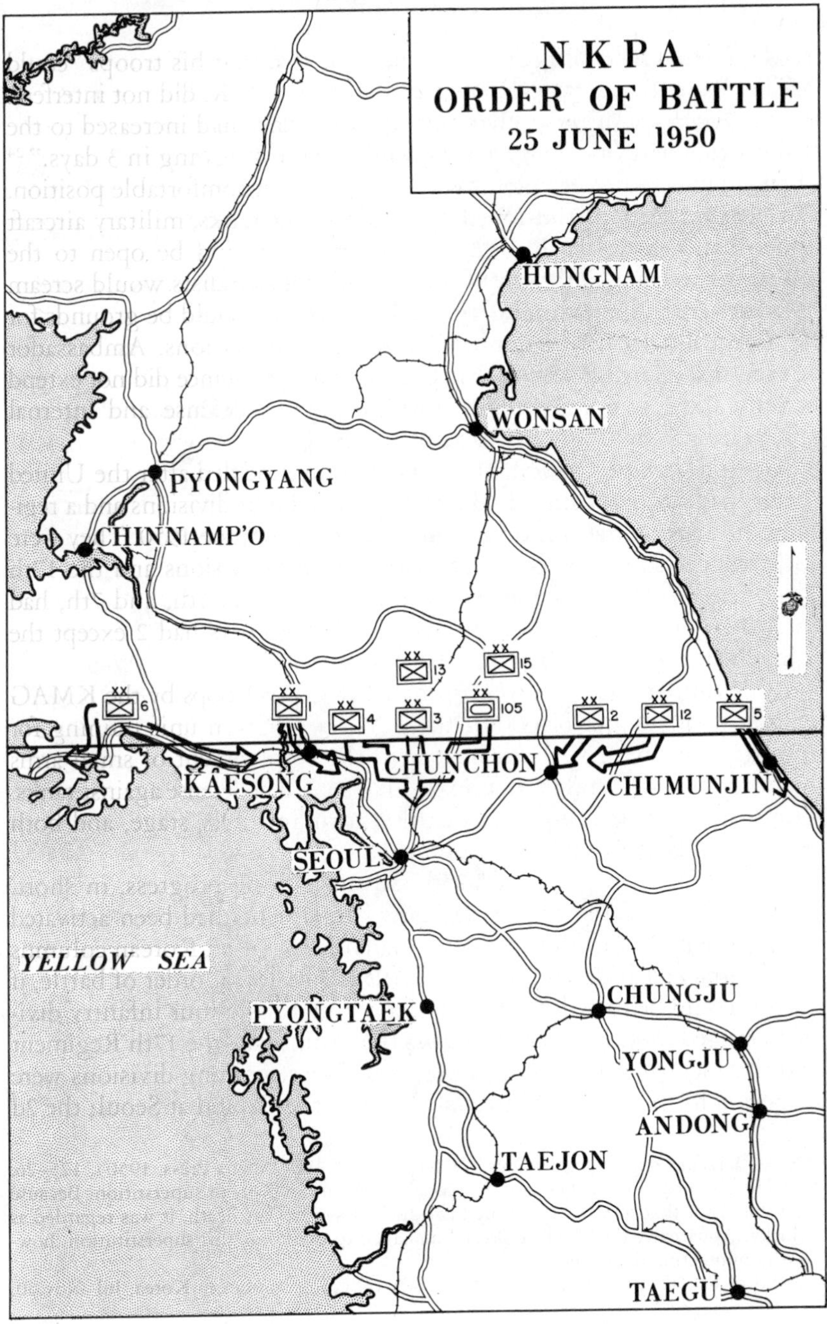
NKPA
ORDER OF BATTLE
25 JUNE 1950
HUNGNAM
WONSAN
PYONGYANG
CHINNAMP'O
13
15
6
1
4
3
105
2
12
5
KAESONG
CHUNCHON
CHUMUNJIN
SEOUL
YELLOW SEA
PYONGTAEK
CHUNGJU
YONGJU
ANDONG
TAEJON
TAEGU

at Chongju and Taejon; the 3d at Taegu; and the 5th at Kwangju.

The ROK frontier forces were not well disposed for defense in depth. Taken by surprise, they put up an ineffectual resistance despite brave fights here and there against odds. On other occasions the sight of an enemy tank or armored car was enough to scatter ROK riflemen, and the progress of the invading columns resembled an occupation rather than an attack.

Before sundown on the day of invasion it appeared that NKPA leaders had not erred in allowing a timetable of 10 days for overrunning the Republic of Korea. The question now was whether the conflict could be confined to that Asiatic peninsula. Communist aggressions were no novelty, to be sure, either in Asia or Europe. But in the past there had always been some show of peaceable intentions, however hypocritical, or some shadow of legality. This was the first time that a Soviet puppet nation had been permitted to go as far as open warfare. Matters had come to a showdown, and it could only be interpreted as a challenge issued by Communism to the free nations of the world.

CHAPTER III

The Marine Brigade

NKPA Gains of First Week—Early United States Decisions—Geography of Korea—United States Ground Forces in Korea—Requests for United States Marines—Activation of the Brigade—Brigade Leadership

AT THREE O'CLOCK in the morning of 25 June 1950 the telephone rang in the New York suburban home of Trygve Lie, secretary-general of the United Nations. He was informed that North Korean forces had crossed the 38th Parallel to invade the Republic of Korea.

The news had just been received by the United States Department of State directly from Seoul. Ambassador Muccio had emphasized that this was not one of the large-scale North Korean raids into ROK territory which had become an old story during the past 2 years. For his report concluded:

> "It would appear from the nature of the attack and the manner in which it was launched that it constitutes an all-out offensive against the Republic of Korea." [1]

The implications were disturbing. Every middle-aged American could recall the failure of the League of Nations to halt Japanese, Italian, and German aggressions of the 1930's with moral suasions. Even when economic sanctions were invoked, the aggressors went their way defiantly without respect for anything short of armed force. And now history seemed to be repeating itself with dismaying fidelity as new aggressors challenged the new union of nations striving to maintain peace after World War II.

There was even an ominous parallel in the fact that another civil conflict in another peninsula had been the prelude to Armageddon in the 1930's. For it might well have been asked if the Korea of 1950 were destined to become the Spain of a new world war.

---

[1] U. S. Dept of State, *Guide to the U. N. in Korea* (Washington: GPO, 1951).

305713 O-F-55—4

The answer of the United Nations was prompt and decisive. At 2 o'clock in the afternoon on 25 June 1950, a meeting of the Security Council was called to order at New York. A dispatch had just been received from UNCOK—the United Nations Commission on Korea—reporting that four Soviet YAK-type aircraft had destroyed planes and jeeps on an airfield outside of Seoul. The railway station in the industrial suburb of Yongdungpo had also been strafed.[2]

By a unanimous vote of nine member nations (with the U. S. S. R. being significantly absent and Yugoslavia not voting) the blame for the aggression was placed squarely upon the North Korean invaders. They were enjoined to cease hostilities immediately and withdraw from ROK territory.

The United Nations had no armed might to enforce its decisions. But the Security Council did not intend to rely merely upon moral suasion or economic sanctions. At a second meeting, on 27 June, the Council proclaimed the NKPA attack a breach of world peace and asked member nations to assist the Republic of Korea in repelling the invasion.

For the first time in the war-racked 20th century, a group of nations banded together for peace had not only condemned an aggression but appealed to armed force to smite the aggressor. On the same day that the Security Council passed its historic resolution, the United States announced that it was giving immediate military aid to the Republic of Korea.

President Truman, as commander in chief, ordered American naval and air forces into action. Fifty-two other members of the United Nations approved the recommendations of the Security Council. Their pledges of assistance included aircraft, naval vessels, medical supplies, field ambulances, foodstuffs and strategic materials.

Only 3 of the 56 nations responding to the Council were opposed to the majority decision. They were the Soviet Union and her two satellites, Poland and Czechoslovakia, which had been brought into the Communist orbit by compulsion after World War II.

On 29 June President Truman authorized General MacArthur to send certain supporting United States ground force units to Korea. An American naval blockade of the entire Korean coast was ordered, and Japan-based Air Force planes were given authority to bomb specific military targets north of the 38th Parallel.

These decisions were upheld by the wholehearted approval of nearly

---

[2] *Ibid.*

all Americans, according to contemporary newspapers.[3] Virtually the only dissenters were such left-wing extremists as the 9,000 who attended a "Hands off Korea" rally held early in July 1950 under Communist auspices in New York.[4] Barring such rule-proving exceptions, Americans had long been smoldering with indignation at Soviet cold-war tactics. They applauded the resolute stand taken by the United Nations, and they were proud of their country for its response. Unfortunately, they did not anticipate that anything more serious than a brief "police action" would be necessary to settle affairs. Never in their wildest imaginations had it occurred to them that an Asiatic peasant army might be more than a match for all the United States ground forces in the Far East.

NKPA Gains of First Week

It was by no means a contemptible army, judged even by Western military standards, which ripped through ROK defenses after crossing the 38th Parallel. The major effort was the two-pronged attack on Seoul, conducted with precision by the 1st NKPA Infantry Division, advancing through Kaesong and Munsan while the 4th and 3d united south of the frontier with elements of the 105th Armored to proceed by way of the Yonchon-Uijongbu and Pochon-Uijongbu corridors.

On the right the 6th Infantry Division made short work of overrunning the isolated Ongjin Peninsula and thrusting eastward toward Kaesong. On the left the offensive was covered by the drive of the 2d and 12th Infantry Divisions on Chunchon while the 5th made rapid gains along the east coast.

In this area the North Koreans initiated the first amphibious operations of the war with four Soviet-manufactured torpedo boats. Built entirely of aluminum, of about 16 gross tons displacement when fully loaded, these craft measured slightly over 19 meters in length and were powered by two 10-cylinder engines rated at 850 horsepower each. With a crew of 8 men, a cruising speed of 20 to 25 knots and a range of 15 hours, the boats carried 2 torpedoes and were armed with a 12.7-mm. heavy machinegun and 2 submachineguns.[5]

During the first 5 days of the invasion, the 4 torpedo boats escorted

[3] *Newsweek,* 10 Jul 50, 17.
[4] *Ibid,* 29.
[5] FECOM, ATIS, *North Korean Forces, op. cit.,* 45–6.

convoys which transported NKPA troops down the east coast for unopposed landings as far south as Samchok. But on 2 July 1950 the tiny North Korean "navy" was almost literally blown out of the water when it encountered UN Task Group 96.5 off Chuminjin while escorting 10 converted trawlers. With more bravery than discretion, the small North Korean craft accepted battle with the American light cruiser *Juneau* and two British warships, the light cruiser *Jamaica* and the frigate *Black Swan.* Evidently the enemy hoped to score with a few torpedoes at the cost of a suicidal effort, but the U. N. guns sank 2 of the aluminum craft and drove a third to the beach, where it was soon destroyed along with 7 of the convoy vessels. The North Koreans were credited with "great gallantry" in the British dispatch after the fourth torpedo boat escaped.[6] But it was the last naval effort of any consequence by an enemy strangled in the net of the UN blockade.

On land the NKPA columns advanced almost at will during the first 4 days. Nearly a hundred tanks and as many planes were employed by the two main columns advancing on Seoul, and on 27 June 1950 the ROK seat of government was removed to Taejon while Far East Air Force planes were evacuating United States citizens. ROK fugitives, winding southward in an endless stream of humanity, choked every road and multiplied the difficulties of the defense. To add to their misery, one of the bridges across the river Han was blown prematurely when masses of Koreans were crossing.

The fall of Seoul on the 28th ended the first stage of the offensive as the NKPA forces halted for regrouping. Chunchon had surrendered in east-central Korea, so that the invaders held a ragged line stretching from Chumunjin on the east coast through Chunchon, Kapyong and Seoul to the port of Inchon on the west coast.

The beaten and in some instances shattered ROK forces were meanwhile falling back through Suwon in the hope of establishing new positions of defense.

Early United States Decisions

A strategy of delaying actions was the only course open to General MacArthur for the time being. One of his first decisions led to the estab-

---

[6] Capt Walter Karig, USN, *Battle Report: The War in Korea* (New York: Rinehart, 1952), 58–59.

lishment on 27 June of the GHQ Advanced Command Group at Suwon under the command of Brigadier General John H. Church, USA. This group had as its primary mission the reorganization of the demoralized ROK forces, which were already reporting thousands of men missing in action. Secondary missions were to keep Tokyo informed as to military developments and expedite the delivery of supplies. As early as 27 June, 119 tons of emergency supplies had been sent to Korea by air, and an additional 5,600 tons were being loaded on ships in Japan.[7]

American naval and air forces lost no time at getting into action after President Truman's authorization. United States Naval Forces in the Far East, under the command of Vice Admiral C. Turner Joy, had as their principal element the Seventh Fleet, commanded by Vice Admiral Arthur D. Struble. Its tactical organization, Task Force 77, immediately clamped down a blockade on the Korean coast after wiping out enemy naval opposition. Other warships of the Seventh Fleet were meanwhile blockading Formosa to guard against the possibility of Chinese Communist intervention by means of an attack on the last Nationalist stronghold.

The United States Far East Air Forces, commanded by Lieutenant General George E. Stratemeyer, USAF, consisted of eight and a half combat groups responsible for the defense of Japan, Okinawa, Guam and the Philippines. Primary missions assigned to the fighter and bomber squadrons were the elimination of NKPA air opposition and the retarding of enemy ground forces by means of interdictory air strikes on bases and supply routes.

Geography of Korea

Geography being a first cousin of strategy, maps of Korea were almost literally worth their weight in diamonds both in Tokyo and at the Pentagon. For that matter, they were nearly as rare as diamonds, and it became necessary in many instances to work with outdated Japanese maps.

On the map of Asia the Korean peninsula resembles a thumb dipping down into the Yellow and Japan seas. For centuries it has been the sore thumb of Asiatic power politics, so that trouble in Korea resulted in a twinge being felt in the capitals of Europe. But small as Korea appears on the map, it is actually about 575 miles in length—a peninsula

[7] U. S. MilAcad, *op. cit.*, 7–8.

resembling Florida in shape but having about the area of Minnesota.

Variations in climate are comparable to the gradient from Maine to Georgia along the Atlantic seaboard of the United States. Extremes ranging from summer weather of 105° F. to winter temperatures of 40° below zero have been recorded. A monsoon season of floods is to be expected in July and August, followed by a period when typhoons are a possibility. Altogether, it is a climate which can contribute no little to the difficulties of a mechanized invader.

It would be almost an understatement to say that Korea is mountainous. Few areas of the earth's surface are so consistently rugged. Bleak cliffs seem to thrust themselves dripping out of the sea on the East Korean littoral. The peaks become higher and more perpendicular as they march inland, until altitudes of 9,000 feet are reached.

The principal chain of mountains extends from the Yalu in the north along the east coast to the Pusan area. Just south of the 38th parallel a spur branches off diagonally to southwest Korea in the region of Mokpu. The remainder of the peninsula consists largely of smaller ranges and foothills.

The few broad valleys are found chiefly on the west coast, which has a good many indentations and estuaries. Here also are most of Korea's large rivers, flowing west and south. Of little aid to navigation, these streams are broad and deep enough to hamper military operations; and in the monsoon season, floods become a menace.

As if the west coast were paying a penalty for being less mountainous, mud flats and islands hamper navigation. And here the tides are among the highest in the world, with an extreme range of about 30 feet existing at Inchon in contrast to unusually moderate tides along the east coast.

The west and south are the agricultural areas of Korea. Nothing is wasted by peasants who till every inch of the lowland flats, rice paddies, and terraced hills. Due to their back-breaking toil rather than many natural advantages, Korea was able to export as much as half of its two food staples, rice and fish, under the Japanese administration.

The population, estimated at 25,000,000 in 1945, increased both by immigration and a high birth rate during the next 5 years until as many as 29,000,000 inhabitants were claimed. Seoul was a capital of a million and a half residents, and the two leading seaports, Pusan and Inchon, had not far from a quarter of a million each. Modern office buildings, factories and street railways were found in combination with muddy streets and thatched huts on the outskirts.

A standard-gauge rail network, built largely by the Japanese, linked the principal cities and connected in the north with the Manchurian railways. The highway system was good for an Asiatic country but inadequate for the purpose of an invader on wheels and tracks. Hard-surfaced roads were few and far between, and the ordinary earth roads were churned into bogs during the monsoon season. Air transportation was limited to only a few large airfields and emergency landing facilities.

Altogether, Korea promised to be a tough nut to crack, when it came to geography, for the officers poring over maps in Tokyo.

United States Ground Forces in Korea

The United States ground forces in the Far East comprised the understrength 7th, 24th, and 25th Infantry Divisions and the 1st Cavalry (dismounted) Division of the Eighth United States Army, which had been stationed in Japan since the end of World War II. These divisions had only about 70 percent of their personnel, the regiments being limited to two battalions.

The explanation of these deficiencies goes back to the end of World War II. Popular clamor for the speedy discharge of the victorious United States forces had resulted in American military sinews becoming flabby during the next few years. Strenuous recruiting had been necessary to maintain the small army of occupation in Japan at part strength, and it was no secret that many of the men were attracted by the expectation of travel and light occupation duties. The possibility of battle had scarcely been anticipated when the invasion began, and combat readiness left a good deal to be desired. Training on the company level had been good on the whole, but both officers and men were handicapped by the lack of maneuvers for units larger than a battalion.

Shortages in equipment were equally serious. There were not enough mortars, recoilless rifles and other weapons even if there had been enough maintainance parts and trained maintenance technicians. Most of the arms, moreover, consisted of worn World War II equipment which had seen its best days. Finally, the divisional armored units had been provided with light M24 tanks, instead of the heavier machines normally employed, because of the weak bridges in Japan.[8]

It was, in brief, an unprepared and ill-equipped little army of

[8] U. S. MilAcad, *loc. cit.*

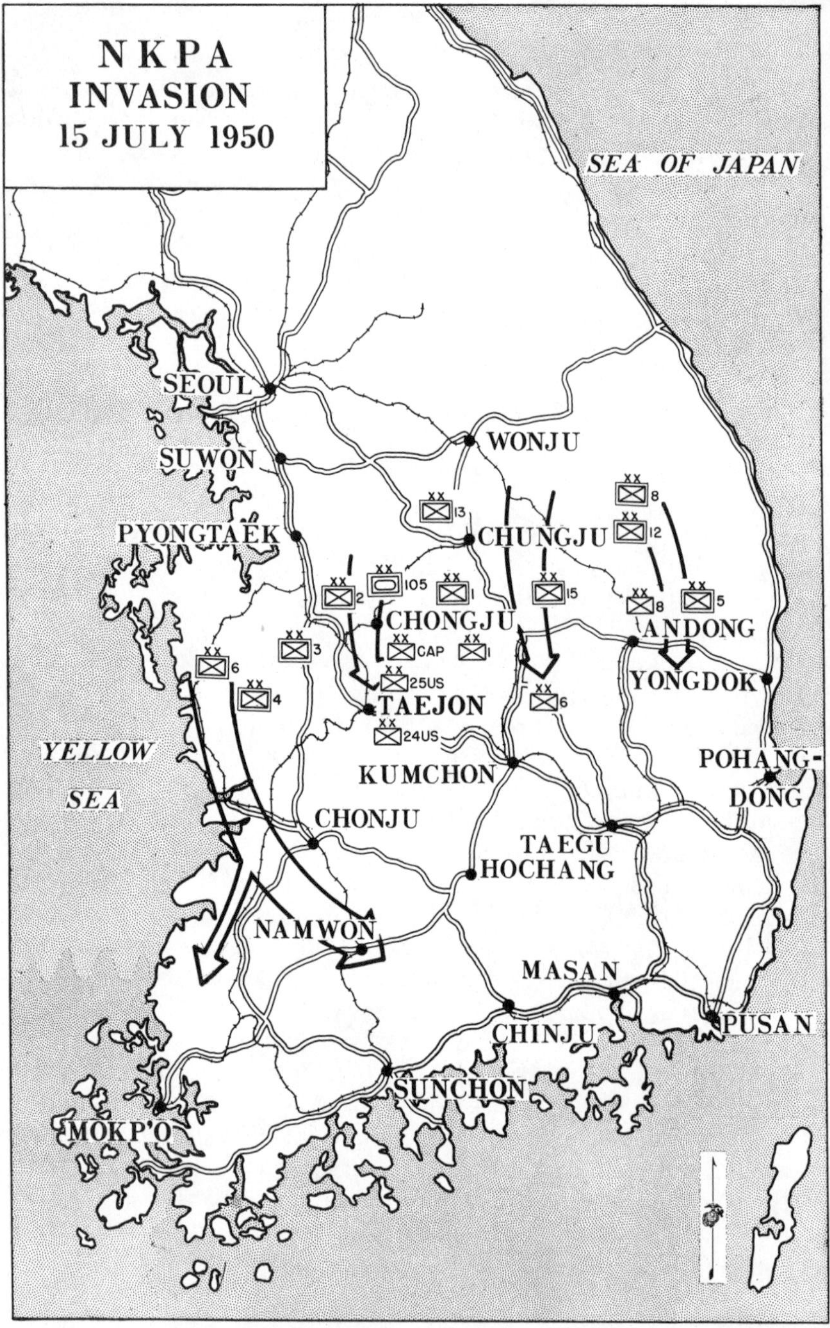

NKPA INVASION 15 JULY 1950

occupation which represented the first line of United States defense in the Far East.

On 2 July the advance elements of the 24th Infantry Division, commanded by Major General William F. Dean, were flown from Japan to Korea. Two days later, on the American national holiday, the first contact of the United States ground forces with the enemy was made near Osan, about 8 miles south of Suwon.

The American force consisted of 2 infantry companies, a battery of artillery, two 4.2″ mortar platoons, a platoon of 75-mm. recoilless rifles, and six 2.36″ rocket-launcher teams. Named Task Force Smith after its commanding officer, Lieutenant Colonel Charles B. Smith, the first United States contingent collided on the morning of 5 July with a whole NKPA division supported by 30 T–34 tanks. Despite the odds against it, Task Force Smith put up a good delaying fight of 4 or 5 hours before pulling out with the loss of all equipment save small arms.[9]

On 7 July, the UN Security Council passed a resolution calling for a unified command in Korea, and President Truman named General MacArthur as commander in chief. Lieutenant General Walton H. Walker, who had been one of Patton's best officers in World War II, was appointed commander of the Eighth United States Army in Korea (EUSAK) on 12 July, and 4 days later he assumed control of all ROK ground forces.

The ROK army, as might be supposed, was badly battered and much in need of reorganization. At the end of the first week of invasion, the ROK missing in action had reached a total of about 34,000. Whole battalions had been scattered like chaff, yet it speaks well for the spirit of the troops that most of the missing eventually returned to their units.[10] The odds against them had made it a hopeless fight, but these Korean soldiers would give a good account of themselves when they had better training and equipment.

The United States forces were finding it hard sledding, for that matter. The remaining units of the 24th Infantry Division were in action by 7 July, having arrived by sea from Japan. They were followed by the 25th Infantry Division, commanded by Major General William B. Kean, which completed the movement to Korea on 14 July.

These first outweighed United States forces had no choice except to trade space for time in a series of delaying actions. Although the units

[9] 24th InfDiv, Supporting Documents, 24 Jul–16 Aug 50, 6–7.
[10] Appleman, *op. cit.*

had to be employed piecemeal at first, they slowed up the main thrust of the enemy—the advance of three NKPA divisions, well supported by armor, down the Seoul-Taejon axis.

Seldom in history have American forces ever endured a worse ordeal by fire. Unprepared morally as well as materially, snatched from soft occupation duties in Japan, they were suddenly plunged into battle against heavier battalions. The "Land of the Morning Calm" was to them a nightmare land of sullen mountains and stinking rice paddies. There was not even the momentary lift of band music and flag waving for these occupation troops, and they were not upheld by the discipline which stiffens the spines of old regulars.

Considering what they were up against, the soldiers of the 24th and 25th have an abiding claim to a salute from their countrymen. They fought the good fight, even though they could keep militarily solvent only by withdrawals between delaying actions.

Officers as well as men were expendables in this Thermopylae of the rice paddies. Because of the large proportion of green troops, colonels and even generals literally led some of the counterattacks in the 18th-century manner. Colonel Robert R. Martin, commanding the 34th Infantry of the 24th Division, fell in the thick of the fighting while rallying his troops. General Dean stayed with his forward units, personally firing one of the new 3.5″ bazookas until the enemy broke through. He was reported missing for months, but turned up later as the highest ranking United States military prisoner of the conflict in Korea.

American light tanks could not cope with the enemy's T-34's; and even when the first few medium tanks arrived, they were equipped only with 75-mm. guns against the heavier NKPA armament. Not until the third week of ground force operations, moreover, did the United States artillery units receive 155-mm. howitzers to supplement their 105's.

There was nothing that the ground forces could do but withdraw toward the line of the river Kum. Here a stand was made by 24th Division units at Taejon, an important communications center. But the enemy managed to establish bridgeheads, and the fall of the town on 20 July marked the end of the first phase.

Two days later the 24th Division, now commanded by General Church, was relieved south of Taejon by Major General Hobart R. Gay's 1st Cavalry (dismounted) Division, which had landed at Pohang-dong on the 18th. And on 26 July the separate 29th Infantry RCT disembarked at Chinju on the south coast after a voyage from Okinawa.

The reinforced Eighth Army was still too much outnumbered to vary its strategy of delaying actions with sustained counterattacks. While the new American units and the 25th Division fell slowly back toward the line of the Naktong, the regrouped ROK divisions were assigned sectors toward the north and east, where a secondary NKPA offensive threatened Pohang-dong. Meanwhile, the exhausted 24th Division went into Eighth Army reserve.

The ground forces would doubtless have been in a worse situation if it had not been for hard-hitting United States naval and air support. Major General Emmett O'Donnell's B-29 Superforts of the FEAF Bomber Command took off from Japanese bases to fly strikes on enemy supply routes, communications hubs, marshaling yards and other strategic targets all the way back to the Yalu.

Task Force 77, ranging along the west coast, gave Pyongyang its first large-scale bombing on 3 July. Gull-winged F4U Corsairs, leading off from the *Valley Forge* flight deck with 5-inch rockets, were followed by AD Skyraiders and new Douglas dive bombers. Bridges and railway yards were destroyed by raiders who shot down two YAK-type planes in the air and destroyed two on the ground.

Along the east coast the *Juneau* and other warships of the Anglo-American blockading force patrolled the enemy's MSR, which followed the shoreline. Salvos from the cruisers, fired at the sheer cliffs, loosed avalanches of earth and rock to block the highway. Railways were mined and tunnels dynamited by commando parties landing from ships' boats.

The combined U. N. efforts inflicted heavy material and personnel losses while slowing up the NKPA offensive. But it is a testimonial to Soviet and Red Korean preparations for aggression that the army of invasion kept on rolling. There was even some prospect late in July that the enemy would yet make good his boast of being able to take Pusan within 2 months in spite of United States intervention.

Requests for United States Marines

Upholding their long tradition as America's force-in-readiness, the Marines have usually been among the first troops to see action on a foreign shore. Thus it might have been asked what was holding them back at a time when Army troops in Korea were hard-pressed.

The answer is that the Marines actually were the first United States ground forces to get into the fight after completing the long voyage from the American mainland. There were no Marine units of any size in the Far East at the outset of the invasion. But not an hour was lost at the task of assembling an air-ground team at Camp Pendleton, California, and collecting the shipping.

The spirit of impatience animating the Marine Corps is shown by an entry on the desk calendar of General Clifton B. Cates under the date of 26 June 1950. This was the day after the news of the invasion reached Washington, and the Commandant commented:

"SecNav's policy meeting called off. Nuts."[11]

On the 28th General Cates had his first conference with Admiral Forrest P. Sherman, Chief of Naval Operations. He noted on his calendar the next day: "Recommended to CNO and SecNav that FMF be employed." Two days later General Cates "attended SecNav's conference." And on 3 July his calendar recorded more history:

"Attended JCS meeting. Orders for employment of FMF approved."[12]

The steps leading up to this decision may be traced back to the conference of 28 June, when Cates gave Sherman a summary of the strength of the Marine Corps. Along with other branches of the service, it had taken cuts in appropriations since World War II, so that total numbers were 74,279 men on active duty—97 percent of authorized strength. The Fleet Marine Force had a strength of 27,656—11,853 in FMFPac (1st Marine Division, Reinf., and 1st Marine Aircraft Wing) and 15,803 in FMFLant (2d Marine Division, Reinf., and 2d Marine Aircraft Wing).[13]

Neither of these understrength divisions, General Cates pointed out, could raise much more than an RCT of combat-ready troops with supporting air.

Admiral Sherman asked CinCPacFlt on 1 July how long it would take to move (*a*) a Marine BLT and (*b*) a Marine RCT from the Pacific Coast. Admiral Radford replied the next day that he could load the BLT in 4 days and sail in 6; and that he could load the RCT in 6 days and sail in 10.[14]

Next, a dispatch from CNO to Admiral C. Turner Joy announced that a Marine RCT could be made available if General MacArthur desired it. COMNAVFE called personally on the general, who had just returned from a depressing inspection of the invasion front. Not only

---

[11] Gen Clifton B. Cates ltr to authors, 7 Apr 54 (Cates, 7 Apr 54).

[12] *Ibid.*

[13] Ernest H. Giusti, *The Mobilization of the Marine Corps Reserve in the Korean Conflict* (Washington, HQMC, G-3, HistSec, 1951), 1–2.

[14] CNO disp to CinCPacFlt, 1 Jul 50; and CinCPacFlt disp to CNO, 2 Jul 50.

did CINCFE accept immediately, but he showed unusual enthusiasm in expressing his appreciation.[15]

Sunday 2 July was the date of the message from General MacArthur requesting the immediate dispatch of a Marine RCT with supporting air to the Far East. CNO acted that same day. With the concurrence of JCS and the President, he ordered Admiral Radford to move a Marine RCT with appropriate air to the Far East for employment by General MacArthur.[16]

Later, when General Cates asked CNO how the historical decision had been accomplished, Admiral Sherman replied cryptically in baseball language, "From Cates to Sherman, to Joy, to MacArthur, to JCS!"[17]

Activation of the Brigade

Even at this early date there was talk both in Washington and Tokyo of forming an entire Marine division after mobilizing the Reserve. For the present, however, it sufficed to organize the RCT requested by General MacArthur. There could be little doubt that the assignment would be given to an air-ground team built around the two main West Coast units, the 5th Marines and Marine Aircraft Group 33. They were activated along with supporting units on 7 July as the 1st Provisional Marine Brigade, commanded by Brigadier General Edward A. Craig, senior officer at Camp Pendleton. The air component, consisting of three squadrons of MAG-33, was placed under the command of Brigadier General Thomas H. Cushman, who was named deputy commander of the Brigade.

Lieutenant General Lemuel C. Shepherd, Jr., commanding general of FMFPac, and a G-3 staff officer, Colonel Victor H. Krulak, had been ordered on 4 July to proceed immediately to Tokyo and confer with General MacArthur. Before leaving, Shepherd found time to recommend formation of third platoons for rifle companies of the 5th Marines, and CNO gave his approval the following day.[18]

Unfortunately, there was not enough time to add third rifle companies

---

[15] Marine Corps Board, *An Evaluation of the Influence of Marine Corps Forces on the Course of the Korean War* (4 Aug–15 Dec 50) (MCBS) I–B–1, I–B–2.

[16] CINCFE disp to CNO, 2 Jul 50; CNO disp to CinCPacFlt, 2 Jul 50; and JCS disp to CINCFE, 3 Jul 50.

[17] Cates, 7 Apr 54.

[18] CNO disp to CinCPacFlt, 5 Jul 50.

to the battalions of the 5th Marines which had been training with two companies on a peacetime basis. Camp Pendleton and its neighboring Marine Air Station, El Toro, hummed with day and night activity as the Brigade prepared to sail in a week. Weapons and clothing had to be issued, immunization shots given, and insurance and pay allotments made out. Meanwhile, telegrams were sent to summon Marines from posts and stations all over the United States.

Among these Marines were the first helicopter pilots of the United States Armed Forces to be formed into a unit for overseas combat service. Large-scale production of rotary-wing aircraft had come too late to have any effect on the tactics of World War II, though a few Sikorsky machines had been used experimentally both in the European and Pacific theaters toward the end of the conflict. But it remained for the United States Marine Corps to take the lead in working out combat techniques and procedures after organizing an experimental squadron, HMX–1, at Quantico in 1947.

Seven pilots, 30 enlisted men and 4 HO3S–1 Sikorsky 2-place helicopters were detached from HMX–1 on 8 July 1950 for service with the Brigade. Upon arrival at El Toro, these elements were combined with 8 fixed-wing aircraft pilots, 33 enlisted men and 8 OY planes to form the Brigade's air observation squadron, VMO–6.

This is an example of how units were assembled at Pendleton and El Toro. Major Vincent J. Gottschalk, appointed commanding officer of VMO–6 on 3 July, had orders to ready his squadron for shipment overseas by the 11th. Thus he had just 48 hours, after the arrival of the Quantico contingent, in which to weld the elements of his outfit together. Among his other problems, Gottschalk had to grapple with the fact that there were not enough OY's in good condition at El Toro. He found a solution by taking eight of these light observation planes overseas with a view to cannibalizing four of them for parts when the need arose.[19]

There was not enough time in most instances for weapons familiarization training. Company A of the 1st Tank Battalion had been accustomed to the M4A3 Medium tank with either the 75-mm. gun or the 105-mm. howitzer. Activated on 7 July for service with the Brigade, the unit was equipped with M–26 "Pershing" tanks and 90-mm. guns. Captain Gearl M. English, the commanding officer, managed to snatch 1 day

---

[19] Lynn Montross, *Cavalry of the Sky* (New York: Harper, 1954), Chapter VII. This book is devoted entirely to the operations of the U. S. Marine helicopter units organized from 1947 to 1953 for service both in the United States and overseas.

in which to take his men to the range with 2 of the new machines. Each gunner and loader was limited to 2 rounds, and the 90-mm. guns were never fired again until they were taken into combat in Korea.[20]

Support battalions were cut down to company size, generally speaking, for service with the Brigade. Thus Company A of the 1st Motor Transport Battalion numbered 6 officers and 107 men; and Company A of the 1st Engineer Battalion (reinf.) totaled 8 officers and 209 men.

The largest unit of the ground forces, of course, was the 5th Marines with 113 officers and 2,068 men commanded by Lieutenant Colonel Raymond L. Murray. Next came the 1st Battalion (reinf.) of the 11th Marines, numbering 37 officers and 455 men under the command of Lieutenant Colonel Ransom H. Wood.

Altogether, according to a report of 9 July 1950, the Brigade ground forces reached a total of 266 officers and 4,503 men.[21]

On this same date, the Brigade's air component amounted to 192 officers and 1,358 men. The principal units were as follows:

VMF-214	29 officers, 157 men, 24 F4U4B aircraft.
VMF-323	29 officers, 157 men, 24 F4U4B aircraft.
VMF(N)-513	15 officers, 98 men, 12 F4U5N aircraft.
VMO-6	15 officers, 63 men, 8 OY and 4 HO3S-1 aircraft.[22]

Adding the ground force and air figures gives a grand total of 6,319—458 officers and 5,861 men—on 9 July 1950. Before sailing, however, the activation of third rifle platoons and the last-minute attachment of supporting troops brought the strength of the Brigade and its air components up to 6,534.

Most of the equipment came from the great Marine supply depot at Barstow in the California desert. Here were acres of "mothballed" trucks, jeeps, DUKW's and amphibian tractors dating back to World War II. It has been aptly remarked, in fact, that "there were more veterans of Iwo and Okinawa among the vehicles than there were among the men who would drive them." [23]

Rail and highway facilities were taxed to the limit by the endless caravan of equipment moving from Barstow to Pendleton and El Toro

---

[20] 1st Tank Bn Special Action Report (SAR), 7 Jul–29 Aug 50, in 1st Provisional Marine Brigade (Brig) SAR, 2 Aug–6 Sep 50.

[21] CinCPacFlt disp to CINCFE, 9 Jul 50.

[22] *Ibid.*

[23] Andrew Geer, *The New Breed* (New York: Harper, 1952), 2–7. This book about U. S. Marine operations of 1950 in Korea contains an excellent account of the mounting out of the Brigade from Camp Pendleton.

after being hastily reconditioned and tested. Not all the arms were of World War II vintage, however, and the Marines of the Brigade were among the first American troops to be issued the new 3.5″ rocket launcher.

Brigade Leadership

It appeared to be a scene of mad confusion at Pendleton as Marines arrived hourly by train, bus, and plane. But the situation was kept well in hand by General Craig, who had seen many other departures for battle during his 33 years in the Corps. Born in Connecticut and educated at the St. Johns Military Academy, Delafield, Wis., he was commissioned a Marine second lieutenant in 1917 at the age of 21. Throughout the next 3 decades he served with distinction both as a line and staff officer, and both as student and instructor at the Marine Corps Schools.

During World War II he was executive and later commanding officer of the 9th Marine Regiment, which he led in the landing at Empress Augusta Bay on Bougainville and the recapture of Guam in the Marianas. Awarded the Bronze Star and Navy Cross for gallantry in these operations, Craig became operations officer of the V Amphibious Corps in time to help plan the Iwo Jima operation. After the war he returned to Guam for 2 years in 1947 to command the 1st Provisional Marine Brigade, Fleet Marine Force, before becoming ADC to Major General Graves B. Erskine, CG 1st Marine Division, in 1949.

The white hair and slender, erect figure of the dynamic Brigade commander would soon become a familiar sight to every platoon leader at the front. His assistant, General Cushman, was born in St. Louis, Mo. in 1895 and attended the University of Washington. Enlisting in the Marine Corps shortly after the outbreak of World War I, he completed flight training and was designated a naval aviator. Subsequent tours of aviation duty in Haiti, Nicaragua, and Guam were varied with assignments as instructor at Pensacola and administrative officer with BuAer in Washington. Cushman was a wing commander in World War II and was awarded a Bronze Star and Legion of Merit while serving in that capacity and later as chief of staff to the CG of Marine Aircraft Wings, Pacific. After the war he became commander of the Marine Corps Air Bases and CG of Aircraft, FMFPac.

Lieutenant Colonel Murray, CO of the 5th Marines, was born in Los Angeles in 1913. He graduated from Texas A. and M. College in 1935 and was commissioned a Marine second lieutenant. After prewar service in China and Iceland, he became a troop leader in three of the hardest-fought Marine operations of World War II—Guadalcanal, Tarawa, and Saipan. Awarded the Navy Cross, two Silver Stars, and the Purple Heart medal, Murray made a name for heroism that was noteworthy even in Marine circles.

This was no light achievement, for both CMC and CG FMFPac—General Cates and General Shepherd—had distinguished themselves as Marine combat leaders. Both were wounded in Marine operations of World War I, and both won later honors during Caribbean actions of the Marine Corps.

On 11 July, as Brigade preparations for sailing neared a climax, General Shepherd sent the first report of his visit to Korea. He and Colonel Krulak had held conferences with General MacArthur, Admiral Joy and Rear Admiral James H. Doyle, commanding Amphibious Planning Group 1. The commander in chief, said Shepherd, already envisioned a great amphibious operation with a complete Marine division and air components as his landing force. Not only was he "enthusiastic," about the employment of Marines, but he believed in the necessity for employing them as an air-ground team.[24]

MacArthur was "not sanguine" about the situation in Korea. He felt that the nature of enemy resistance, combined with the rugged terrain and the possibilities of Soviet or Red Chinese intervention, threatened to protract operations. Thus he favored a Marine amphibious landing far in the enemy's rear to cut off and destroy the North Korean columns of invasion.[25]

General Shepherd's report made it seem likely, just before the Brigade sailed, that its units would probably be absorbed soon into a Marine division with an amphibious mission. For the present, however, it was enough to start the movement from Pendleton and El Toro to San Diego, where the convoy awaited. MAG-33 had orders to embark in the transports *Anderson* and *Achernar* and the carrier (CVE-116) *Badoeng Strait.* The ground forces would make the voyage in the LSD's *Fort Marion* and *Gunston Hall,* the AKA's *Alshain* and *Whiteside,* and the APA's *Pickaway, Clymer* and *Henrico.*[26]

General Cates was on hand at the docks from 12 to 14 July when

---

[24] CG FMFPac memo for record, "Visit to Far East Command," 11 Jul 50.

[25] *Ibid.*

[26] For the Brigade's task organization in detail, with names of commanding officers and strength of units, see Appendix B.

305713 O-F-55——5

the Brigade sailed. His long cigarette holders were famous, and no second lieutenant in the Corps could throw a more military salute. As he eyed the ground forces filing past, the Commandant could only have felt that Marine traditions would be upheld. A good many of the PFC's, it is true, were too young to have seen action in World War II, though nearly all had been well grounded in fundamentals. Perhaps at the front they might become victims at first of their own over-anxiety. But they would doubtless grin sheepishly about it afterwards and become combat-hardened in a short time.

A glance at the NCO's, the platoon leaders and company commanders of the Brigade could only have brought a gleam of pride to the Commandant's battlewise eye. With few exceptions, they were veterans of World War II who could be relied upon to get the best out of their men. And it may be that the Commandant was reminded of the remark attributed to General William T. Sherman during the Civil War:

"We have good corporals and sergeants and some good lieutenants and captains, and those are far more important than good generals." [27]

Nobody could give a more smooth and eloquent talk than General Cates before a Washington audience. But when it came to saying farewell to the Brigade troops, he addressed them in the language of Marines.

"You boys clean this up in a couple of months," said the Commandant, "or I'll be over to see you!" [28]

---

[27] Quoted in Lynn Montross, *War Through the Ages* (New York: Harper, 1946), 609.
[28] Geer, *op. cit.*, 6.

CHAPTER IV

The Advance Party

Conference With CINCFE—The Washington Scene—The Advance Party in Japan—Voyage of the Brigade—The Advance Party in Korea—Crisis of the Eighth Army

As the ships of the Brigade vanished over the horizon, Generals Craig and Cushman rushed to complete final administrative details at their respective West Coast bases. Then, in the early morning of 16 July, the advance party, consisting of the two commanders and parts of their staffs, boarded a transport plane at the Marine Corps Air Station, El Toro, and began the long journey westward.

The first stop was Pearl Harbor, T. H., island "Pentagon" of America's vast defensive network in the Pacific. On arrival, Craig and Cushman immediately reported to General Shepherd. In company with him, the two visitors called briefly on Admiral Radford. Later, Shepherd, his staff, and the advance party met at Fleet Marine Force Headquarters for a conference on the problems incident to the Marine commitment in combat.[1]

The Brigade commander painted a vivid picture of his provisional fighting force, stressing both its potential and its handicaps. He repeatedly emphasized the necessity for the addition of a third rifle company to each infantry battalion. With equal fervor he spoke of the need for two more 105-mm. howitzers in each battery of his artillery battalion. He told how the Brigade had been forced to leave behind much of its motor transport because of limited shipping space, and he requested that replacement vehicles be provided as soon as possible.

His presentation was not falling on deaf ears; for combat-wise officers knew only too well how such shortages would restrict the maneuverability, firepower, and mobility of the Brigade. Finally, Craig repeated his

---

[1] LtGen E. A. Craig ltr to authors, 25 Jan 54 (Craig, 25 Jan 54).

earlier request that steps be taken immediately to provide for monthly replacement drafts of 800 men. If the peace-strength Marine unit were committed to combat in the near future, he said, it could ill afford to watch its already thin ranks dwindle indefinitely.[2]

Leaving behind a maze of support and reinforcement problems for FMFPac Headquarters, the Brigade advance party boarded its plane and set out for Japan. On 19 July the big aircraft discharged its passengers at the Haneda Airport, near Tokyo. General Craig immediately reported to his naval superior, Admiral Joy. Later the Brigade commander, General Cushman, and the other officers of the advance party, assembled at General Headquarters, Far East, where they would get their first glimpse of the war through the eyes of the United States Army.

They conferred first with Major General Edward A. Almond, USA, and Brigadier General Edwin K. Wright, USA. The former was Chief of Staff to General MacArthur, while the latter served as G-3 on the staff. After Almond and Wright had received a report on the organization and capabilities of the Brigade air-ground team, they ushered the two Marine generals into the office of MacArthur.[3]

Conference With CINCFE

The commander in chief greeted his visitors cordially and expressed his pleasure at having Marines in his command again. He commented briefly on the excellence of the 1st Marine Division and certain Marine air units which had served under him during World War II. The general smiled as he mentioned a rumor to the effect that he had been prejudiced against Marines during the Pacific War. Sweeping aside this tale as being unfounded, he said that he had always held the greatest admiration for the Corps and would welcome its units to his command any time.[4]

Following this reception, MacArthur meticulously briefed Craig and Cushman on the critical situation in Korea, where the war was already entering its fourth week. The commander in chief disclosed his tentative plans for commitment of the Marines: he would hold the Brigade in Japan as a force in readiness until an entire Marine division could be assembled. If he could have this division by September, he intended to launch an amphibious assault against the port of Inchon on the west

[2] Col J. L. Stewart interv with authors, 15 Jan 54 (Stewart, 15 Jan 54).
[3] *Ibid.;* and Col K. H. Weir ltr to CMC, 16 Apr 54 (Weir, 16 Apr 54).
[4] Craig, 25 Jan 54.

coast. Striking deep in the Communist rear, he would sever the long lines of communications linking North Korean bases to the Communist invaders at the front. Thus isolated, the latter would quickly wither, and Walker's Eighth Army could smash out of the Pusan Perimeter.[5]

When MacArthur concluded, he and Craig discussed the organization of the Brigade. The Marine general emphasized that his command was an air-ground team; and though few in numbers, the Brigade had a powerful potential if its air arm remained integral. MacArthur assured him that the Marine combination would remain intact, unless some emergency dictated otherwise.

Craig next mentioned that the infantry and artillery units of the Brigade were at peace strength. MacArthur was surprised to learn that each battalion had just 2 rifle companies, and each battery only 4 guns instead of 6. He was even more surprised to find that each of the 6 infantry companies had 50 men less than the number called for in Marine war tables. The Army leader had been aware of certain shortages when he sent a message to the Pentagon on 10 July, requesting the Joint Chiefs of Staff to authorize expansion of the Brigade to a full war-strength division.[6] He believed at the time, however, that the Brigade itself would be formed on a wartime basis. Now, confronted with reality, he ordered his chief of staff to prepare another dispatch to the Joint Chiefs, asking that the Brigade be expanded to full war strength and reiterating his request for an entire division.[7]

MacArthur concluded the conference by informing Craig that the Marine fighting team would remain in Japan under operational control of Joy's headquarters. This was good news to the Brigade commander. Being attached to the Naval command meant that his Marines would be free to train and otherwise prepare for their future amphibious mission; whereas an assignment to the Eighth Army's rear echelon might have entailed time-consuming occupational and administrative duties.[8]

The Washington Scene

Although the solution to Marine Corps problems had seemed simple enough in MacArthur's office, it was quite another story on the other

[5] *Ibid.;* and Brig SAR, 2 Aug–6 Sep 50, basic rpt.
[6] CINCFE disp to JCS, 10 Jul 50.
[7] CINCFE disp to JCS, 19 Jul 50.
[8] Brig SAR, *loc. cit.*

side of the world in Washington. The Joint Chiefs of Staff had rendered no decision on the general's 10 July request for a Marine division. Nevertheless, General Cates ordered his staff to draw up detailed plans for expansion so that immediate action could be taken if authorization were forthcoming. As a result, Plans Able and Baker were prepared, the one designed to augment the Brigade to war strength, the other to explore the requirements for creating a full division. To cover these possibilities together with the Corps' other irrevocable commitments throughout the world, Marine planners were drawn more and more toward a single basic conclusion—if President Truman and the Joint Chiefs of Staff granted MacArthur's request, the Marine Corps Reserve would have to be mobilized at once.

When the Joint Chiefs received the message which MacArthur had dictated in General Craig's presence, they requested an estimate from the Marine Corps on how long it would take to form a war-strength division. General Cates summed up his case: the Marine Corps, numbering only 74,279 officers and men,[9] was committed on a global basis. There was a brigade on its way to Korea, a peace-strength division on the Atlantic Coast,[10] and a battalion landing team permanently assigned to the Mediterranean Fleet. There were detachments of Marines assigned for domestic security, shipboard duty, and overseas security. Moreover, in order to carry out any expansion program on a sound basis, it would be necessary to maintain cadres of experienced personnel in various training centers. The Commandant's presentation made it clear that any immediate expansion would, as proved by simple arithmetic, be dependent upon mobilization of the Reserve.

Accordingly, the Joint Chiefs of Staff recommended to President Truman that the Organized Marine Corps Reserve be called to active duty. That same morning, 19 July, Admiral Sherman notified General Cates of this decision. The Commandant lost no time at ordering his staff to alert all Reserve units. His grounds for haste were well founded; for in the afternoon a presidential proclamation announced that the "citizen-Marines" would be mobilized. The following day Cates called CNO and submitted Plans Able and Baker, the proposed procedures for building both the Brigade and 1st Marine Division to war strength.

In the meantime JCS had notified MacArthur that his request could not be granted until late fall "without unacceptable weakening [of] the

---

[9] Figure as of 30 Jun 1950.

[10] The 2d Marine Division, Camp Lejeune, N. C.

Fleet Marine Force Atlantic." [11] When the U. N. commander received this message, he countered immediately with the reply:

". . . Most urgently request reconsideration of decision with reference to First Marine Division. It is an absolutely vital development to accomplish a decisive stroke and if not made available will necessitate a much more costly and longer operational effort both in blood and expense.

"It is essential the Marine Division arrive by 10 September 1950 as requested. While it would be unwise for me to attempt in this message to give in detail the planned use of this unit I cannot emphasize too strongly my belief of the complete urgency of my request. There can be no demand for its potential use elsewhere that can equal the urgency of the immediate battle mission contemplated for it.[12]

"Signed MacArthur"

On 22 July the gears of mobilization were already enmeshed. Taking this into account along with the urgency of MacArthur's last communication, the Joint Chiefs showed the first signs of relenting in their reply to Tokyo. This time they informed the Army general that they were reconsidering his problem, but added that he must advise them of the proposed employment of the Brigade up to 10 September and the possibility of adjusting that deadline. The same message carried the encouraging news that a directive had already been issued to bring both the Brigade and its air group to full war strength.[13]

In answer, MacArthur stated his intention to retain the Brigade in Japan, unless a more critical situation developed in Korea prior to 10 September. He described his operation planned for mid-September as an amphibious landing in the rear of the enemy's lines. This seaborne attack, he added, would be designed to envelop and destroy the Communist invader in conjunction with an offensive from the south by the Eighth Army. The General concluded his message on notes of conditional optimism and grave warning:

"Although exact date of D-day is partially dependent upon enemy reaction during month of August, I am convinced that an early and strong effort behind his front will sever his main lines of communications and enable us to deliver a decisive and crushing blow. Any material delay in such an operation may lose this opportunity. The alternative is a frontal attack which can only result in a protracted and expensive campaign to slowly drive the enemy north of the 38th parallel." [14]

On 25 July these exchanges came to a climax when the Pentagon

---

[11] JCS disp to CINCFE, 20 Jul 50.
[12] CINCFE disp to JCS, 21 Jul 50.
[13] JCS msg 86778 to CINCFE, 22 Jul 50.
[14] CINCFE msg C-58473 to JCS, 23 Jul 50.

directed the Marine Corps to build its 1st Division to full war strength.

At this point the change of heart among the Joint Chiefs of Staff is pertinent because of its direct effects on the 1st Provisional Marine Brigade. As previously noted, the Pentagon on 22 July approved the Marine Corps' plan Able which provided for the expansion of the Brigade to war strength. General Cates immediately set machinery in motion to bolster the ranks of that unit. With the approval of Admiral Sherman, he cut into the rosters of Marine security detachments throughout the United States and arranged for the personnel thus released to be channelled to Craig's command. It was also possible now to implement an earlier plan relating to casualty replacements for the Brigade. As far back as 14 July, the Commandant had ordered activation of the First Replacement Draft, fixing its departure for Korea at 10 August.[15] Thus Craig could be assured of early reinforcement by more than 800 officers and men if the course of the war necessitated a premature commitment of his Brigade.

The Advance Party in Japan

Generals Craig and Cushman were meanwhile assigned a large office in General Headquarters, Tokyo. There they cleared away much administrative detail which accumulates in the path of every military operation.

On 20 July the two commanders called on General Stratemeyer. Marine Air was the focal point of discussion as they again explained the organization of their fighting team. When they informed Stratemeyer of MacArthur's decision to keep the Brigade intact, the air officer gave them further assurance that MAG-33 would always be available to support the Marine ground force.[16]

Originally, the Army planned to base the Marine ground elements at Sasebo, Japan, and the air group 400 miles away at Itami Field, near Kobe. Craig and Cushman realized that the resulting large gap would give rise to problems in liaison, training, and supply. Hoping to change such an undesirable arrangement, the Brigade staff carefully studied the layout of available land and facilities. Armed with the results of this research, Craig proposed to General Headquarters that all Marines be based in the Kobe-Osaka-Kyoto area. After he outlined the advantages of keeping the Brigade and its supporting aviation close together,

[15] CMC disp to FMFPac, 22 Jul 50.
[16] Craig, 25 Jan 54.

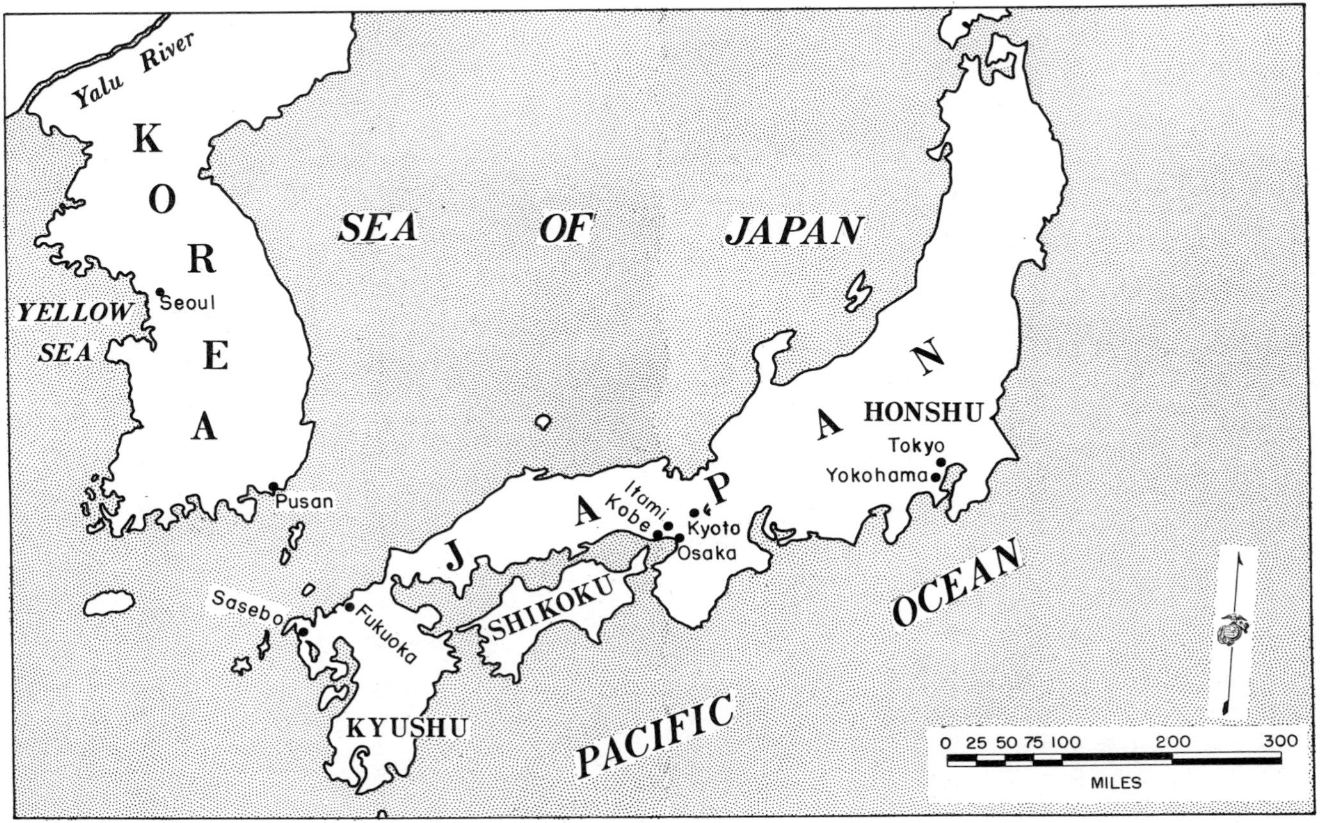

Yalu River
KOREA
Seoul
YELLOW SEA
Pusan
SEA OF JAPAN
JAPAN
HONSHU
Tokyo
Yokohama
Itami
Kobe
Kyoto
Osaka
SHIKOKU
Sasebo
Fukuoka
KYUSHU
PACIFIC OCEAN
0 25 50 75 100 200 300
MILES

Wright responded encouragingly to the recommendation.[17]

Confident that the suggestion would be favorably considered, the advance party flew to Itami on 21 July and made a detailed reconnaissance of debarkation, billeting, and training sites. While Craig inspected the area and prepared a report, Cushman examined the air base facilities and established his headquarters according to the initial plan. The Marine officers then returned to Tokyo 2 days later to push the request for getting both air and ground forces located in the same area. To support his proposal, Craig submitted a complete "floor plan" not only for the Brigade but also for the entire 1st Marine Division. MacArthur's staff promptly approved.[18]

On the 25th the advance party again set out for Itami, this time to prepare for the arrival of the Brigade. Their plane was a scant 20 minutes out of Tokyo when an urgent message from General Headquarters directed their return to that city at once. The big aircraft roared back to the field, and a few minutes later the Marines were driving through the Japanese capital.

At headquarters, Wright summed up the most recent reports from the front. The American forward wall was crumbling under continuous hammering. A wide envelopment had just netted the whole southwestern tip of the peninsula for the Communists, who were now pressing in on Pusan from the west as well as north. Lacking sufficient troops to defend its broad frontage, the Eighth Army was falling back. If the Red tide continued unabated, there was imminent danger of losing Pusan, the one remaining major port in American hands. Should this coastal city fall, South Korea would be lost.

Wright told Craig that all available troops had to be thrown into the line to meet this threat. Therefore, General MacArthur had diverted the seaborne Brigade from Japan to Korea, where it would join General Walker's beleaguered forces.[19]

Obviously, the Marines were not far from a fight.

Voyage of the Brigade

At sea the 1st Provisional Marine Brigade was unaware of the decisions and difficulties developing on higher levels. Nevertheless, that tactical

---

[17] *Ibid.*

[18] *Ibid.;* LtGen E. A. Craig ltr to authors, 15 Apr 54 (Craig, 15 Apr 54); Weir, 16 Apr 54; and Brig SAR, *loc. cit.*

[19] Stewart, 15 Jan 54; and Brig SAR, *loc. cit.*

organization was having enough trouble of its own. On 12 July, Company A, 1st Tank Battalion, and the 1st Amphibious Tractor Company departed San Diego on board the LSD's *Fort Marion* and *Gunston Hall.* Designated Task Unit 53.7.3, the twin amphibious ships sailed 2 days before the rest of the Brigade and were scheduled to join the main convoy, Task Group 53.7, before crossing 160° east longitude.[20]

At noon on 13 July, the well deck of the *Fort Marion* accidentally flooded, the water rising to a height of 5 feet among the Brigade's M-26 tanks. An hour passed before the ship's pumps could drain the compartment, and briny water damaged 14 of the new armored vehicles, 300 90-mm. projectiles (then in critical supply), and 5,000 rounds of .30-caliber ammunition.

When news of the flood damage reached Brigade headquarters, then still at San Diego, the message was rushed to Craig. He immediately sent a dispatch to Captain English, authorizing him to jettison the ruined ammunition. He added that replacement armor would be requisitioned from the Barstow depot without delay. Craig then contacted the supply base and was promised that 14 M-26's would be commissioned and on their way to San Diego within 24 hours. The Brigade commander was preparing to request additional shipping for the vehicles when messages from the *Fort Marion* reported that 12 tanks could be restored to operating condition at sea. The remaining two would require new parts and 72 hours of repair work upon debarkation.[21]

As already noted, the Marines were placing heavy reliance on their armor, confident that it was a match for the enemy's Russian-built T-34 tank in Korea. Consequently, Craig's staff reacted to the flood reports with concern. Headquarters FMFPac was asked to include four M-26's in its first resupply shipment to the Brigade; arrangements were made for new parts to be flown to the port of debarkation, and ammunition to replace that damaged in the flood was loaded on board the larger convoy.

Misfortune struck again a few hours after Task Group 53.7 steamed from San Diego on 14 July. The transport *Henrico* developed a serious mechanical failure and was declared temporarily unseaworthy. This ship was carrying Lieutenant Colonel Murray, his regimental staff, and the entire 1st Battalion Landing Team.[22] After Murray and his headquarters transferred to the APA *Pickaway* off San Clemente Island, the *Henrico* limped back toward California with about one-third of the Brigade's

[20] Brig SAR, *loc. cit.*

[21] *Ibid.;* and Craig, 15 Apr 54.

[22] 1st Bn, 5th Marines, with supporting units.

fighting force. The vessel docked at the United States Naval Supply Depot, Oakland, on the 16th. Repairs were started in urgent haste, since there was no other ship available. For security reasons, the Marines were forbidden to leave ship except for training on the dock. On the nights of the 16th and 17th, they sat on deck and gazed longingly at the beckoning lights of San Francisco. Twice during this time the *Henrico* weighed anchor and passed westward under the Golden Gate bridge; twice it was forced to return for additional repairs. Finally, on the evening of the 18th, the vessel steamed under the great bridge for its third attempt. This time it kept going, but it would not overtake the convoy until the morning of the very day the ships reached their destination.

During the voyage, strict wartime security measures, including radio silence, were enforced on all ships. While the North Koreans were believed to have no warships left afloat, their naval capabilities remained hidden from the outside world by a blur of question marks. No one realized more than the commander of Task Group 53.7 [23] that it was much too early to take Soviet Russia for granted.

The *Henrico,* now travelling independently, had a spine-chilling experience during her second night out of Oakland. The ship's radar picked up two "unidentified submarines" which appeared to be converging on the stern of the lone vessel. General Quarters was sounded. While sailors peered into the darkness from their battle stations, several hundred Marines joked weakly in the troop compartments below the waterline. After an anxious hour, the persistent spots on the electronic screen vanished.

Shipboard life for the Brigade was otherwise uneventful. The troops took part in physical drills as vigorously as the limited confines of vessels would allow. Daily classes and conferences emphasized those subjects most relevant to the news reports trickling back from the front. Success of North Korean armor stimulated keen interest in land mines and the new rocket launchers. Press commentaries on the battleground's primitive environment made even field sanitation a serious matter. Since there was no military intelligence available on the North Korean forces, officers and NCO's turned to publications on Russian tactics and weapons.

As previously noted, Sasebo, Japan, was the original destination of the ships transporting the Brigade's ground elements. The *Achernar, Anderson,* and *Badoeng Strait* were bound for Kobe with MAG-33. When Craig's proposal for consolidation was approved by General Headquar-

---

[23] Capt L. D. Sharp, Jr., USN.

ters, the entire convoy was ordered to Kobe. Then, on 25 July, Colonel Edward W. Snedeker, Chief of Staff, received the dispatch sending the ground force directly to Pusan.

.This announcement came as no surprise to the majority of officers and men. Day by day, news reports had been outlining the course of the war. The shrinking perimeter of Walker's army was traced on maps and sketches throughout every ship. After the Communist "end run" in southwest Korea, Marines began to wonder if there would be any front at all by the time they arrived. In the captain's mess of the *Pickaway,* senior Marine and naval officers were giving odds that the Brigade would reach the South Korean port only in time to cover a general evacuation of the peninsula.[24]

The Advance Party in Korea

With the Brigade well beyond the halfway point in its Pacific voyage, Craig and his staff could not afford to waste a minute. At 1700 on 25 July they left Tokyo by plane for Korea. En route they landed at Itami, where the Brigade commander and Cushman made hurried adjustments to meet the new situation.[25]

Leaving Itami on the 26th, they flew to Fukuoka, Japan. There they transferred from their 4-engine Marine aircraft to a smaller Air Force plane which could be accommodated on the primitive landing fields of Korea. On the last lap of their journey, they reached Taegu at 1400.

Taegu was a dismal place during this crucial phase of the UN delaying action. Hastily chosen as a headquarters by General Walker, the ancient town gave the appearance of a remote outpost. Its airstrip was crude. The fewness of the airmen and soldiers among the handful of transport and fighter planes served only to emphasize the critical situation of the UN forces.[26]

General Craig reported to General Walker immediately, while the Brigade G-3, Lieutenant Colonel Joseph L. Stewart, met with his Eighth Army opposite, Colonel William E. Bartlett. Later, Walker's chief of staff, Colonel Eugene M. Landrum, assembled all the Marine officers for an official briefing. He explained that the Brigade had not been earmarked for any specific mission. The battle situation was too fluid for

---

[24] Col R. L. Murray interv with author, 15 Feb 54 (Murray, 15 Feb 54).
[25] Craig, 25 Jan 54.
[26] Stewart, 15 Jan 54.

firm plans. Information from the field was sketchy and unreliable, as outnumbered Army forces slowly retreated. From the time of first contact by American units, the front had been more of a blur than a distinct line. Landrum concluded by saying that the Brigade must be prepared to move anywhere after debarkation—and on a moment's notice.[27]

After he and his officers had been assigned rooms in a temporary barracks, Craig requested permission to reconnoiter the combat zone.[28] Walker assented, providing his own plane and pilot for the trip. Accompanied by Stewart and Lieutenant Colonel Arthur A. Chidester, his G-4, Craig flew first to Pusan, where he checked harbor facilities, roads, and railways. There he conferred with Brigadier General Crump Garvin, USA, to initiate preparations for the Brigade's arrival.[29]

Leaving Pusan, the Marine officers flew over Chinhae, which they discovered to be a suitable base, if necessary, for VMO-6 and the Brigade's air support control unit. Cruising westward, they passed over Masan, then continued toward Chinju. From the latter vicinity, the enemy's envelopment was then threatening the western approaches to Pusan. Veering northward, the reconnaissance party paralleled the Naktong River. The pilot, who was familiar with the ground, briefed his passengers along the way. By the time the plane returned to Taegu, the Marines had a broad picture of the critical areas most likely to become Brigade battlefields.[30]

General Craig and his ground officers remained at Taegu 4 days. Attending daily briefings of the Eighth Army staff, they acquired a sound knowledge of the tactical situation. At a conference with Major General Earle E. Partridge and his Fifth Air Force staff,[31] the Marines were brought up to date on the disposition of aviation and its policy for supporting UN ground forces.[32]

In the fight for time, ground force units in line were frequently withdrawn and shuttled to plug gaps in the sagging front. Reports from the battlefield more often were food for the imagination rather than fact for the planning room. All of this created confusion among Eighth Army staff officers.[33]

---

27 *Ibid.*

28 The *combat zone* comprises that part of the theater of operations required for the conduct of war by field forces. In this case it included all of Korea remaining in UN hands.

29 Craig, 25 Jan 54.

30 *Ibid.*

31 Hq 5th AF was also locatd at Taegu.

32 Craig, 15 Apr 54.

33 *Ibid.;* and Stewart, 15 Jan 54.

In the Taejon area the 24th Infantry Division had lost 770 officers and men during the single week of 15–22 July. Of these casualties, 61 were known dead, 203 wounded, and 506 missing in action.[34] Among the missing was General Dean, and the wounded included a regimental commanding officer, a regimental executive officer, and a battalion commander.[35]

Following this ordeal, the 24th had been relieved by the recently arrived 1st Cavalry Division, which went into line alongside the 25th Division in the Kumchon area. ROK divisions held to the north and east, where NKPA forces were driving toward Pohang-dong.

The shape of strategic things to come was indicated late in July when two NKPA divisions completed a much publicized "end run" past the open UN left flank to the southwest tip of the peninsula, then wheeled eastward for a drive on Pusan.

General Walker reacted promptly to the danger by recalling the 24th Division from Eighth Army reserve and moving it southward from Kumchon to block the enemy near Hadong. With the recently landed 29th Infantry attached, the division totalled only 13,351 officers and men.[36] Its front extended from the southern coast near Hadong to the town of Kochang, 40 miles north.[37] In addition to manning this mountainous line, the 24th had troops in action at Pohang-dong, more than 100 miles away on the east coast. There some of its units fought as Task Force Perry, under direct control of Eighth Army headquarters.[38]

The 24th Division and 29th Infantry had no more than deployed when they found themselves plunged into a confused 5-day fight. Although they sold ground as dearly as possible, the Army units were compelled to give up Hadong and fall back toward Chinju.[39]

As the threat to Pusan grew more serious, the Eighth Army commander shifted units. In order to protect the approaches from Chinju to Pusan, he pulled the 25th Infantry Division back across the river Naktong near Waegwan and moved it from the northern to the southern

---

[34] 24th InfDiv Periodic Personnel Rpt No. 2, 15–22 Jul 50.

[35] *Ibid.*

[36] *Ibid.*, No. 3, 29 Jul 50. Actually, as the report itself states, this figure is a meaningless statistic, and exceeds the *real* total by several hundred. It was the practice not to subtract missing-in-action casualties until 30 days after losses were reported. Also, casualty reports from far-flung subordinate units were received irregularly, and some of these undoubtedly were not available when this tally was made.

[37] 24th InfDiv Op Instr, 24–28 Jul 50.

[38] Hq EUSAK Op Dir, 29 Jul 50.

[39] 24th InfDiv Op Instr, 24–28 Jul 50.

front in 48 hours. The next day saw the 1st Cavalry withdrawing across the Naktong in the Waegwan area and blowing the bridges.

After being relieved in the south by the 25th Division, the 24th joined the 1st Cavalry withdrawal to hastily organized defensive positions east of the Naktong. ROK divisions continued to defend the northeast approaches, while the 25th Division stood guard to block any enemy move toward Chinju.[40]

At this juncture General Craig became increasingly concerned about prospects of maintaining the Brigade's integrity as a Marine air-ground team. He and his staff were aware that elements of the 29th Infantry had been rushed from their ships directly into combat in the Chinju area, and some units were badly mauled. Craig took occasion, therefore, to remind Army leaders once more of the Marine tactical concept of the indivisible air-ground team.[41]

MAG-33, said Craig, would have to unload its planes and prepare them for action; and the control squadron would need an interval to set up co-ordinated tactical air support.[42]

Crisis of Eighth Army

As July drew to an end, the situation both on the northern and southwestern fronts was developing into a crisis. Hourly it grew apparent that the Eighth Army's perimeter would have to shrink even more, so that defenses could assume some depth in sensitive areas. Landrum indicated for the first time that the Brigade was being considered primarily for a mission on the left flank.[43] Guided by this possibility, Craig and his staff officers devoted a day to drawing up a flexible operation plan. The purpose of this directive was to advise the Brigade's subordinate commanders of possible commitment in the Chinju, Kochang, or Kumchon areas, in that order of probability. Also included were detailed instructions for movement to forward assembly areas, broad missions for supporting units, security measures to be taken, and a general outline of the situation ashore.[44]

---

[40] Hq EUSAK Op Dir, 29 Jul 50.

[41] Stewart, 15 Jan 54.

[42] *Ibid.;* and Craig, 15 Apr 54.

[43] Craig, 25 Jan 54.

[44] Brig Op Plan No. 3-50, 31 Jul 50; Craig, 25 Jan 54. The "Kochan" and "Kumwan" referred to in the operations plan are actually Kochang and Kumchon. The odd assortment of maps available in the early days of the war offered a variety of spelling along with far more serious inaccuracies.

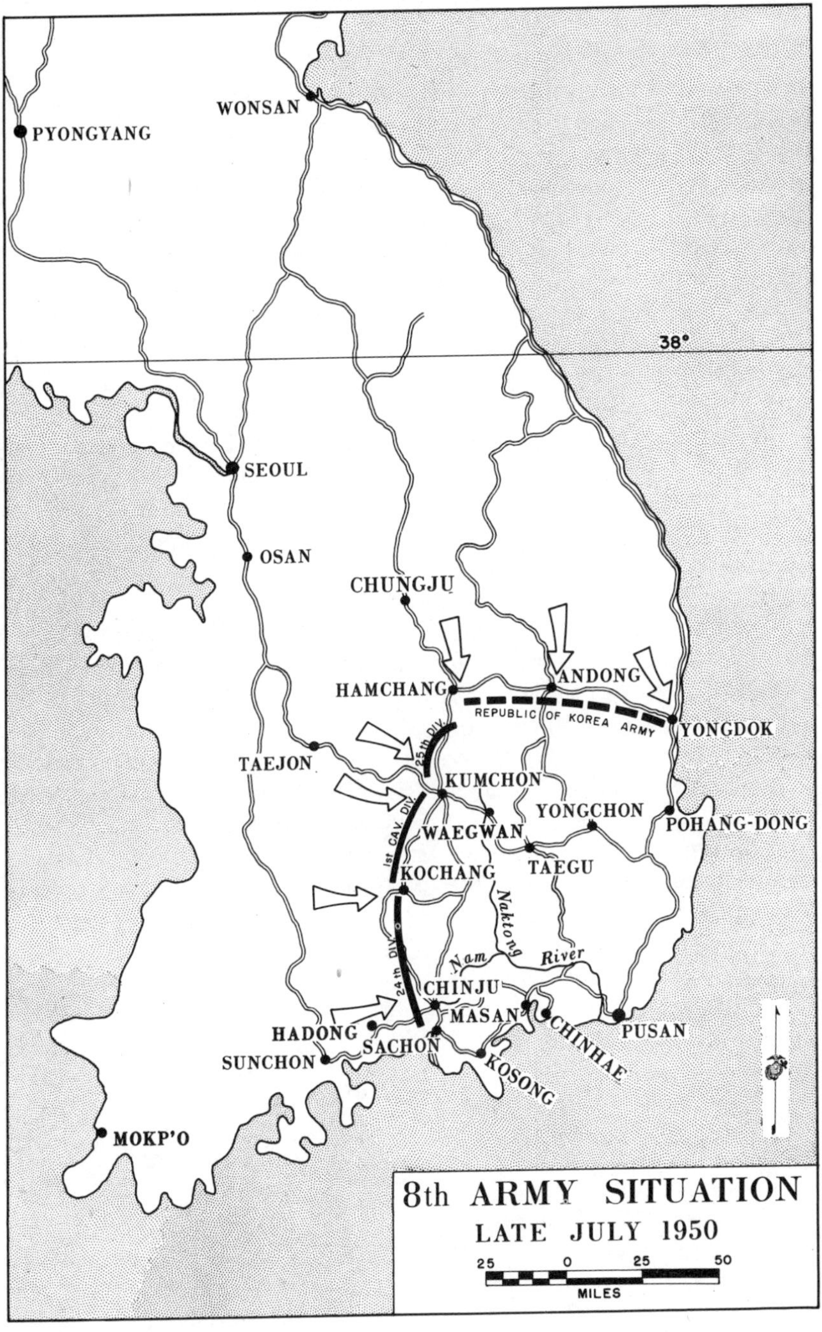
WONSAN
PYONGYANG
38°
SEOUL
OSAN
CHUNGJU
HAMCHANG
ANDONG
REPUBLIC OF KOREA ARMY
YONGDOK
25th DIV.
TAEJON
KUMCHON
1st CAV. DIV.
YONGCHON
POHANG-DONG
WAEGWAN
TAEGU
KOCHANG
Naktong
Nam
River
24th DIV.
CHINJU
MASAN
CHINHAE
PUSAN
HADONG
SACHON
SUNCHON
KOSONG
MOKP'O
8th ARMY SITUATION
LATE JULY 1950
25 0 25 50
MILES

The advance party extracted from the plan a fragmentary warning order suitable for radio transmission. This message was delivered to Eighth Army headquarters with a request that it be sent immediately to the Brigade at sea.[45] Now Craig assumed that Snedeker and Murray would have a reasonable impression of the situation awaiting them.[46]

At an Army briefing on the 29th, the Marines learned that the UN left flank was collapsing. An air of uneasiness pervaded Taegu, and Eighth Army headquarters began preparations for displacement to Pusan. Craig was told that the Brigade definitely would be committed in the southwest, unless a more critical situation suddenly sprang up elsewhere. Again the Army officers added that the Marine unit actually must be prepared to move in any direction on short notice.[47]

With the approval of the Eighth Army, the Brigade commander immediately sent a message to COMNAVFE requesting that the Marine air group be made available to support the ground force by 2 August, and that VMO-6 be transported to Korea as quickly as possible.[48] Time was drawing short.

On 30 July, General Craig had a final conference with Generals Walker and Partridge. This time, Walker himself told the Marine leader that the Brigade would be sent to the southwest; and that the unit, once committed, would be free to push forward without interference from Eighth Army.[49] Partridge interjected that his planes would be available to support Craig's ground troops if Marine air did not arrive in time.[50]

Immediately after the conference, the Marine officers set out for Pusan by jeep. While their vehicles bounced southward on the ancient road, army headquarters in Taegu was sinking to new depths of dejection. Chinju had just fallen, and the Red column was pounding on toward Masan.[51]

---

[45] Stewart, 15 Jan 54.
[46] *Ibid.*
[47] Craig, 25 Jan 54 and 17 Apr 54.
[48] *Ibid.*
[49] *Ibid.*
[50] *Ibid.*
[51] *Ibid.*

Commandant Says Farewell—General Clifton B. Cates visits San Diego for embarkation of 1st Provisional Marine Brigade (Marine Corps Photo).

All Aboard—Marines of the Brigade waiting to embark at San Diego for the Far East (Marine Corps Photo).

Mountains of Supplies—Hundreds of tons of equipment ready for loading aboard ships taking Marines to the Far East (Marine Corps Photo).

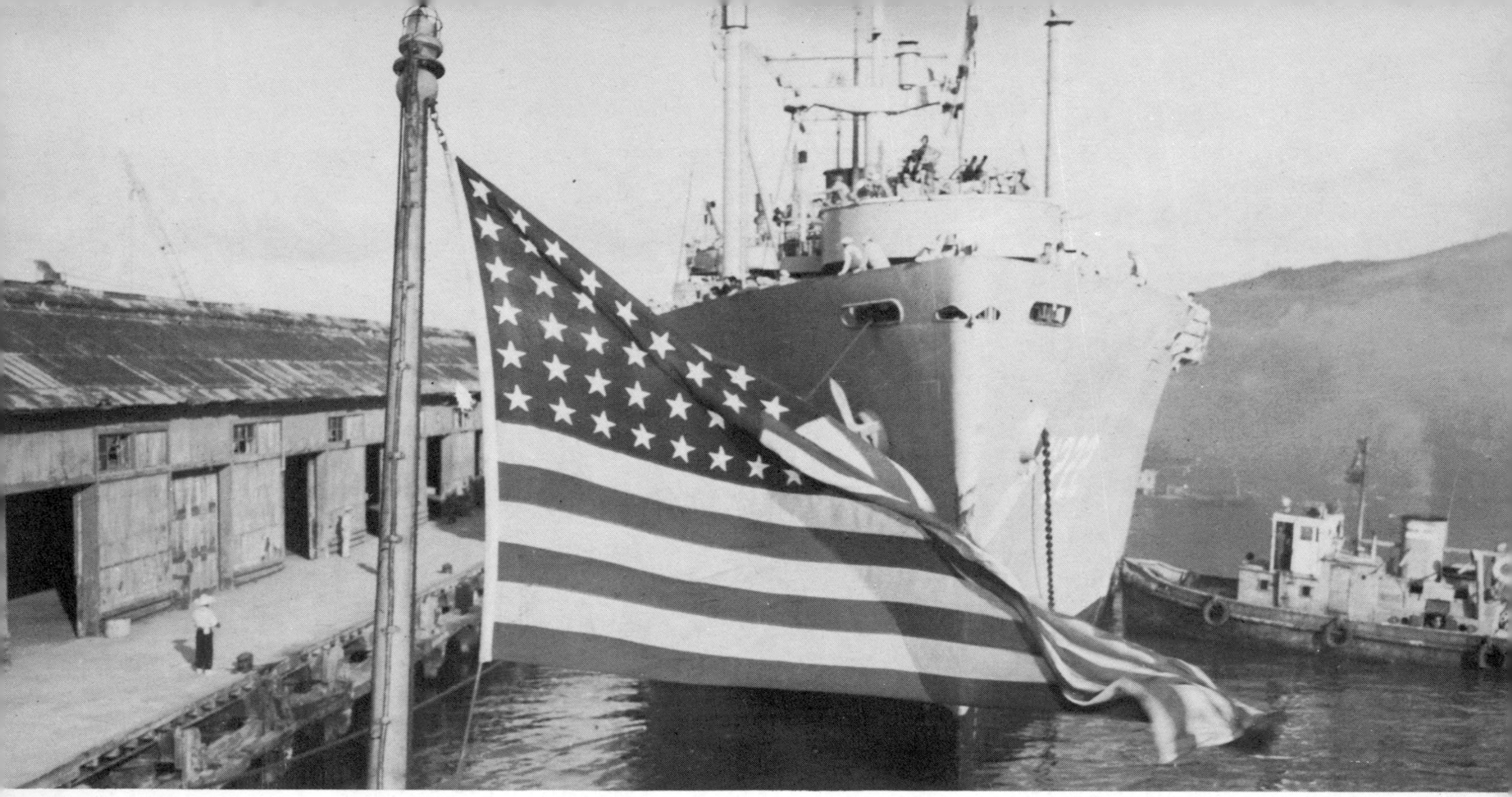

Arrival at Pusan—Marines catch their first glimpse of Korea as the U. S. S. Pickaway *docks (Marine Corps Photo).*

Movement to the Front—Brigade troops preparing to entrain at Pusan for the Changwan bivouac area (Marine Corps Photo).

Visit to the Front—Above, General of the Army Douglas MacArthur with Ambassador John J. Muccio and Major General Edward M. Almond, Chief of Staff, GHQ, FEC; and, below, with Lieutenant General Walton H. Walker, commanding the Eighth U. S. Army in Korea (U. S. Army Photo).

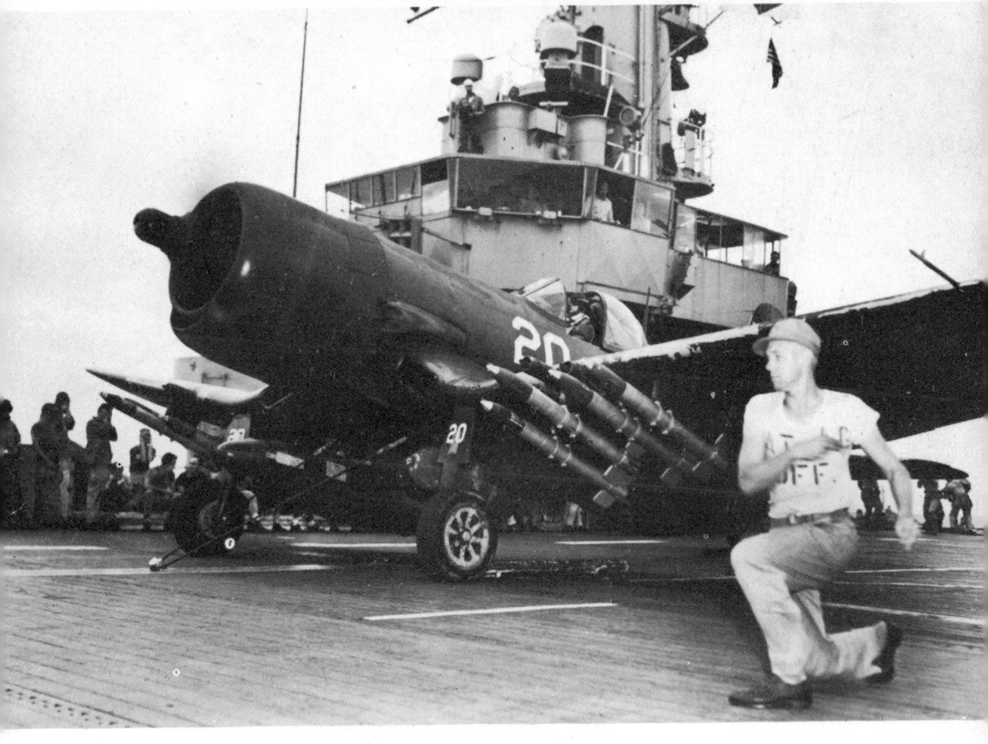

Marine Air Strikes First—Above, the U. S. S. Badoeng Strait *(CVE 116) nearing Japan with Corsairs on deck; and, below, an F4U armed with eight rockets and a 500-lb. bomb takes off from the U. S. S.* Sicily *(CVE 118) (U. S. Navy Photo).*

Korea the Vertical—Marines of the Brigade literally climb into battle during their first fights in the Chindong-ni area (Marine Corps Photo).

Marines in Action—Above, Brigade infantry and M–26 tank, advancing under fire, pass body of dead United States soldier on left; and, below, ambushed Marines are pinned down temporarily by enemy machinegun fire at Naktong Bulge (Marine Corps Photo).

At the Brigade CP- Lieutenant Colonel Joseph L. Stewart, Brigade G–3 and Brigadier General Edward A. Craig, with Colonel Edward W. Snedeker, Brigade chief-of-staff, in background (Life Magazine Photo).

Combat Leaders of 5th Marines—Front row, Lieutenant Colonel Raymond L. Murray, regimental commander, and Lieutenant Colonel L. C. Hays, Jr., Executive Officer; rear, Lieutenant Colonel H. R. Roise, CO 2d Battalion, Lieutenant Colonel G. R. Newton, CO 1st Battalion, and Lieutenant Colonel R. D. Taplett, CO 3d Battalion (Marine Corps Photo).

Marine Air in Action—Above, rocket-laden planes of VMF–214 warming up on the flight deck of the Sicily; *and, below, a Corsair takes off for the front in Korea (U. S. Navy Photo).*

Marine Mortar Crew—Supporting the infantry advance with 81-mm. shells are, left to right, Private First Class Jesse W. Haney, Jr., Bakersfield, Calif.; Private First Class Bennie M. John, Ardmore, Okla.; Private First Class Richard A. Robey, Houston, Tex.; and an unidentified Marine in background (Marine Corps Photo).

Introducing the Enemy—No prisoner of war appears at his best, but Marine veterans of the Brigade can attest that some of the tough well-trained NKPA soldiers put up a good fight in Pusan Perimeter operations (Marine Corps Photo).

Crest of the Ridge—Two Marine PFC's, Harold R. Bates (left) of Los Angeles, and Richard N. Martin, of Elk River, Minn., take a break after fighting their way to the top of a ridge in the Naktong Bulge (Marine Corps Photo).

The Flying Windmills—Above, Generals Craig (left) and Cushman waiting for the pilot to take them aloft in an HO3S–1 helicopter; and, below, a VMO–6 helicopter lands near the artillery positions of the 1st Battalion, 11th Marines (Marine Corps Photo).

CHAPTER V

Prelude to Battle

Reconnaissance by Jeep—Brigade Air Lands—Landing of Ground Force—Bedlam on Pusan Water Front—The Brigade at Changwon—The Pusan Perimeter—Brigade Air Strikes First—Planning the Sachon-Chinju Offensive

AFTER THE ADVANCE party reached Pusan, General Craig established a temporary command post in the headquarters building of General Garvin's Base Command. Then the Marine officers plunged into the final phase of planning and preparation for the Brigade, although they were still handicapped by the undisclosed secret of the convoy's arrival date. Staff gears were meshing smoothly by this time, with solutions being ground out for one problem after another.

On the night of 30 July, Lieutenant Colonel Stewart and other staff officers were discussing whether MAG-33 would be able to get its planes airborne in time to support the Brigade in its initial combat. Acting on a hunch, Stewart picked up a telephone in the slim hope of placing a call through to Japan. The long shot paid off. After some wrangling by startled operators, he managed to contact Itami Air Force Base and talk to Colonel Kenneth H. Weir, Cushman's chief of staff.

Stewart briefed the Marine aviator on the latest developments, emphasizing that the Brigade would undoubtedly get into the fight soon after arrival. He asked Weir to send the Air Support Section and helicopters to Korea by LST as quickly as possible after unloading in Japan.[1]

Craig received a radio message that same night from FMFPac, informing him that the replacements for the Brigade would not be sent directly to Pusan, as requested. They were to be assembled at Camp Pendleton for travel with the 1st Marine Division, and this meant a delay which could be critical. Craig immediately insisted that the reinforcements be

[1] Stewart, 15 Jan 54.

sent to Pusan to replace Brigade battle losses and form the third rifle companies.[2] The Marine leader's determination in this instance proved to be a blessing a few weeks later.

Reconnaissance by Jeep

On the morning of 31 July, Craig and Stewart set out by jeep to reconnoiter the rear areas of the crumbling southwestern sector. Kean's 25th Division, having just replaced the 24th in line, was now blocking the threatened western approaches to Pusan. Since all indications pointed to the Brigade's commitment in this area, Craig wanted to walk and ride over the terrain he had previously scouted from the air.[3]

He returned to Pusan just in time to receive a telephone call from Colonel Landrum of Eighth Army Headquarters. The chief of staff told him of General Walker's intention to attach the Army's 5th Regimental Combat Team, newly arrived from Hawaii, to the 1st Provisional Marine Brigade. With two regiments under his command, Craig would be assigned a vital area of responsibility along the Nam River, near its confluence with the Naktong north of Masan.[4] Unfortunately, the Brigade reached Korea 1 day too late. When the 5th RCT debarked at Pusan on 1 August, it was earmarked for the 25th Division and placed in Eighth Army reserve.[5]

Also debarking on the 1st was the Army's skeletonized 2d Division. This unit cleared Pusan and hurried to the hard-pressed Taegu area where it also passed into Eighth Army reserve.[6]

During the last hours before the Brigade's arrival, Lieutenant Colonel Chidester was diligently engaged in the task—or art—of procurement. It has already been explained why the Marine ground force would debark for combat with little more than what its troops could carry on their backs. In order to offset partially the deficiencies, the G-4 successfully negotiated with Army authorities for 50 cargo trucks, several jeeps, some radio vans, and various other items of equipment. Officers of the Pusan Base Command reacted to all of Chidester's requests with as much generosity as their meager stocks of materiel would allow.[7]

---

[2] Craig, 25 Jan 54.
[3] *Ibid.*
[4] *Ibid.*
[5] MCBS, II–A–7.
[6] Hq EUSAK Op Dir, 3 Jul 50.
[7] Craig, 25 Jan 54.

Not until the morning of 2 August did General Craig learn that Task Group 53.7 was scheduled to dock at Pusan that very evening. The last-minute disclosure relieved him of considerable anxiety, but he was still disturbed for want of specific orders concerning departure of the Brigade from Pusan. His instructions from General Walker were to debark the ground force immediately and have it prepared to move forward by 0600 the following morning. The same orders advised him that a specific destination "would be given later." [8]

"Later" did not come soon enough for the Marine commander. As the long column of ships steamed into Pusan Harbor in the early evening, he still did not know where he would lead his Brigade the next morning.[9]

Brigade Air Lands

When Task Group 53.7 entered Far Eastern waters, the ships transporting the forward echelon of the 1st Marine Aircraft Wing veered toward Japan, while the others continued to Korea. The Brigade's air arm arrived at Kobe late in the afternoon of 31 July.

Within three hours debarkation had been completed and unloading was in full swing. A waiting LST took on Marine Tactical Air Control Squadron Two and the ground personnel and equipment of VMO-6. By the next morning it was steaming toward Pusan, carrying the vital link in General Craig's air-ground team. Cushman and Weir were making good their promises.[10]

Since harbor facilities at Kobe were unsuitable for offloading aircraft, the *Badoeng Strait* stood out to sea on 1 August and catapulted 44 of its Marine fighter planes into the air. The aircraft sped to the field at Itami, where they were quickly checked by pilots and crews for their imminent role in combat. On the following day, the other 26 fighters left the carrier and joined the first group ashore for maintenance and testing.[11]

To achieve maximum mobility and striking power, Marine and Navy commanders agreed to base VMF's 214 and 323 aboard aircraft carriers for initial operations over Korea. After only 1 day of refresher flights at Itami, the pilots of VMF-214 landed their planes aboard the U. S. S.

---

[8] *Ibid.*

[9] *Ibid.*

[10] Annexes Charlie and Fox to MAG-33 SAR, 5 Jul–6 Sep 50.

[11] Annex Charlie, *ibid.*

Sicily. Two days later, on 5 August, Major Arnold Lund led his VMF-323 back to the *Badoeng Strait.*[12]

The squadron of night fighters, VMF(N)-513, was land-based. Having been assigned to the Fifth Air Force, it would be controlled by the Itazuke field for night heckler missions over Korea. This unit had time for only a few night training flights before being committed to combat.[13]

Kobe's waterfront was the scene of feverish activity around the clock. The light observation planes and helicopters of VMO-6 were unloaded, assembled, and—to the amazement of local Japanese—flown from the very streets of the city to the base at Itami. There they were hurriedly checked by mechanics and prepared for the short ferry flight to Korea.[14]

Headquarters and Service Squadrons of MAG-33 were left with the task of unloading supplies and equipment from the *Achernar* and *Anderson.* Since the three fighter squadrons were farmed out to the carriers and Air Force, Group headquarters turned its attention to administrative and maintenance matters. For the next month it would be hard-pressed to keep the carrier squadrons supplied with spare parts while providing replacement aircraft for the sea-borne units, handling a variety of airlift requests with its lone transport plane, and making arrangements for the support of VMF(N)-513 at Itazuke.[15]

Landing of Ground Force

The hapless *Henrico* finally overtook Task Group 53.7 in the Tsushima Straits on the morning of 2 August. A few hours later the Marines of the Brigade got their first glimpse of Korea's skyline. Seen from a distance, the wall of forbidding, gray peaks was hardly a welcome sight to men who had been broiled and toughened on the heights of Camp Pendleton.

For reasons unknown, neither Colonel Snedeker nor anyone else had received the operations plan which Craig had sent via Eighth Army at Taegu. Although every Marine in the convoy realized the gravity of the situation ashore, there could be no specific preparations by troop leaders whose only source of information was an occasional news broadcast.

Having heard nothing from his superiors, Lieutenant Colonel Murray was thinking in terms of a purely administrative landing. Had he known

[12] VMF-323 SAR, 3 Aug–6 Sep 50.
[13] Annex Charlie, *op. cit.*
[14] *Ibid.*
[15] *Ibid.*

what awaited his 5th Marines ashore, he would have had his troops draw ammunition and rations while still at sea. Throughout the sleepless night that followed, he had ample time to reflect sourly on the fortunes of war.[16]

Shortly after 1700 on 2 August, the first ship steamed into Pusan Harbor. As it edged toward the dock, Leathernecks crowding the rail were greeted by a tinny and slightly tone-deaf rendition of the Marine Corps Hymn, blared by a South Korean band. Army troops scattered along the waterfront exchanged the usual barbed courtesies with their webfooted brethren aboard ship, and old salts smiled while noting that tradition remained intact.

When the *Clymer* approached its berth, Craig waved a greeting to Snedeker and shouted, "What battalion is the advance guard?" [17]

The chief of staff registered an expression of astonishment.

"Did you get my orders?" Craig called to Murray when the *Pickaway* slid against the dock.

"No, sir!" [18] replied the CO of the 5th Marines.

Craig ordered a conference at 2100 for the Brigade staff, Murray, battalion commanders, and the leaders of supporting units. When the officers entered the wardroom of the *Clymer* at the specified time, the last ship of Task Group 53.7 was being moored in its berth.

After introductory remarks by the general, his G-2, Lieutenant Colonel Ellsworth G. Van Orman, launched the briefing with a grim narrative of the enemy situation. Next came Stewart, who outlined tentative operations plans. The Brigade would definitely begin moving forward at 0600 the next morning, although a specific destination had yet to be assigned by the Army. Travel would be by road and rail. The necessary trains were already awaiting in the Pusan terminal, and the 50 trucks procured by Chidester were standing by, complete with Army drivers.[19]

Craig then summed up his earlier discussions with Walker. The Army leader had voiced a strong desire to use the Marines in an attack, for he felt it was high time to strike back at the Red invader. Employment of the Brigade as an offensive force was a natural conclusion to its commander, and he told his subordinates how he had won assurances for the integrity of the air-ground team. This was an encouraging note on which to close one of the strangest combat briefings in the history

[16] Murray, 15 Feb 54.
[17] BrigGen E. W. Snedeker ltr to CMC, 21 Apr 54.
[18] Murray, 15 Feb 54.
[19] Stewart, 15 Jan 54.

of the Corps. The leaders of over 4,000 Marines rushed from the ship to alert their units for movement into a critical tactical situation. They would leave in a few hours, but didn't know where they were going.[20]

Bedlam on Pusan Waterfront

It is not surprising that the Pusan waterfront turned into a bedlam. As darkness settled, thousands of Marines poured onto the docks. Cranes and working parties unloaded vehicles, supplies and equipment, while a chorus of commands and comments was added to the roar of machinery. Supply points were set up under searchlights, and long lines of Marines formed on the docks, in buildings and along streets. Armfuls of C-rations, machinegun belts, grenades, and bandoleers gave men the appearance of harried Christmas shoppers caught in a last-minute rush.

The activity and din continued all night. Few men could sleep through the noise, crowding, and shuffling. Before dawn, new lines began to form in reverse as groggy Marines filed back aboard ships to get their last hot meal for many a day.

After the conference aboard the *Clymer,* Brigade headquarters resumed its efforts to obtain specific information from Taegu. Finally, at 2325, Landrum telephoned Craig and announced Walker's decision—the Brigade would go westward to the vicinity of Changwon, where it would remain for the time being in Eighth Army reserve. Only Walker himself could order any further move. If some extreme emergency arose and communications with Eighth Army were lost, the Brigade would then come under the control of the CG, 25th Infantry Division.[21]

The long-awaited message gave added impetus to the unloading operations. Major William L. Batchelor's shore party company devoted one of its principal efforts to the big howitzers and vehicles of 1/11, while English and his tankmen struggled to get their steel monsters ashore from the LSD's. Engineer heavy equipment, mobile maintenance shops of the Ordnance Detachment, fuel, ammunition, and medical supplies swung from decks to docks, where waiting Marines rushed them off to staging areas around the waterfront.

Altogether, 9,400 tons of supplies were unloaded, and the vast majority were turned over to Army quartermaster authorities in Pusan. Four officers and 100 men of Major Thomas J. O'Mahoney's Combat Service

---

[20] *Ibid.*

[21] Craig, 25 Jan 54.

Detachment were designated as the Brigade rear echelon. This group would remain in the port city to handle logistical and administrative matters. Supplies were moved into Army warehouses, where they became part of the common pool shared by all units at the front. This led to confusion later, when the Brigade requested its own Class II and IV items, only to discover that they had already been issued to other outfits. But the Army divisions had already been fighting for a month in a war which caught the nation unprepared, so that the Pusan Base Command had no alternative but to issue supplies on the basis of immediate need, not ownership.[22]

The Brigade was prepared to travel light. Not only the bulk of supplies but also all personal baggage was left behind in Pusan, to be stored and safeguarded by the rear echelon. When dawn broke on 3 August, each Marine carried only his pack, weapon, ammunition, and rations.[23]

The Brigade at Changwon

Despite the tumult of the sleepless night at Pusan, Lieutenant Colonel George R. Newton's 1st Battalion set out for Changwon shortly after 0600 on 3 August. As advance guard for the Brigade, it made the 40-mile trip in Marine and Army trucks, reaching a point 1 mile west of the town at 1400. There the battalion took up defensive positions astride the Changwon-Masan road in order to cover the arrival of the remainder of the Brigade.[24]

Although he had orders to bivouac at Changwon, General Craig decided to deploy the Brigade defensively to the west of the town. This decision was prompted by the enemy situation west of Masan, which was a scant 6½ miles from Changwon. Then, too, the Marine commander saw the layover as a final opportunity to check the field discipline of the Brigade.[25]

Between 0630 and 0700, the main body of the Marine ground force moved out of Pusan by road and rail. Vehicles over 2½ tons, all heavy equipment, and the M-26 tanks were transported on flatcars.

The roads were narrow and bumpy, and the churning wheels of the trucks threw up clouds of stifling dust that hung in the air and painted Marines and equipment a ghostly gray. Aboard the primitive trains,

---

[22] Brig SAR, basic rpt.
[23] Annex Queen, *ibid.*
[24] Annex How.
[25] Craig, 25 Jan 54.

which frequently jolted to stops for no apparent reason, men tried vainly to fit themselves to miniature wooden seats constructed in perfect right angles. And always, the troops inhaled that characteristic odor drifting in from well-fertilized rice paddies.

By 1600, all combat and support elements of the Brigade, with the exception of one tank platoon, had arrived in the Changwon area. Southwest of the city the 1st Battalion was relieved of its responsibility on the left side of the Changwon-Masan road, when 3/5 occupied the high ground in that area. Newton was then able to extend his right flank farther along the towering ridge north of the road.[26]

South of the MSR, a wide rice paddy stretched between 3/5's positions and the town. Almost in the center of this low ground was a hill commanding a good all-around view of the entire area. It was on this dominating height that Lieutenant Colonel Harold S. Roise deployed his 2d Battalion. Behind Roise, General Craig established his CP in a small basin among hills in the immediate vicinity of Changwon. Close-in protection for his headquarters was provided by the engineer company and various headquarters units. Throughout the interior of the bivouac area were tank platoons and the batteries of Lieutenant Colonel Wood's artillery battalion.

As night settled on 3 August, an army of phantoms invaded the Brigade perimeter and drove to the very fringe of Craig's CP. The reaction of green troops was typical of men new to combat. Shortly after 2200, a rifle shot cracked. Many Brigade Marines had never heard a weapon fired in combat, so they concluded that likely targets were present in the perimeter area. As nerve-taut men stared fixedly into the blackness, forms that had been harmless bushes and rocks took on the guise of Communist infiltrators.

The first shot was soon followed by others. Toward midnight, the firing developed into a continuous crackle, particularly in the immediate vicinity of the Brigade CP. Palpitating hearts pounded even more strenuously when two Marine machineguns began chattering in positions occupied by Brigade headquarters troops.

Anxiety also spread to the foxholes of the 5th Marines. In 2/5's area one man was shot. The 1st Battalion suffered 2 casualties, 1 resulting from mistaken identity during challenging, the other inflicted when a weapon discharged accidentally.[27]

---

[26] Annex How.

[27] *Ibid.*

The commotion finally died down around 0300, after cursing NCO's convinced the military novices that they had been firing at delusions of their own overwrought imaginations.

Although such a reaction is not uncommon among untried troops, this realization was no balm to a wrathful Brigade commander at dawn on 4 August. Craig called in leaders of the most obvious offenders and severely reprimanded them. He made it known in no uncertain terms that such conduct would not be tolerated again; and from that time on, every man in the Brigade took him at his word.

The remainder of the stay at Changwon was relatively calm. On one occasion a group of seven unidentified persons was spotted atop a mountain overlooking the Brigade area. Closer scrutiny disclosed that the individuals had radios and were carefully observing all activity within the Marine perimeter. A platoon of infantry was dispatched to destroy what was apparently an enemy observation post; but by the time the rifleman scaled the height, both intruders and radios had disappeared.

The climb caused a number of heat prostration cases within the platoon, for Korean terrain and heat were giving Marines their first bitter taste of a crippling combination. Brigade helicopters, flown to Pusan on 2 August, set a combat precedent by delivering rations and water to the infantrymen on the mountain, and by evacuating the more severe heat casualties.[28]

While Craig's ground force spent its time patrolling and training around Changwon, VMO-6 and the Air Support Section (MTACS-2) were readying themselves. Accompanying the 4 HO3S helicopters in the flight to Pusan from Japan on 2 August were 4 of VMO-6's OY-2 observation planes. The other 4 light aircraft remained in Japan, to be used as spares. On 4 August the LST which had been dispatched by Cushman and Weir also arrived at the South Korean port. While two helicopters flew to Changwon to operate from Craig's CP, the others, together with the rest of VMO-6 and the Air Support Section, moved to the airfield at Chinhae. By 5 August, MTACS-2 had established communications with the *Sicily* and *Badoeng Strait* and was ready for business.

The Pusan Perimeter

The big picture, militarily speaking, was outlined in somber colors during the first few days of August 1950. Only the southeast corner of

[28] Brig SAR, basic rpt.

Korea was left to the Eighth Army and its battered ROK allies. Space had been traded for time until there remained in effect merely a UN beachhead about 90 miles long and 60 wide.

Unremitting enemy pressure throughout July had pushed the UN forces back to positions stretching raggedly from Pohang-dong on the east coast to Masan on the south coast by way of Taegu in the center. The logistical lifeline extended from Pusan to Taegu both by road and rail, and some 300,000 tons of supplies were moved in July by the Pusan Logistical Command.

The vital seaport had to be held if the UN forces were to retain a foothold in the peninsula, and the enemy was already threatening both Pohang-dong and Masan, each within 50 miles. Only by courtesy could the irregular chain of UN positions have been called a line. Gaps were the rule rather than exception, and an entire enemy corps might have driven through the mountainous area between Andong and Yongdok without meeting serious opposition. Nor was this the only spot where the dangerously stretched UN forces had to depend on the terrain for support. Yet the time had come to make a stand, and this final UN beachhead has gone down in history by the name of the Pusan Perimeter.

From Taegu in the center to the eastern coast, five depleted ROK divisions were arrayed during the first week in August. East of the Naktong, from the Taegu-Waegwan area southward, the 1st Cavalry and the 24th Infantry Division held defensive positions. This left the southern sector to the 25th Division, reinforced by the Army 5th RCT and the 1st Provisional Marine Brigade.

The principal enemy units pressing toward Masan and Pusan in the southern sector were identified as the NKPA 6th Infantry Division and the 83d Motorcycle Regiment. Composed entirely of Chinese civil war veterans in July 1949, the 6th Division had at that time been the 166th Division, 56th CCF Army, which later entered Korea as a completely equipped unit. Its three infantry regiments, the 13th, 14th, and 15th, were distinguished throughout the invasion for a high esprit de corps. After capturing Yongdungpo, an industrial suburb of Seoul, the 6th had pushed southward and won fresh honors by forcing the river Kum and taking Kunsan by storm.[29]

On the eve of the Kunsan operation, according to a captured enemy document, troops of the 6th were informed that they were facing a

[29] FECOM, ATIS, *North Korean 6th Infantry Division* (InterRpt, Sup No. 100), 33–6.

United States Army regiment. "Since this unit is planning to advance to the north, it is our mission to envelop and annihilate it. . . . We are fully prepared and confident of success in this operation."[30]

A numerical superiority as well as good combat discipline enabled the initial assault waves to cross the Kum in pneumatic floats and establish a bridgehead before noon on 16 July 1950. Half of the town of Kunsan was occupied before nightfall, and the United States and ROK defenders withdrew under cover of darkness.

Next came the "end run," with 6th Division units racing toward the capture of Namwon, Kwangju, Yosu, and Mokpu in the southwest corner of the peninsula. No opposition awaited except ineffectual delaying actions by ROK constabulary troops. After mopping up a few small pockets of resistance, the 6th Division pushed eastward to lead the North Korean drive toward Pusan.

The capture of Sunchon gave the division an assembly area for the attack on Chinju. And on 28 July the commander, Major General Pang, issued a message to his troops:

> "Comrades, the enemy is demoralized. The task given to us is the liberation of Masan and Chinju and the annihilation of the remnants of the enemy. We have liberated Mokpu, Kwangju and Yosu and have thereby accelerated the liberation of all Korea. However, the liberation of Chinju and Masan means the final battle to cut off the windpipe of the enemy. Comrades, this glorious task has fallen to our division! Men of the 6th Division, let us annihilate the enemy and distinguish ourselves!"[31]

Up to that time the division's total casualties had been remarkably few. Only 400 killed and wounded were reported from 25 June until after the capture of Kunsan, and the 6th had met scarcely any opposition since that action. It was just prior to the assault on Chinju, moreover, that the 83d Motorcycle Regiment was attached to reinforce the drive toward Pusan.

This unit had been part ot the 105th Armored Division until June 1950, when it was given a separate existence. Equipment consisted of motorcycles with sidecars and jeeps of Soviet manufacture. Fixed machineguns on both types of vehicles were operated by the crews in addition to submachineguns. Not much is known about the numbers of the 83d at this time, but it had experienced little combat since the beginning of the invasion.[32]

---

[30] *Ibid.*

[31] *Ibid.*

[32] *Ibid., Enemy Forces, op. cit.,* 36–7.

During the advance on Chinju the NKPA column ran into elements of the United States 24th Infantry Division and was stopped by machinegun fire at Hadong. All three regiments of the 6th Division had to be committed before this halfway point could be secured, and the 83d Motorcycle Regiment was blooded in the attack. More hard fighting awaited on the road to Chinju, but the two NKPA outfits battled their way into the town on or about 30 July 1950.

Brigade Air Strikes First

These North Korean units were destined to become the opponents of the Brigade a few days later. Before the Marine ground forces could get into action, however, the air components struck the first blow.

When Lieutenant Colonel Walter E. Lischeid's VMF-214 landed on board the *Sicily* on 3 August, eight of its Corsairs were immediately refueled and armed. At 1630, the initial Marine offensive action of the war was launched as the fighter planes roared up from the carrier's flight deck. Minutes later their incendiary bombs and rockets were hitting Red-held Chinju and the village of Sinban-ni. A series of strafing runs concluded the Marines' greeting to the North Korean People's Army.[33]

While the 2 Red bases were erupting in smoke and flame, 2 other pilots of the squadron flew from the *Sicily* to Taegu to be briefed on the broad tactical situation. They returned from their visit with maps and intelligence material for guidance in future operations.[34]

The squadron flew 21 sorties on 4 August against enemy bases controlling the pressure on Eighth Army's southern flank. Racing in from the sea, gull-winged Marine planes struck at bridges, railroads, and troop concentrations in the Chinju and Sachon areas.

On 5 August, the *Sicily* steamed into the Yellow Sea. Marine planes descended on Inchon, Seoul, and Mokpo, battering airfields, factories, warehouses, railroads, bridges, and harbor facilities. The same pattern of destruction was repeated the following day.[35]

On 6 August came a thundering bid for fame by VMF-323, as its sleek Corsairs streaked toward Korea. Operating from the deck of the *Badoeng Strait,* the squadron flew 30 sorties in deep support forward of Eighth Army lines. Carrying the mail with 500-pound bombs, 20-mm.

---

[33] VMF-214 SAR, 14 Jul–6 Sep 50.
[34] *Ibid.*
[35] *Ibid.*

cannon and 5-inch rockets, Marine pilots struck at Communist troop concentrations, vehicles, supply dumps, bridges and railroads.[36]

Planning the Sachon-Chinju Offensive

As early as 3 August, during the Brigade move from Pusan to Changwon, General Craig and Lieutenant Colonel Stewart had flown by helicopter to Masan for a conference of troop commanders There they joined General Walker and General Kean at the latter's 25th Division command post. Also present was Brigadier General George B. Barth, artillery officer of the 25th.[37]

Craig suggested to the Eighth Army commander that some ROK army trainees be attached to the Brigade. There were thousands of such Korean recruits, and a few serving as scouts, interpreters, and rear-area guards would be of great value to the Marines. Walker agreed to provide the native troops and arm them as well.[38]

The Army leader confirmed the previous night's telephonic orders which had caused the Brigade's move to Changwon. After the four generals had discussed the tactical situation on the southern flank, Walker directed Craig to have the Brigade prepared for commitment to combat any time after the evening of 5 August.[39]

This schedule worked out perfectly from Craig's point of view. The Air Support Section at Chinhae had just established communications with the two carrier-based squadrons. Army-Navy-Marine co-operation thus enabled the Brigade commander to lead his entire air-ground team into battle.

On 5 August Craig and Stewart flew to Masan for a final meeting with Walker and Kean. The Eighth Army commander outlined his plans for the first UN counteroffensive. In forceful terms, he expressed his dissatisfaction with the course of the war up to that time. He announced that the strategy of trading space for time had come to an end, and he did not mince words in referring to past UN defeats. With firm conviction in the cause, he had ordered all units to stand to the death. The Eighth Army could not and would not lose more ground or equipment.[40] Advances had been made by the enemy with such rapidity that

---

[36] VMF-323 SAR, *op. cit.*
[37] Craig, 25 Jan 54.
[38] *Ibid.*
[39] *Ibid.*
[40] *Ibid.*

he had extended his supply lines almost to the breaking point, concluded Walker. The time had come to strike back [41]

To the 25th Division, 1st Provisional Marine Brigade, and 5th RCT would go the honor of launching the counterattack from Chindong-ni, a small coastal village 8 miles southwest of Masan on the road to Chinju. In its effort to roll up the southern UN flank, the NKPA 6th Division was exerting heavy pressure on Chindong-ni from both the west and north.

A few miles west, the irregular coastline takes a sharp turn to the south to form a stubby peninsula about 25 miles wide and 15 miles long. Near the western base is the important town of Sachon. About 10 miles above this western junction of peninsula and coast lies Chinju. Both Sachon and Chinju were the targets of Walker's counteroffensive.

Approximately 3½ miles west of Chindong-ni is the tiny thatched-hut hamlet of Tosan, an unimpressive road junction which could be easily overlooked. The western fork is merely the continuation of the main route leading directly to Chinju, some 25 miles distant. The other fork branches south from Tosan and also goes to Chinju; but it skirts the coastline of the peninsula just described, passing through the communication hubs of Paedun-ni, Kosong, and Sachon. Thus, while both roads lead to Chinju, the southern or peninsular route is 17 miles longer.

Since it was known that enemy forces were present on the small peninsula, any UN thrust astride the main road to Chinju would be exposed to a constant flanking threat from the left. To eliminate this danger, Walker had decided to send the 1st Provisional Marine Brigade around the southern route from Tosan to Sachon. After the peninsula was secured, the 5th RCT would strike out for Chinju along the main road, while the 35th Infantry of the 25th Division guarded its right flank in the mountains to the north.[42]

Craig and Stewart opposed this plan, arguing that the Brigade itself would be exposed to flanking danger on the right, if it made the initial advance alone.[43]

After further discussion, it was decided that all three units would attack simultaneously along the routes already designated. However, the 5th RCT was given a preparatory mission of uncovering the Tosan junction before the Brigade began its advance.[44] D-day was scheduled for 7

---

[41] Stewart, 15 Jan 54.

[42] Stewart, 15 Jan 54.

[43] *Ibid.*

[44] Annex How; and Brig Op Plan 4–50.

August. All participating units were to be part of Task Force Kean, so named after the 25th Division commanding general who would exercise overall control.

Craig hurried from the conference to alert the Brigade. In a past military age a general might have sprung into the saddle, but the Brigade commander had discovered a steed that covered more ground. He and Stewart climbed into a HO3S-1 helicopter piloted by Lieutenant Gustave F. Lueddeke of VMO-6, and a few minutes later they landed at Lieutenant Colonel Murray's CP to brief him on the forthcoming action.

305713 O-F—55——8

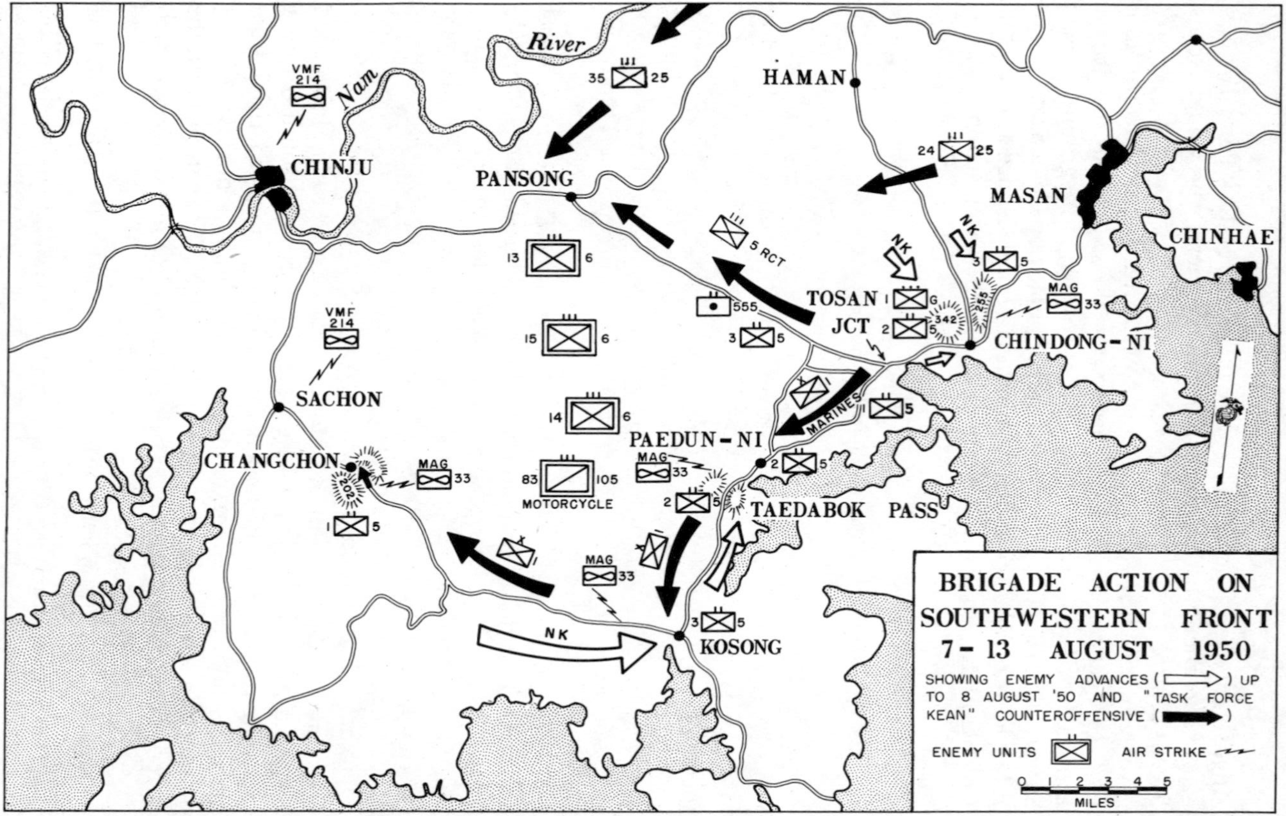

BRIGADE ACTION ON SOUTHWESTERN FRONT
7 – 13 AUGUST 1950
SHOWING ENEMY ADVANCES ( ) UP TO 8 AUGUST '50 AND "TASK FORCE KEAN" COUNTEROFFENSIVE ( )
ENEMY UNITS
AIR STRIKE
0 1 2 3 4 5
MILES
CHINJU
Nam
River
VMF 214
PANSONG
HAMAN
MASAN
CHINHAE
TOSAN
JCT
CHINDONG - NI
MAG 33
NK
5 RCT
555
SACHON
CHANGCHON
PAEDUN - NI
TAEDABOK PASS
KOSONG
MARINES
MOTORCYCLE

CHAPTER VI

Action on Hill 342

First Platoon Fight—The Perimeter on Hill 342—Call for Artillery Fires—Task Force Kean Stalled—General Craig Assumes Control—Enemy Attack at Dawn

ON 6 AUGUST 1950 the Brigade was attached to the 25th Infantry Division and ordered forward to Chindong-ni. The area from that village westward toward the Tosan junction was occupied by thinly spread elements of the 5th RCT and the 27th Infantry. While the former took over front line positions preparatory to launching the main attack on the next day, the latter was gradually displacing rearward to go into Eighth Army reserve.[1]

To facilitate the early relief of the 27th Infantry, Lieutenant Colonel Robert D. Taplett's 3d Battalion, 5th Marines, departed from Changwon at 1040, 6 August, and arrived at Chindong-ni less than 2 hours later. The infantry unit was accompanied by the 1st Battalion, 11th Marines; the 2d Platoon, 75-mm. Recoilless Guns; and the 3d Platoon, Company A Engineers. After assembling in a schoolyard north of the village, 3/5 relieved the 2d Battalion, 27th Infantry, on and around Hill 255.[2]

One and a half miles out of Chindong-ni, the road from Masan takes a sharp turn so that it is running generally north and south before it enters the village. Hill 255 borders the west side of the road, rising from the valley floor just above Chindong-ni and climbing northward to its summit in a series of prominent steps. Its ridgeline is narrow, with the eastern slopes falling steeply to the Masan route while its western wall

[1] Annexes 1 and 2 to 25th InfDiv War Diary, Sep 50, Book VIII; and Brig SAR, basic rpt.

[2] All hill numbers given in this text refer to the highest peak of the specific high ground being considered. Numbers indicate height in meters above sea level, and Hill 255 is therefore more than 800 feet high. Chindong-ni, being almost at the water's edge, may be taken as sea level.

plunges sharply to the valley and road connecting Chindong-ni and Haman.

Taplett set up his CP, headquarters units, and weapons company along the first step of the hill. Higher up, at the top of the second rise, Captain Joseph C. Fegan deployed Company H in defensive positions facing generally north. Forward, a long narrow plateau stretched for 250 yards before the third step of the ridge rose abruptly to the second highest peak on the hill. Noting the advantages of the commanding ground to his north, Fegan requested permission to move his company forward to that area. Since this would have placed him 500 yards from the nearest 3/5 unit, the request could not be granted.[3]

The battalion commander intended to keep his defenses as tightly knit as possible in order to discharge his mission of blocking the approaches to the Masan-Chindong-ni MSR. Despite vigorous patrolling by 25th Division units in the mountains between the coastal village and Haman, intelligence reported increasing numbers of enemy troops, heavy weapons, and equipment in the area to the north. It appeared that large NKPA forces were slipping through and descending on Chindong-ni to "cut off the windpipe" of Walker's southern flank.

First Lieutenant Robert D. Bohn, commander of Company G, deployed his 2d and 3d Platoons on Hill 99, to the west and across the valley from 255. He arranged his defenses to block the approaches from the high ground on his north (actually an extension of Hill 99) and from the valley to the west, separating him from massive Hill 342.[4]

On a small knoll at the base of Hill 255 was deployed Company G's 1st Platoon, commanded by Second Lieutenant John H. Cahill. With the 75-mm. recoilless gun platoon attached, this unit guarded the Haman road 600 yards from Chindong-ni.[5]

On high ground east of the MSR and beyond the village sat the 2d Platoon of Company H, with the mission of defending against infiltration from the direction of the sea and the mountains southeast of the road to Masan.[6]

This completed the infantry deployment. Company H had its three platoons spread over 1,500 yards, while those of Company G ranged at least an equal distance. Due to the lack of a third company, Taplett had no reserve other than a handful of headquarters troops. Thus 3/5 got its

---

[3] Maj Joseph C. Fegan interv with authors, 17 Apr 54 (Fegan, 17 Apr 54).

[4] Capt R. D. Bohn interv with authors, 17 Apr 54 (Bohn, 17 Apr 54).

[5] *Ibid.*

[6] Fegan, 17 Apr 54.

taste of things to come in a strange war of mountains and men.

As the riflemen were digging their hilltop holes with traditional distaste, other supporting elements of the Brigade and 5th Marines began to arrive at Chindong-ni and set up for business. These included the Brigade Reconnaissance Company and a platoon of the regimental 4.2-inch Mortar Company.[7] All Marine units in the area temporarily came under control of 3/5's Battalion Commander. Taplett was given the added responsibility of handling all area requests for tactical air support.[8]

For the time being, the 3d Battalion itself was under operational control of Colonel John H. Michaelis, USA, commander of the 27th Infantry "Wolfhounds." Verbal instructions from Major General Kean on 6 August had given the Army officer control of all troops in the Chindong-ni area. When a second Marine battalion arrived in the locale, command would then pass to General Craig.[9]

By 1600, Taplett had reported his command post location and defensive positions to Michaelis. Immediately afterwards he ordered mortars and artillery to lay registration fires on the northern approaches to Chindong-ni.[10] Having left the phantoms of Changwon far behind, the Marines of the reinforced battalion settled down for the night.

First Platoon Fight

Shortly after midnight, the 3d Battalion received an unexpected message which precipitated the first Marine infantry action of the war. Colonel Michaelis radioed Taplett and passed on a directive from 25th Division, ordering the Marine battalion to commit immediately one reinforced platoon for the defense of Hill 342. He explained that this unit was to relieve a beleaguered Army company being slowly eaten away in a private war of attrition. Taplett informed the regimental commander that he could ill afford to spare 1 of his 6 rifle platoons, but was told in return that General Kean had ordered 342 held at all costs.[11]

Tagged with the ominous sounding name "Yaban-san" by Koreans,

---

[7] Annex How.

[8] LtCol R. D. Taplett interv with authors, 20 Apr 54 (Taplett, 20 Apr 54).

[9] Brig SAR, basic rpt.

[10] *Ibid.;* and Annex How.

[11] This section of the narrative is derived from: LtCol R. D. Taplett interv with the author, 18 Nov 53 and 19 May 54; Annexes Easy and How to Brig SAR; and Capt J. H. Cahill ltr to authors, 9 Dec 53.

this hill resembles a huge molar whose roots rise from the MSR west of Chindong-ni and lead to a tremendous mass about 2,000 yards north of the road. There the ground climbs sharply, culminating in a peak 1,100 feet high. Beyond, a long saddle extends a few thousand yards northwest, connecting 342 with a height of almost 2,000 feet. The latter was a stronghold of NKPA 6th Division elements, making a determined bid to carry 342 and cut the MSR.

Assigned the mission of making the Brigade's first ground contact was young Lieutenant Cahill of Company G. His 1st Platoon was reinforced with a machinegun squad and SCR–300 operator before he led it from 3/5's perimeter.

Moving westward on the MSR, the platoon reached Michaelis' CP, located near the bridges south of Hill 99. Cahill was told that he would be met by a guide at a road junction 700 yards farther down the MSR. From this point the platoon followed a soldier who escorted Cahill to the CP of the 2d Battalion, 5th RCT. This headquarters was situated just north of the road, on the tip of 342's eastern "root," 1 of the 2 long ridges leading to the hill itself.

The Marine officer was told to relieve the Army company on the summit and hold the hill with his platoon. Following a quick briefing, Cahill and the guide led the column northward from the CP, skirting the western base of the ridge. A few hundred yards along the way, the guide discovered that he had miscalculated in the darkness. More time was lost while the platoon descended to resume the correct route.

As the men threaded their way along the unseen trail, a few enemy artillery shells burst nearby. The column reached the end of the valley separating the two long spurs of 342, and a volley of rifle fire cracked in the darkness. Two of Cahill's Marines were painfully wounded.

Since the column was still in friendly territory, the guide advised Cahill not to climb 342 until dawn shed light on the mystery. It was then 0500, 7 August, and the Marine platoon had marched 3 miles from its original position.

Shortly after first light, it was discovered that soldiers of the 2d Battalion, 5th RCT, had fired on the Marines, not realizing that friendly units were moving within the area.

As the sun rose in a cloudless sky, Cahill took the lead. First, he climbed the high ground joining 342 with its eastern spur, then crossed over and continued toward the peak from a southeasterly direction.

The platoon made good progress at the outset, but the heat became stifling; and all the while the slopes of 342 stretched ahead like a

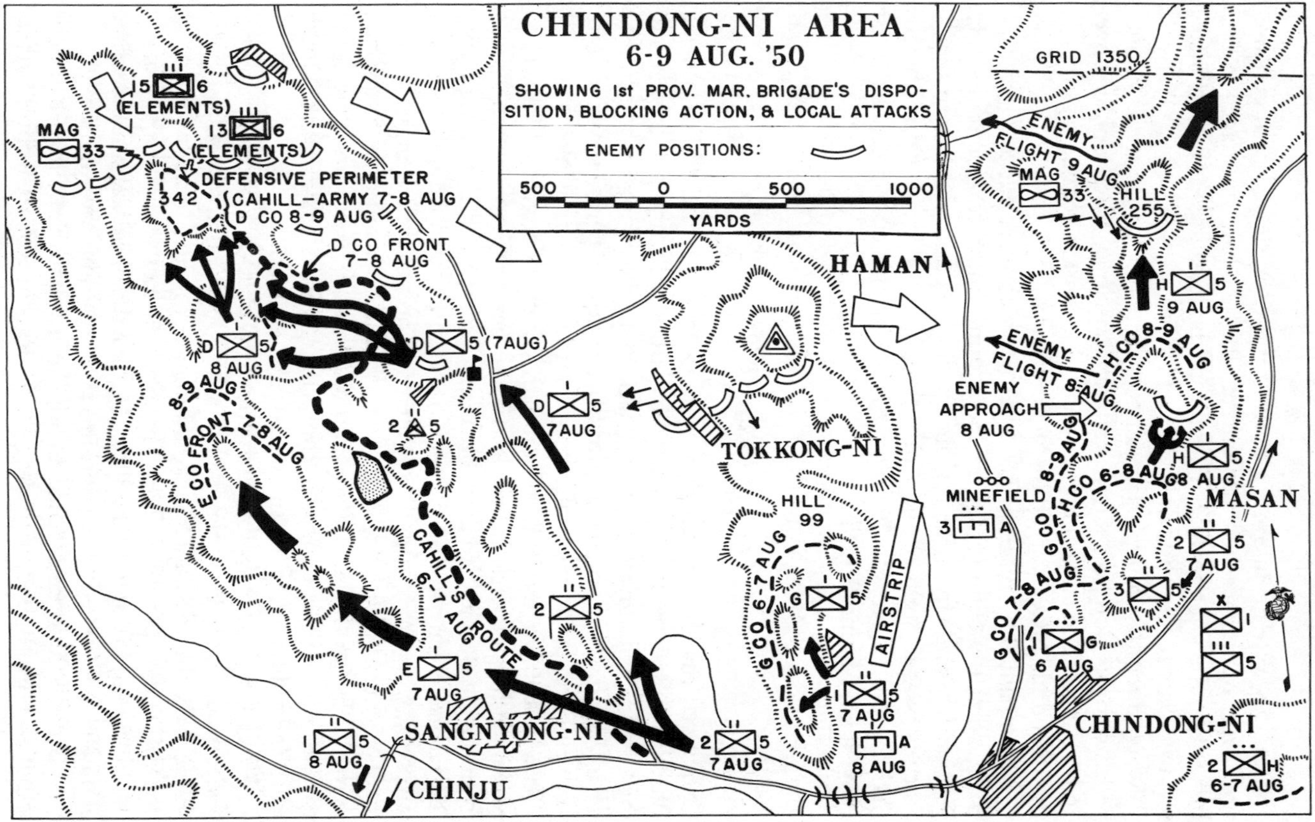

CHINDONG-NI AREA
6-9 AUG. '50
SHOWING 1st PROV. MAR. BRIGADE'S DISPOSITION, BLOCKING ACTION, & LOCAL ATTACKS
ENEMY POSITIONS:
500
0
500
1000
YARDS
GRID 1350
ENEMY FLIGHT 9 AUG
MAG 33
HILL 255
9 AUG
HAMAN
ENEMY FLIGHT 8 AUG
H CO 8-9 AUG
ENEMY APPROACH 8 AUG
TOKKONG-NI
H CO 6-8 AUG
8 AUG
MINEFIELD
MASAN
HILL 99
7 AUG
G CO 8-9 AUG
G CO 7-8 AUG
AIRSTRIP
G CO 6-7 AUG
6 AUG
CHINDONG-NI
6-7 AUG
8 AUG
(ELEMENTS)
(ELEMENTS)
DEFENSIVE PERIMETER
342
CAHILL-ARMY 7-8 AUG
D CO 8-9 AUG
D CO FRONT 7-8 AUG
(7AUG)
8 AUG
8-9 AUG
E CO FRONT 7-8 AUG
7AUG
CAHILL'S 6-7 AUG ROUTE
7AUG
SANGNYONG-NI
8 AUG
CHINJU
7AUG

continuous wall. Stumbling, gasping for breath, soaked with perspiration, every Marine reached the point at which he barely managed to drag himself up the steep incline. There were choked curses as men gained a few feet, only to slip and fall back even farther.

Water discipline collapsed as canteens were quickly emptied. Marines began to drop along the slope, some unconscious, others doubled over and retching. The tactical formation of the platoon became ragged, but Cahill and his NCO's urged the men upward.

Accompanied by Sergeant Lee Buettner, Cahill set out to contact the Army company commander on the summit and reconnoiter the area. Seventy-five yards from the top, he was fired on from the eastern slopes. Since he was in sight of the Army troops on the crest, it was obvious that the North Korean People's Army had officially greeted the 1st Provisional Marine Brigade.

The Perimeter on Hill 342

Convinced that he was encountering only sniper fire, Cahill ordered Buettner to stay behind and keep the platoon moving up a draw affording cover. Then, ignoring enemy marksmen, the young officer climbed up to the crest and entered a grim little company perimeter under constant rifle and machinegun fire from its front and both flanks.

It was 0830 when the Army company commander greeted Cahill and explained his defenses. It had been customary, he said, to man a broad front during the day and draw back into a tight perimeter at night. But the intense enemy fire of the previous night had not diminished after daybreak, with the result that his men still occupied their night perimeter. The Army officer added that he had returned his mortars to the base of the hill, since they had drawn too much fire to be effective. Deployed around a triangular perimeter conforming to the shape of 347's peak were the remnants of his three shattered platoons.

While Cahill appraised the situation, his platoon labored up the hill under prodding by Buettner and other NCO's. Well up the southeastern slope, the column suddenly came under automatic weapons fire from invisible enemy positions. The exhausted Marines set up weapons along the hillside and fired at area targets. Despite the blistering sun and whine of bullets, NCO's led their fire teams and squads up toward the peak.

When the Marines reached Cahill, he learned that 1 man had been killed and 6 wounded, including Staff Sergeant Robert Robinson, platoon sergeant, and Sergeant Thomas Blackmon, platoon guide. A number of heat casualties were recuperating far down the slope, and one Marine had suffered an emotional collapse. Blackmon, despite a mortal wound, had been so intent on joining his platoon leader at the crest that four weary men were required to carry him down the hillside to safety. Three other able-bodied Marines also had to assist wounded men down the hill.

Of the 52 men who had set out the previous night, only 37, including those recovered from heat sickness, finally reached Cahill. As they assembled on the reverse slope of 342, a group of soldiers on the crest broke under a heavy volume of enemy fire and bolted from the perimeter. The Army company was on the verge of panic until a young Army lieutenant restored order and led the men back to their foxholes.

Cahill and his remaining NCO's crawled around the perimeter to insert Marines in positions among those of the Army troops. This psychology was sound, for each infantryman, eyeing his Army or Marine neighbor, prided himself on setting a high standard of military conduct. From that time on, every man discharged his responsibility in a most exemplary manner.

Two more Marines had been killed instantly while being led to their positions by Sergeant Jack Macy. These casualties brought the platoon's total to 3 KIA and 8 WIA.

It is not likely that Cahill's men were interested enough in historic dates to recall that it was the eighth anniversary of the Marine landing on Guadalcanal in World War II. For at noon, the fight on Hill 342 took on aspects of a siege. Swarms of North Koreans inched upward toward the crest, taking advantage of cover and concealment as they kept a steady stream of rifle and machinegun fire cutting across the hilltop. Despite the visual handicap resulting from the enemy's use of smokeless powder, the Marines and soldiers returned the fire with determination.

Due to the urgency of the situation on 342, the 2d Battalion, 5th RCT, ordered its company to remain on the crest with Cahill's platoon. Plans were already underway for a larger Marine force to clear the high ground.

Call for Artillery Fires

In the meantime Cahill used his initiative to improve the situation. With his SCR-300, he called for Army artillery fire to silence the Communist mortars. When the first shells were fired for registration, he searched the perimeter and located an artillery forward observer. Accurate bursts were laid on likely looking mortar OP's in enemy territory, yet the Communist tubes continued to fire.

With ammunition and water in critical supply, the Marine officer radioed 3/5's CP and requested an air drop. Taplett's Tactical Air Control Party relayed the message to the Brigade Air Section, and an Air Force R4D transport flew over the restricted drop area atop Hill 342. The precious supplies tumbled from the big plane—into enemy territory. A single recovered packet contained carbine cartridges, the one type not needed.

The Brigade Air Section then turned the mission over to VMO–6. Every 5-gallon water can owned by the squadron was donated, and the more maneuverable OY–2's were able to drop them within the confined perimeter. Unhappily, the containers burst upon striking the ground, so that the parched hill defenders were able to salvage only a few mouthfuls of water apiece.

Sergeant Macy reacted with vigor. With Cahill's permission, he organized a few volunteers into a patrol to search for water. Descending the perilous southeastern slope under fire, the little group struck out for the village of Taepyong-ni, located along the base of 342's eastern spur and facing Hill 99 across the valley.

As the afternoon wore on, the Army-Marine defenders clung to their precarious perch, despite swollen tongues and Communist fire. The enemy had succeeded in surrounding the entire peak with a ring of fire. Several more casualties were inflicted on the infantry company, and a Marine machinegunner was killed instantly by a sniper who had worked his way to the south of the perimeter.

Task Force Kean Stalled

Although the night of 6–7 August had been uneventful for 3/5's front lines around Chindong-ni, Taplett's CP near the base of Hill 255 came under sporadic shelling between 0100 and 0400. The first messages from Cahill, received about 0600, caused anxiety over the fate of his platoon.[12]

At 0200 that morning, a long column of trucks had set out from Changwon, carrying Lieutenant Colonel Harold S. Roise's 2d Battalion, 5th Marines. The head of the convoy reached Chindong-ni about 0500

[12] Annex How.

and entered the truck turn-around in a schoolyard at the base of Hill 255.[13] As 2/5 unloaded, the turn-around became a bottleneck of vehicles, men, and equipment which slowed movement on the MSR itself almost to a standstill. To make matters worse, the heavy traffic gradually pounded the schoolyard into a quagmire, so that trucks bogged down and added to the confusion.

While Roise was assembling his battalion, the entire area came under heavy mortar and artillery fire from the north. The sudden shelling, which caused 2/5's first battle casualties, brought all traffic on the road from Changwon to an abrupt halt.

Although the Marines of the 2d Battalion were well covered behind Hill 255, bursts from shells striking the trees high on the ridge filled the air with fragments. Before the enemy mortars ceased, 1 Marine had been killed and 11 wounded, including Captain George E. Kittredge, Jr., commander of Company E.[14]

Lieutenant Colonel Murray, whose headquarters was behind Roise's unit in the convoy, was still north of Chindong-ni when the column slowed almost to a standstill. He radioed 2/5's commander and told him to keep the trucks moving despite the shelling. Roise replied that the muddy schoolyard, not enemy fire, was the main cause of the delay. Thus Murray received the first of many object lessons in Korean geography. He sat patiently in his jeep, while the column inched into Chindong-ni.[15]

After the regimental commander arrived in Chindong-ni, the 3d Battalion, less Cahill's platoon, reverted to his control. Because of the battle in progress on Hill 342 and enemy activity to the north of the village perimeter, Murray ordered 2/5 to occupy and defend an expanse of 255 above Company H's positions. He directed 1/5 (following his headquarters in the column from Changwon) to occupy Hill 99, thus relieving Company G to bolster Taplett's lines on lower 255.[16]

General Craig arrived at Chindong-ni shortly after 0700, just in time to be warmly greeted by the enemy shelling as he stepped from his helicopter. Since the Brigade attack scheduled for 7 August hinged on the 5th RCT's success at the Tosan junction, Craig quickly arranged for a telephone line to that unit, so that his CP would be in constant contact.[17]

News from the front was not good. At 0630, after air and artillery

---

[13] *Ibid.;* and LtCol H. S. Roise ltr to authors, 5 Feb 54 (Roise, 5 Feb 54).

[14] *Ibid.*

[15] Murray, 15 Feb 54.

[16] Annex How.

[17] LtGen E. A. Craig ltr to authors, 12 Jan 54 (Craig, 12 Jan 54).

preparations, the 5th RCT had jumped off on schedule. Just beyond the line of departure, it came to a sudden halt as a result of increased enemy activity north of the road. Elements of the NKPA 6th Division, paying little attention to the plans of Task Force Kean, had launched an attack of their own above the MSR.

The situation on Hill 342 kept the entire 2d Battalion, 5th RCT, tied down in a fight to hold the Chinju road open. With the help of Cahill's platoon on the crest, this mission was being accomplished; but the battalion was temporarily lost to its regiment, and the road itself was choked with men and vehicles unable to move.[18]

General Craig Assumes Control

The Brigade was ordered to provide a battalion for the relief of the Army unit on Yaban-san, so that the 5th RCT could strike harder at the road junction 2½ miles to the west.[19]

Just as 2/5 was ascending Hill 255, Lieutenant Colonel Murray received word from Brigade of the Marine commitment. The 5th Marines commander canceled Roise's orders and directed him to relieve both Cahill's platoon and the 2d Battalion, 5th RCT, and to seize the remainder of Hill 342.[20]

At 1120 on 7 August, General Craig received a telephone message from General Kean directing the Brigade commander to assume control of all troops in the Chindong-ni area until further orders. With this overall responsibility, Craig went forward to observe the 5th RCT in action. He ascertained by personal reconnaissance that enemy resistance was light, although few friendly gains were being made because of the scattered and confused nature of the fighting.[21] The MSR between Sangnyong-ni, at the base of Hill 342's spurs, and the vital Tosan junction was jammed with men, vehicles, and equipment, while infantrymen probed the surrounding high ground in an effort to weed out snipers and infiltrators.

When 2/5 reached the road junction at which Cahill had been met by the Army guide during the night, Lieutenant Colonel Roise ordered Company D to move up the north fork, tracing the base of 342's eastern

---

[18] Brig SAR, basic rpt.
[19] *Ibid.*
[20] *Ibid.;* and Annex How.
[21] Craig, 12 Jan 54.

spur, and seize both the spur and great hill itself. Company E, now commanded by 1st Lieutenant William E. Sweeney, was to pass behind Sangnyong-ni and seize the west spur. Such a deployment would leave the battalion spread thinly, but Roise's orders were to protect the wide valley formed by the two long ridges. This could be done only by occupying both spurs and 342 itself.[22]

Outside of Chindong-ni, Major Morgan J. McNeely, 2d Battalion S–3, had picked up Captain John Finn, Jr., CO of Company D, and the two officers drove ahead by jeep to the village of Taepyong-ni at the eastern base of Hill 342. The staff officer informed Finn that Dog Company was to relieve a 5th RCT unit on the high ground above the clump of thatched huts. Both McNeely and an Army guide said that the Marines would meet no organized resistance in their climb.[23]

Having spent a sleepless night on the road from Changwon to Chindong-ni, Finn's infantrymen were fagged. It was now midafternoon, and the heat began to take its toll of Dog Company.

Just as the leading elements reached Finn at Taepyong-ni—30 minutes after McNeely's departure—the column came under rifle and machine-gun fire from the high ground above the road and from the hamlet of Tokkong-ni across the valley on the right. The Marines thought they were being shot at by Army troops, but the chatter of Communist "burp guns"[24] soon convinced them that they were meeting enemy resistance.[25]

Finn ordered his men into the rice paddies bordering the road. Calling his platoon leaders, he told them that there was no real intelligence, but that the fire from Tokkong-ni would be ignored due to the company's mission on 342. He assigned routes of ascent to each platoon. The 2d, under Second Lieutenant Wallace J. Reid, would push through Taepyong-ni and on up the hill at its juncture with the spur. On the left, Second Lieutenant Edward T. Emmelman would lead his 3d Platoon to the top of the spur. The 1st Platoon, commanded by Second Lieutenant Arthur A. Oakley, would hold the right flank and ascend the southern slopes of 342 itself.[26]

Company D met scattered opposition. By the time it moved over the crest of the spur, five Marines had been wounded. The sun, however, had been more effective; for twelve men were completely unconscious

[22] Roise, 5 Feb 54.
[23] Capt J. Finn, Jr., ltr to authors, 1 Mar 54 (Finn, 1 Mar 54).
[24] PPS-1943, Soviet 7.62-mm. submachinegun.
[25] Capt R. T. Hanifin ltr to authors, 15 Feb 54 (Hanifin, 15 Feb 54).
[26] *Ibid.;* and Finn, 1 Mar 54.

from the 100° heat, and the rest of the company had neared the point of exhaustion.

Finn ordered his executive officer, First Lieutenant Robert T. Hanifin, Jr., to set up headquarters and the 60-mm. mortars on the high ground directly above Taepyong-ni. It was already early in the evening when Hanifin established a thin perimeter of headquarters personnel to safeguard the CP.[27]

In the meantime, Finn was leading his three rifle platoons up the same southeastern approach to 342's summit which Cahill's platoon had scaled 12 hours earlier. The company commander could no longer overlook the combined effects on his men of heat and overexertion. A few hundred yards from the summit, he radioed Roise that Company D was exhausted. During the halt, Lieutenant Oakley climbed to the summit to contact the Army and Marine defenders. He returned just before dark with Cahill and the Army company commander.[28]

In the hurried conference that followed, the Army officer advised Finn against finishing the rugged climb and assured him that his soldiers and Cahill's platoon could defend the peak through the night. Informed of this by radio, Roise allowed Company D to hold its present position and relieve at dawn.[29]

Earlier in the day, Lieutenant Sweeney had led Company E up the lower tip of 342's western spur, then along the ridgeline toward the large hill mass. At intervals the company came under long range, ineffectual machinegun fire. But, as in the case of Finn's unit, the heat and terrain were more damaging than enemy bullets. At dusk, Company E had reached the midway point along the ridge, and there it dug in for the night.

Enemy Attack at Dawn

Under cover of darkness, Red Korean troops wormed their way around the little perimeter on the summit of Hill 342. Just before dawn the soldiers and Marines were greeted by bursts of short-range rifle and machinegun fire. The defenders returned the fire and hurled grenades down the slopes, but a small force of North Koreans succeeded in crawling

[27] Hanifin, 15 Feb 54.
[28] Finn, 1 Mar 54.
[29] *Ibid.*

close enough to launch an assault against the northeast leg of the triangle.[30]

A fierce hand-to-hand struggle ensued at the point of contact, and the Communists were thrown back down the hill. One of Cahill's men died of bayonet and gunshot wounds, and another Marine and several soldiers were wounded.[31]

Finn's men struck out for the summit shortly after daybreak on 8 August. With three platoons abreast along the southern face of 342, Dog Company pushed upward swiftly, brushing aside light resistance. Upon reaching the perimeter, the Marines came under a storm of fire from NK positions which ringed the northern half of the hill.[32]

The relief was effected, nevertheless, and Cahill's thinned squads descended Hill 342 together with the shattered Army company. The Marine platoon had lost 6 killed and 12 wounded—more than a third of the 52 men who had set out from Chindong-ni.[33] But its determined stand with the beleaguered Army unit had saved the height and frustrated the Communist attempts to establish a bastion overlooking the MSR.

Company D fared no better than its predecessors at consolidating the crest of 342 and clearing upper slopes which were crawling with North Koreans. Finn's unit took several casualties in the fire fight that accompanied and followed the relief of the original defenders. Two of those killed in action were Second Lieutenants Oakley and Reid. The only surviving platoon leader, Lieutenant Emmelman, received a serious head wound as he was pointing out targets to a Marine machinegunner.[34]

Captain Finn, seeing Reid's motionless form lying ahead of the company lines, crawled forward to recover the body. Having moved only a short distance with his burden, the company commander himself was struck in the head and shoulder by enemy bullets Barely conscious and almost blinded by blood, Finn crept back to his lines on his hands and knees.

A corpsman administered first aid and Company D's first sergeant helped the officer down the steep slope.[35] On the way the pair met Lieutenant Hanifin, who was leading company headquarters and the mortar

---

[30] Cahill, 9 Dec 53.

[31] *Ibid.*

[32] Finn, 1 Mar 54; and Roise, 5 Feb 54.

[33] Annex Able to Annex How.

[34] Finn, 1 Mar 54; and Hanifin, 15 Feb 54.

[35] *Ibid.*

section to the high ground from their positions of the previous night. Finn informed the executive officer that he was now in command of the company.[36]

Reaching the summit, Hanifin had just enough time to reorganize his defensive positions and emplace the 60-mm. mortars before the Communists launched another attack. Again Marine rifles, machineguns, and grenades scorched the northern slopes. Again the enemy was beaten back, leaving the hillside littered with dead. But Company D's casualties had mounted meanwhile to 6 killed in action and 25 wounded.[37]

About 1130, as the fire fight slackened, Roise phoned Hanifin from his OP on the eastern spur. The conversation had no sooner begun when the company commander collapsed from heat exhaustion. A veteran NCO and a young officer promptly filled the command vacuum. Company D's gunnery sergeant, Master Sergeant Harold Reeves, assumed control of the three rifle platoons with the confidence of long experience. Second Lieutenant Leroy K. Wirth, a forward observer of 1/11, took responsibility for all supporting arms, including the planes of MAG–33 circling overhead. The NCO of almost 30 years service and the young officer repeatedly ranged forward of the front lines to spot enemy positions for air strikes and make new appraisals of the situation. Company D remained steady, and never again did the North Koreans seriously threaten the hilltop.[38]

The 2d Battalion, 24th Infantry, was scheduled to relieve 2/5 on Hill 342 during the afternoon of 8 August; but the Army unit was unable to reach the area for reasons to be explained later. Informed of the change in plans, Roise kept his battalion busy with consolidation of positions and evacuation of casualties.

Company E moved forward a few hundred yards along the western spur of 342 and dug new foxholes. Captain Andrew M. Zimmer reported from regiment, where he had been an assistant S–3, and took command of Company D.[39]

Although the North Koreans continued to harass the "iron triangle" on the crest, there was no more hard fighting. A few additional casualties were taken by Zimmer's company, most of them occurring while Ma-

---

[36] *Ibid.*

[37] Annex How; Hanifin, 15 Feb 54; and Maj A. M. Zimmer ltr to author, 18 Feb 54 (Zimmer, 18 Feb 54). This breakdown of casualties is as nearly correct as can be ascertained from recollections of participants and a comparison with the final total given after 2/5 was relieved on position.

[38] Hanifin, 15 Feb 54.

[39] Annex How.

rines tried to retrieve airdropped supplies which had fallen wide of their mark.[40]

During the fighting on 342, Major Walter Gall, commander of 2/5's Weapons Company, had dispatched a small patrol to eliminate the enemy machineguns in Tokkong-ni. After a brief fire fight which cost three friendly casualties, the withdrawal of the patrol left the Communists still entrenched in the village. When the Marines returned to Weapons Company lines on the eastern spur, First Lieutenant Ira T. Carr turned his 81-mm. mortars on Tokkong-ni and brought the enemy fire to an end.[41]

The night of 8–9 August was relatively quiet on 342. Obviously weakened by casualties, the enemy gave the Marine positions a wide berth. NKPA harassing fires consisted of periodic bursts from long-range machineguns and antitank guns.[42] There was desultory sniping during the morning of the 9th, but Brigade intelligence reported a gradual withdrawal of the enemy northward.[43]

That afternoon Company D was relieved by an Army unit when 2/5 turned over responsibility for the hill to the 2d Battalion, 24th Infantry. The fight had made veterans out of the men Zimmer led down to the road, but the company paid with 8 dead and 28 wounded.[44]

Documents taken from enemy dead disclosed that the defenders of Hill 342 had been opposed by elements of the 13th and 15th Regiments of the NK 6th Division. Lieutenant Cahill qualified his report of 150 enemy dead as "conservative,"[45] and 2/5 set the total at 400 after its fight.[46] The actual number of fatalities inflicted by Marine-Army infantry and supporting arms probably lies somewhere between these two estimates.

At any rate, the Red Korean commander had committed at least two rifle companies supported by machineguns, mortars and artillery. The force thrown against Yaban-san could be estimated at 500 to 600 troops, and they had failed in their attempt to cut the MSR.[47]

---

[40] Zimmer, 18 Feb 54.
[41] Maj Walter Gall interv with authors, 9 Feb 54.
[42] Zimmer, 18 Feb 54.
[43] Brig Periodic IntelRpt No. 6.
[44] Zimmer, 18 Feb 54; and Annex How.
[45] Cahill, 9 Dec 53.
[46] Annex How.
[47] *Ibid.;* and Brig Periodic IntelRpts Nos. 5 and 6.

305713 O-F-55--9

CHAPTER VII

Advance to Kosong

Heavy NKPA Resistance—Assault on Hill 255—Confusion at Tosan Junction—Brigade Artillery in Support—Encounter With Japanese Maps—Ambush at Taedabok Pass—The Seizure of Kosong

WHILE 2/5 AND the 1st Platoon of Company G were fighting the enemy and weather on 7 August, Lieutenant Colonel Taplett's 3d Battalion sat out an ominous calm at Chindong-ni. From their positions on Hills 255 and 99, Captain Fegan and Lieutenant Bohn periodically called for supporting fires to check enemy movement in the northern approaches to the village.

At 1015 Second Lieutenant Lawrence W. Hetrick and his 3d Platoon, Company A Engineers, completed the laying of the first Marine minefield, located across the Haman road a half mile above Chindong-ni.[1]

Lieutenant Colonel Newton's 1st Battalion reached the village in the afternoon of the 7th and relieved Company G's two platoons on Hill 99. Bohn took his company back across the valley and deployed on the lower slopes of 255 facing the Haman road. These positions were hit by close-in sniper fire during the night of 7–8 August, and at dawn the Marine infantrymen were startled to discover four NK soldiers emplaced less than 100 yards away in the valley. Both the enemy position and its occupants were quickly destroyed.[2]

Shortly after daybreak on 8 August—while Cahill was being relieved on Yaban-san—the Marines of Company H noted a column of troops climbing Hill 255 from the direction of the Haman road. Believing the newcomers to be ROK soldiers, Fegan's men watched as the long file reached the high peak beyond the plateau forward of the Marine positions. When the group set up facing Company H, Fegan became skeptical enough to alert his riflemen and machinegunners. His precautions

---

[1] Annex How.
[2] *Ibid.;* and Bohn, 17 Apr 50.

were timely, for the visitors immediately opened fire on the Marines.[3]

This surprise attack had a critical effect on the Task Force Kean sector. In possession of the high ground above 3/5, the North Koreans were able to block the Masan-Chindong-ni stretch of the MSR, leaving most of the American ground forces out on a limb for supply and reinforcement purposes. Thus when the 2d Battalion, 24th Infantry, advanced from Masan to relieve both 3/5 and 2/5 on their respective hills, it was driven off the fire-swept road north of Chindong-ni.[4]

Upon being informed of the enemy's presence, Taplett ordered Company H to attack and destroy the Communist position. Fegan called his two platoon leaders[5] while the Marine infantrymen in the line exchanged shots with the enemy across the plateau. After a quick briefing, Second Lieutenant John O. Williams led his 1st Platoon to the long tableland.[6]

Echeloned to the right, the skirmish line pushed aggressively over the open area, firing on the enemy as it moved forward. The platoon closed to within 30 yards of the Communist-held peak, but showers of hand grenades and continuous machinegun fire pinned down the attackers. Fegan sent a message forward, directing Williams to work around the enemy's left flank. Although one fire team succeeded in reaching the rocks below the NK positions, the flanking maneuver failed.

Heavy NKPA Resistance

The 3d Platoon had taken several casualties. Marines still in the open area were unable to advance, while those who had attempted the envelopment could only cling to the steep slopes above the MSR. When some of this group were struck by enemy fire, the impact sent them rolling helplessly down the sharp incline.

Convinced that Williams could not carry the peak, Fegan ordered him to pull his platoon back toward the line of departure and reorganize. While the withdrawal was in progress, the company commander ordered the 3d Platoon to pass through the 1st and continue the attack. There was no response to the order.[7]

Fegan realized that the men were momentarily unnerved after wit-

---

[3] Fegan, 17 Apr 54.
[4] Brig SAR, basic rpt; and Craig, 12 Jan 54.
[5] The 2d Platoon was still in position east of the MSR.
[6] Fegan, 17 Apr 54.
[7] *Ibid.*

nessing the failure of the first attack. The company commander, therefore, assumed control and personally led the 3d Platoon forward on the plateau. Halfway across the open area, the new skirmish line passed through Williams' outfit as it was reforming.

The Marines of the 3d Platoon responded with confidence to Fegan's leadership. They crossed the tableland in a wedge formation with 1 squad at the apex and the other 2 slightly withheld. Air strikes and artillery preparations had little effect against the rocky crag beyond the plateau, so that the final assault was fought to a finish with small arms and grenades.[8]

Staff Sergeant John I. Wheatley, one of the prime movers, fell wounded along with several of his men. Sergeant Edward F. Barrett, shot in the elbow and hip, lay helpless, exposed to enemy fire, until Captain Fegan carried him back to safety.

The 3d Platoon gained the rocky summit and worked its way through the NKPA position, a foxhole at a time, while the enemy resisted to the death. Corporal Melvin James[9] hit the Red Korean left flank with his squad and drove deep into the enemy position. The NKPA right flank was rolled up by a vigorous assault sparked by Technical Sergeant Ray Morgan and Private First Class Donald Terrio[10] as each knocked out a Communist machinegun and its crew.

Having wiped out the main enemy position, the 3d Platoon advanced northward about 200 yards to a gulf where the high ground fell away abruptly. Beyond this depression rose the highest step of the ridgeline's rugged staircase: Hill 255 with a height of more than 800 feet above the MSR. The three squads held up here to await further orders.

How Company's fight up to this time had cost the Marines 6 dead and 32 wounded.[11]

Assault on Hill 255

A column of NKPA reinforcements bound for Hill 255 was spotted during the action by Company G from its positions facing the Haman road. The enemy platoon struck out across the valley from the high ground north of Hill 99, then attempted to ascend 255 via the same route used by comrades at dawn.

---

[8] *Ibid.;* and Annex How.

[9] James was awarded the Distinguished Service Cross for this action.

[10] Morgan and Terrio received Silver Star medals.

[11] Annex How.

The Marines of Company G and their supporting arms cut loose with a hurricane of fire. And after scattering in panic, the enemy survivors scuttled back to their starting point.[12]

Lieutenant Colonel Murray, upon being informed of the progress made by How Company, directed Taplett to halt the attack and dig in for the night. While Fegan's men were carrying out this order under NKPA artillery and mortar fire, MAG-33 and the Marine artillery roared into action. The saddle north of How Company's lines was pounded so mercilessly that the enemy pulled back from Fegan's immediate front. Throughout the night of 8-9 August, 1/11 and 3/5's mortar platoon dropped a steel curtain across the battalion front, with the result that no enemy activity was noted.[13]

The systematic reduction of enemy positions on Hill 255 the next morning was a triumph of supporting arms. Marine artillery shells led off at 0825, followed by Marine air which worked the enemy over with the first close-support payload of napalm recorded so far in the Korean conflict. And four minutes before Company H launched its final attack on the hill, airborne TAC reported the objective neutralized.[14]

Fegan's men scaled the peak against negligible opposition. Two knocked-out machineguns and a few enemy dead were all that remained at the summit.[15]

The plan for eliminating the threat to the MSR called for a Marine advance along Hill 255 to grid line 1350. North of this boundary, the ridge would be cleared by Army troops approaching from Masan.

Company H sighted soldiers of the 24th Infantry at 1125 as they moved southward to the grid line, and the long ridge was considered secure. It had been no light price, however, that 3/5 paid to open the MSR. Casualties on Hill 255 totalled 16 dead and 36 wounded, and since nearly all had been taken by Company H, Fegan's outfit was reduced by 25 percent.[16]

Confusion at Tosan Junction

On the whole, Task Force Kean's scheduled drive on Chinju and Sachon had not met with much success during the first 48 hours. The

---

[12] Bohn, 17 Apr 54.
[13] Annex How.
[14] *Ibid.*
[15] Fegan, 17 Apr 54.
[16] Annex How.

only advance was made on the right, where the 35th Infantry seized its first objective and inflicted an estimated 350 casualties on the enemy.[17]

In his capacity as provisional commander of all units along the Masan-Chinju axis, General Craig was directing the Army operations at the front and in the rear areas of the Task Force sector. Thus on 8 August he ordered the 5th RCT to continue its attack and take Tosan, so that his Marines could make progress on the road to Sachon.

After preparatory fires, the Army regiment again pushed forward toward its immediate objective. Enemy resistance was much heavier than on the day before; nevertheless, some gains were made from the starting point near the village of Singi. The attack was also slowed by the narrow MSR carrying the entire traffic load for the Task Force. Heavy fighting above the road on Hills 255 and 342 added to the congestion and confusion on the vital artery.

Lieutenant Colonel Newton's 1st Battalion, 5th Marines, had been ordered to move forward from Chindong-ni at 0600, 8 August, with the mission of attacking along the south fork of the Tosan junction preparatory to seizing a regimental objective which would be designated later.[18]

Leaving its positions on Hill 99 at the assigned time, the battalion was stalled immediately at the bridges on the MSR below. The road was still clogged with soldiers and Army vehicles, making it impossible for the Marine unit to proceed.[19]

General Craig, who was in the vicinity, told Newton to hold up until the situation at the front became clarified. Company B, commanded by Captain John L. Tobin, was ordered back up on the hill it had just descended; and the battalion waited, three miles from its line of departure.[20]

Finally the word came to move up. While 1/5 worked its way along the crowded road, Newton walked ahead and reached the CP of the 1st Battalion, 5th RCT, located on a hillside between Singi and Oryong. There he learned that the Army unit's companies were already on the high ground all around the junction and that the rice paddies between the battalion CP and these companies were full of North Koreans. The Army commander considered his subordinate units cut off.[21]

---

17 Annexes 1 and 3 to 25th InfDiv War Diary, Book VIII.

18 Annex How; Brig Op Plan 5–50; and Col G. R. Newton, ltr to author, 3 Jan 54 (Newton, 3 Jan 54).

19 LtCol M. R. Olson, interv with author, 30 Dec 53 (Olson, 30 Dec 53).

20 Col G. R. Newton, ltr to author, 19 Jan 54 (Newton, 19 Jan 54).

21 Newton, 3 Jan 54; and Olson, 30 Dec 53.

Shortly afterwards, at about 1400, the head of 1/5's column reached Newton and again came to a halt, a mile and a half from its line of departure.

Arriving on the scene at this time was a dispirited Army staff sergeant, dripping with mud and water. He said that he had just returned from Hill 308, south of the road junction, where his unit was heavily engaged with the enemy. And he added that Communist machineguns covering the wide rice paddy between 308 and the MSR had forced him to crawl almost the whole distance.[22]

Lieutenant Colonel Murray, while driving from Chindong-ni to the front, was stopped on the road by Major General Kean himself. The 25th Division commander directed the Marine officer to arrange for a night relief of the 1st Battalion, 5th RCT. Kean stated that he would inform Brigade headquarters of this change in plans as soon as possible.[23]

It had become a question as to whether Task Force Kean or the NKPA 6th Division controlled Tosan. Newton radioed the 5th Marines commander and asked for enlightenment. Murray, having just finished his conversation with General Kean, ordered the battalion commander to postpone the jumpoff until nightfall.[24]

After withdrawing to the outskirts of Sangnyong-ni, 1/5 went into an assembly area beneath the western spur of Hill 342. There the battalion commander received specific orders to relieve the 1st Battalion, 5th RCT, on positions southwest of Tosan at midnight, 8 August, and secure the troublesome road junction once and for all.[25]

Newton was to have his battalion at the Army CP no later than 2300, when it would be furnished guides to lead the way across the broad rice paddy to Hill 308. As it proved, the Marine unit actually reached the designated rendezvous at 2200. But even though an hour early, Newton discovered that the soldiers on 308 were already withdrawing. Moreover, no guides had been provided.[26]

The Marine battalion continued westward through Singi and stopped on the MSR about a half-mile short of Tosan. Here a narrow dike branched south from the road, and the soldiers were returning along this trail from Hill 308 to the MSR. Since the footpath was pointed out as Newton's route of approach, he had little choice but to wait until the

---

[22] Olson, 30 Dec 53.

[23] Col R. L. Murray, ltr to author, 7 Jan 54 (Murray, 7 Jan 54).

[24] Newton, 3 Jan 54; and Olson, 30 Dec 53.

[25] Annex How; Brig Op Plan 6–50; and Newton, 3 Jan 54.

[26] Newton, 3 Jan 54 and 19 Jan 54; and Olson, 30 Dec 53.

Army troops made the crossing. This was accomplished shortly after midnight, and the column of Marines was left alone in the night on unfamiliar ground reported to be crawling with enemy.[27]

The promised guides reported for duty at this time. They turned out to be two South Korean civilians. Without further ado, the advance on Sachon was launched when a long single file of skeptical Marines fell in behind two unknown natives whose loyalty had to be accepted on faith.

Following the 1,200-yard trail in the darkness was time-consuming as well as nerve-chilling. A misstep on the narrow, slippery dike usually meant a spill into the muck and filth of the paddy for some hapless infantryman. Not only would he delay all those behind, but he would not be as fragrant as a rose in the nostrils of his comrades when he regained the dike.

Finally the head of the file reached the base of Hill 308, having encountered not a single enemy on the way. As more and more men threaded their way in from the paddy, tactical integrity was slowly regained. Dawn of 9 August was already breaking when the rear of the column completed the crossing.[28]

Daybreak brought a radio message from Murray, directing 1/5 to continue the attack to the southwest immediately and seize Hill 308. With Tobin's company leading, the battalion ascended the northern slopes in a long column. The climb took the Marines more than 1,000 feet upward and 2,000 yards to the south. Before the summit was reached, the relentless sun and terrain had taken its toll of Newton's infantrymen. Fortunately, enemy resistance amounted to mere sniping; and by noon, 9 August, the massive terrain feature belonged to the Brigade.[29]

At 1700 that afternoon Craig's operational control of all troops in the area came to a close. At the end of the 54-hour period of the Marine general's overall command, the road junction had been cleared, and both Army and Marine columns were making progress toward the objective.

Brigade Artillery in Support

Nearly all the infantry actions of the first 3 days owed a good deal to the support of the 1st Battalion, 11th Marines. Consisting of three 4-gun

---

[27] *Ibid.*

[28] Olson, 30 Dec 53.

[29] *Ibid.*

batteries, Lieutenant Colonel Ransom M. Wood's outfit had relieved the 8th Field Artillery Battalion at Chindong-ni on the eve of D-day. Since the terrain afforded no suitable alternate areas, the Marine gunners moved into the positions vacated by the Army artillery, partly in the village and partly on the outskirts.

A total of 87 rounds were fired that first night in support of the 5th Marines, with the FO's reporting good results. Before long, however, enemy counterbattery fires searched out friendly positions in the village. Early the next morning a Marine battery took a direct hit from an NKPA 122-mm. shell. Two men were killed and 8 wounded by a blast which destroyed a 105-mm. howitzer. Thus, reversing the usual rule, the artillery suffered heavier casualties than the infantry at the jumpoff of the Brigade attack.[30]

The gunners needed no further admonitions to dig foxholes, gunpits and ammunition pits. During the confused fighting around Chindong-ni, it was not unusual to have one battery laid on an azimuth generally east, another west, and a third to the north.

"I think that this is one of the most important lessons we learned in fighting infiltrating troops," commented Wood; "artillery must be able and always prepared to fire in any direction on a moment's notice."[31]

From 7 to 9 August, with the battalion displacing forward as the infantry advanced, 89 missions and 1,892 rounds were fired. Targets consisted largely of enemy mortar positions. The terrain offered some knotty problems in firing close support missions, due to steep slopes; but the OY's of VMO-6 did a good job of spotting.

Fifty ROK policemen were attached to 1/11 at this time to be used as security troops. Wearing bright green uniforms and rubber shoes upon arrival, they became the responsibility of the battalion to feed, equip and train in marksmanship, sanitation and ammunition handling. The rice-eating Koreans turned up their noses at American food for a few days, but soon they could compete with any chow-hounds in the outfit.[32]

Another difficulty was experienced in convincing the newcomers that NKPA prisoners were to be brought in alive. Many personal scores remained to be paid off in war-torn Korea, but eventually the ROK's learned to control their hatred for the invaders.

---

[30] Annex Item to Brig SAR.

[31] LtCol Ransom M. Wood, "Artillery Support for the Brigade in Korea," *Marine Corps Gazette,* 35, No. 6:16–17 (Jun 51).

[32] *Ibid.*

Encounter With Japanese Maps

As the men of 1/5 were consolidating their hilltop and searching for water to relieve heat prostration cases, Murray radioed Newton to withdraw his unit to the road below and continue the attack to Paedun-ni. The regimental commander was determined to speed up the advance to the south, since intelligence had reported no enemy on the high ground south of Hill 308.[33]

With almost half of Companies A and B stricken by heat sickness, Newton had no choice but to leave them in position on the high ground for the time being. He descended the hill to form a tactical column with Headquarters and Weapons Companies and an attached platoon of tanks.

Reaching the low ground northwest of Hill 308, the battalion commander discovered that his Japanese maps, as usual, bore only a slight resemblance to the actual ground.

During the early weeks in Korea, the map situation was a thorn in the side of every tactical commander. Not only were maps of local areas extremely scarce, but the few available were of early Japanese vintage, almost consistently at variance with the terrain. Grid systems were confusing, villages misnamed and misplaced, and roads either not illustrated at all or else plotted inaccurately. Lack of contouring left the conformation and extent of ridges entirely to the imagination of the map reader. These shortcomings were a constant source of concern; for troop leaders often were misled, even to the extent of getting completely lost.

On the ground itself, there is an intersection called Oso-ri some 600 yards south of the Tosan junction. The routes leading both south and west from this crossroads go to Paedun-ni. An unimproved road, the southward passage is more rugged, while the other, being good by Korean standards, follows a smoother course through the town of Taesil-li.

Newton s map showed only the latter improved road, so he formed his column and headed it toward Taesil-li, a thousand yards west of the intersection.[34] Murray's map showed both roads, but in this case the southern route was erroneously drawn in as the better road. It was thus Murray's intention that 1/5 use this avenue of approach. And since he had spoken of it as the "improved" road, Newton was misled into choosing the route to Taesil-li.[35]

---

[33] Murray, 7 Jan 54.
[34] Newton, 3 Jan 53.
[35] *Ibid.;* and Murray, 7 Jan 54.

The quickly formed column of tanks and infantry had gone only a few hundred yards when the point stopped at a stretch of road littered with land mines. A call went out for a demolitions team. From his CP near Chindong-ni, Captain George W. King dispatched his 1st Platoon, Able Company Engineers. Arriving at the scene, the Marine troubleshooters discovered the obstacles to be merely American antitank mines, apparently spilled on the road from an Army vehicle.

About this time, Lieutenant Colonel Murray arrived at Oso-ri and informed 1/5's commander that he was on the wrong road. Newton reasoned that his unit was following the correct route. After comparing the conflicting maps, the regimental commander studied the terrain and directed Newton to pull his column back and take the road to the south. Then Murray returned to Sangnyong-ni, climbed into an observation plane, and was flown over the route to confirm his decision.[36]

There was no small amount of confusion as the long column of tanks, infantrymen, and engineers pulled back along the narrow road to the intersection. And it was unfortunate for 1/5 that General Craig reached the area while the milling was at its worst. Unaware of what had taken place earlier, the Brigade commander did not refer to the delay and congestion in the most soothing terms.[37]

While the column was being reformed on the southern road, villagers from Taesil-li informed the Marines that a badly wounded American was lying in the hamlet. Craig's jeep driver sped to the clump of thatched huts and returned with a soldier who was more dead than alive, having been left behind by retreating NKPA forces. The man was rushed to the rear for medical attention, while Craig stayed forward to supervise the attack.[38]

The long file of Marines and tanks began moving southward along the winding road below Hill 308. Newton had notified his company commanders of the change, so that they could meet him by descending the western slope of the high ground.

About a mile south of the confusing intersection, the point of 1/5's column rounded a sharp curve. It was greeted by a lone North Korean machinegun hidden in a native hut at the center of the bend. While a Marine brigadier watched with professional satisfaction, a team of infantrymen with a rocket launcher closed on the hut and quickly destroyed the enemy position.

---

[36] Murray, 7 Jan 54.
[37] Craig, 12 Jan 54.
[38] *Ibid.;* and Newton, 19 Jan 54.

It was late afternoon as the column resumed its march to the south. Covering several hundred more yards without incident, it reached the top of a 400-foot pass where the road knifed between Hills 308 and 190. There Newton was joined by Companies A and B from Objective One.[39] The 1st Battalion was ordered to hold up and take defensive positions astride the pass.

Thus, the drive toward Sachon had finally taken shape, and the Brigade was entering its own zone of responsibility. As darkness fell on 9 August, 1/5 was in position 2 miles south of the Tosan line of departure, and General Craig had already set in motion plans for a night attack.

Ambush at Taedabok Pass

On 9 August the Brigade commander was convinced that the absence of resistance in 1/5's path indicated unpreparedness on the part of the enemy. To exploit the advantage, he ordered Murray to execute a night attack and capture Paedun-ni before daylight, 10 August.[40]

At 1600 on 9 August, the Brigade was relieved of mopping up duties in the Chindong-ni area, leaving 2/5 immediately available to the 5th Marines commander. The 3d Battalion was delayed overnight by several hours of security duty until Army units could take over.[41]

Lieutenant Colonel Roise's battalion, having been relieved on Hill 342, entrucked at Sangnyong-ni in the evening and reached its assembly area near Hill 308 at 2100. Two hours later the unit marched southward on the new MSR to make the night attack on Paedun-ni. Passing through 1/5's lines at 0115, 10 August, the weary Marines pressed on toward their target against no resistance.

The point of the column included three M–26's of First Lieutenant William D. Pomeroy's tank platoon. At 0500, with the advance elements only a short distance from Paedun-ni, the lead tank crashed through a concrete bridge. The badly damaged vehicle proved to be wedged immovably between the two abutments.

The second tank, while attempting to negotiate a narrow bypass next to the bridge, threw a track in the center of the stream and stalled the long column behind. Two hours elapsed before the advance could be

---

[39] Olson, 30 Dec 53.
[40] Brig Op Plan 7–50.
[41] This section is derived from: Annex How; Craig, 12 Jan 54; Zimmer, 18 Feb 54; Fegan and Bohn, 17 Apr 54; and Gall, 9 Feb 54.

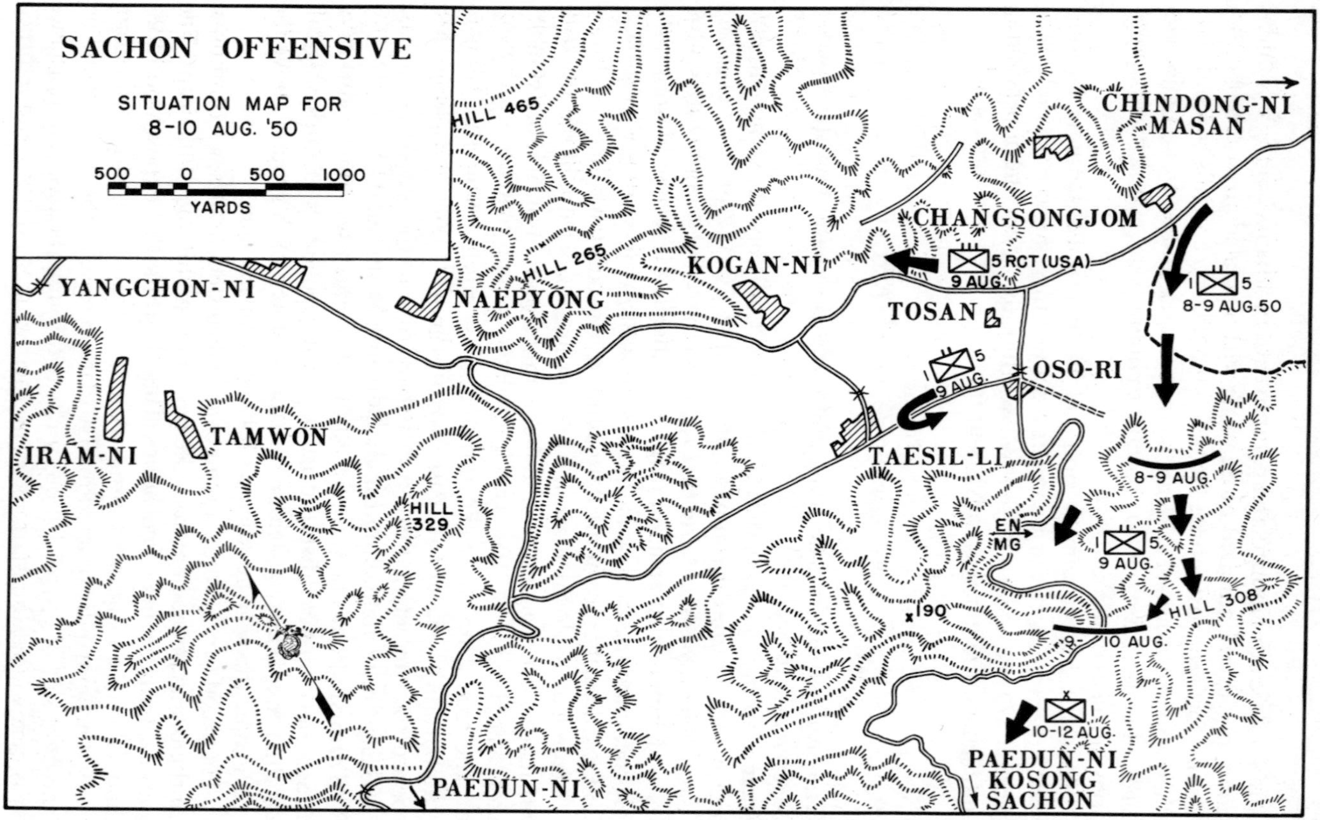
SACHON OFFENSIVE
SITUATION MAP FOR
8-10 AUG. '50
500 0 500 1000
YARDS
HILL 465
HILL 265
CHINDONG-NI
MASAN
CHANGSONGJOM
5 RCT (USA)
9 AUG.
KOGAN-NI
YANGCHON-NI
NAEPYONG
TOSAN
1 5
8-9 AUG. 50
1 5
9 AUG.
OSO-RI
TAESIL-LI
IRAM-NI
TAMWON
HILL
329
8-9 AUG.
EN
MG
1 5
9 AUG.
HILL 308
x190
9-10 AUG.
1
10-12 AUG.
PAEDUN-NI
KOSONG
SACHON
PAEDUN-NI

resumed. South Korean laborers constructed a bypass for light vehicles next to the bridge, and an engineer tractor-dozer arrived to build a detour for heavy trucks and tanks.

Reaching Paedun-ni at 0800, 2/5 reconnoitered the town and found it clear of enemy. By 0930 the battalion column was reformed and pounding the dusty road south.

Murray decided to shuttle troops by truck from Paedun-ni to Kosong, since the 8-mile stretch was believed to be free of enemy. The heavier vehicles being tied up at the collapsed bridge, some delay resulted in motorizing the first increment of 2/5.

General Craig arrived on the scene by helicopter in mid-morning. Not satisfied with the progress of the advance, he ordered Murray and Roise to march on Kosong with "all speed." When the infantry column was a short distance out of Paedun-ni, the 5th Marines commander managed to get five 2½-ton trucks forward to help transport the first serial to the target.

A motorized column was formed of 4 lead jeeps carrying a Reconnaissance Company detachment, followed by part of Company D aboard 6 more jeeps and the 5 trucks. Owing to the shortage of vehicles, Captain Zimmer's first echelon included only the 1st and 2d Platoons, the 60-mm. mortars, an assault squad, and one machinegun section.

Lacking either air or artillery support, the column rolled southward with orders to occupy Kosong and coordinate a defense of the city with its mayor. The remainder of 2/5 continued on foot until more vehicles could be provided

The road makes a sharp turn 2½ miles southwest of Paedun-ni to climb through Taedabok Pass, a defile about 1,000 yards long. Just beyond, at the village of Pugok, a sharp turn to the left skirts the base of a large hill overlooking the entire length of the pass.

The first jeep of the reconnaissance detachment was almost abreast of Pugok at 1500 when NKPA machineguns opened up from the big hill at the bend. Enemy automatic weapons on the high ground above the pass raked the vehicles filled with Dog Company men.

As the Marines were taking cover in roadside ditches, a Communist antitank gun opened fire from the large hill and hit one of the jeeps. The reconnaissance troops gradually withdrew from their exposed positions and fell back on Zimmer's group. After sizing up the situation, the Company D commander ordered his 1st Platoon to seize the high ground on the right side of the road about midway through the pass. No resistance was met, so that the Marines set up their weapons quickly and returned the Communist fire. Meanwhile the 2d Platoon moved up on the right after clearing small enemy groups from the high ground on both sides of the road at the entrance to the defile.

Zimmer had spotted the location of the enemy's antitank gun, and Marine 60-mm. fire put an end to this nuisance. The effort used up all the mortar ammunition, and the Company D commander decided to wait in position for Brigade supporting arms. Two tanks arrived at 1630, and their 90-mm. guns drove the enemy into hiding.

While Marine tanks and air were working over the hill, 3/5 reached Paedun-ni after being relieved of its final security mission in the Chindong-ni area. Murray ordered Taplett to be prepared to pass through 2/5 and continue the attack.

The 3d Battalion reached the entrance to Taedabok Pass in trucks shortly after the arrival of the 2d Battalion troops who had followed their motorized column on foot. Some confusion resulted on the narrow road after Murray's arrival while he waited to confer with Taplett. Unable to find Roise, the two officers climbed the high ground on the left. From this vantage point they could see Kosong, 5 miles away. The regimental commander ordered Taplett to pass through 2/5 immediately and continue the attack.

Company G had already crossed the line of departure and was deploying to assault the hill at the road bend when Murray located Roise in Zimmer's area to the right of the road. The exact location of enemy positions remained in some doubt. In order to clear up the uncertainty, Major McNeely volunteered to lead out a patrol. About 1730, therefore, Roise's S/3 took off in a jeep with a radio operator and a fire team from Dog Company.

By this time, Taplett had a fairly accurate picture of the situation in mind. From his OP on the high ground to the left of the road, he saw that McNeely was headed for danger. The 3/5 commander radioed Bohn to stop the jeep, but it was too late. McNeely and his men vanished from sight around the bend where the road skirted the large hill, and the Marines heard a furious clatter of machinegun and small arms fire.

The fate of the patrol remained in doubt as Company G moved out to the attack, with First Lieutenant Jack Westerman's platoon in the lead. Communist fire held up the advance, but Bohn sent Second Lieutenant Edward F. Duncan's platoon on a sweeping envelopment to the right which outflanked the enemy and drove him from the high ground. Westerman was then able to reach the crest with his platoon. From this position he could see McNeely's bullet-riddled jeep, but that officer and

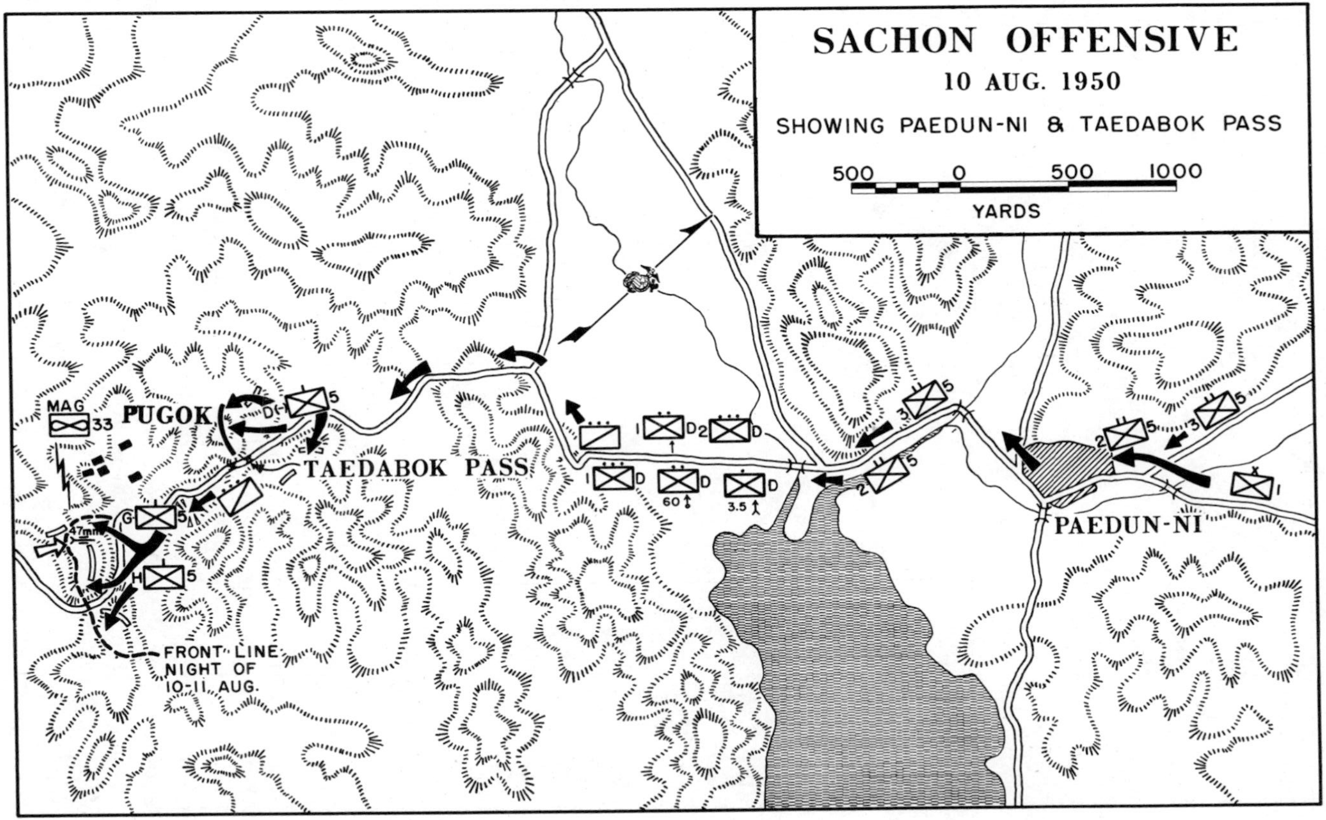
SACHON OFFENSIVE
10 AUG. 1950
SHOWING PAEDUN-NI & TAEDABOK PASS
500 0 500 1000
YARDS
PAEDUN-NI
TAEDABOK PASS
PUGOK
MAG 33
FRONT LINE
NIGHT OF
10-11 AUG.

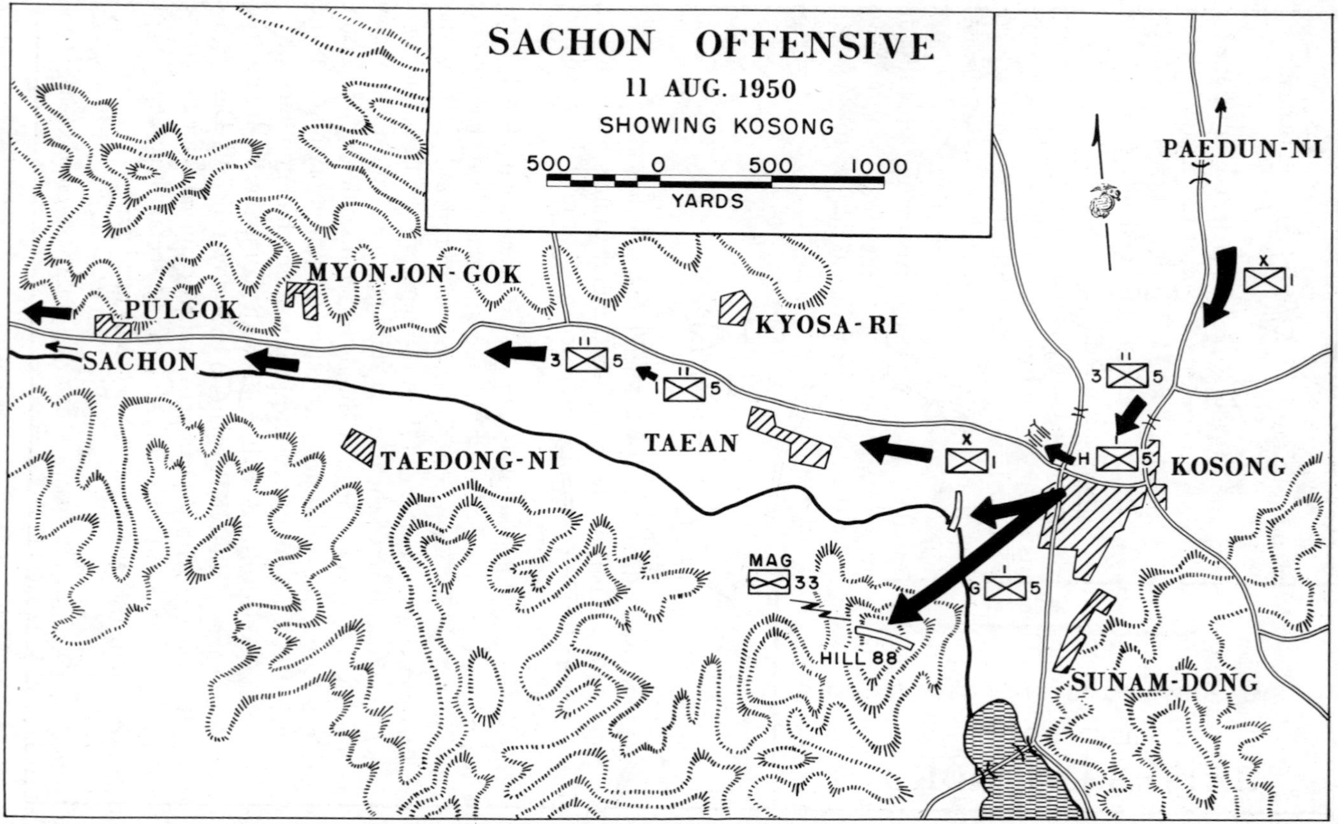
SACHON OFFENSIVE
11 AUG. 1950
SHOWING KOSONG
500 0 500 1000
YARDS
PAEDUN-NI
MYONJON-GOK
PULGOK
KYOSA-RI
SACHON
TAEAN
TAEDONG-NI
KOSONG
MAG 33
HILL 88
SUNAM-DONG

his five men were stretched out motionless on the ground beneath and behind the vehicle.

At great risk, Westerman made a dash to the jeep and brought back McNeely, mortally wounded. Enemy fire prevented further rescues, but it was ascertained that 3 men had been killed outright and 2 severely wounded. These survivors could only continue to take cover behind the wrecked vehicle until 3/5 troops advanced.

When Company G jumped off again, the men were held up by two concealed machineguns at the far end of the road bend. Taplett committed How Company on the left side of the MSR, and Fegan seized the hill opposite Bohn's position. It was almost dark before the Marines could silence the 2 enemy machineguns around the bend, and at 2015 Murray ordered 3/5 to secure for the night and defend the 2 hills already occupied. On the premise that the enemy had prepared an ambush for rescue parties approaching the wrecked jeep, it was decided to wait until morning to bring back the wounded men.

The Seizure of Kosong

The night passed quietly except for scattered rifle fire along the 3d Battalion's 700-yard front. To carry out General Craig's orders for 11 August, the two rifle companies prepared to continue the attack on Kosong at first light.[42]

The enemy had different plans. At the crack of dawn a small force of North Koreans emerged from the fog and charged recklessly into Company G's front. There was a furious hand-to-hand clash as the attackers converged on Bohn's OP in the center of the line. The company commander directed the defense amid grenade explosions, one of which drove a fragment into his shoulder. At his side Staff Sergeant Charles F. Kurtz, Jr., called down effective 60-mm. mortar fire on the Reds while throwing grenades and ducking submachinegun bursts.

The melee ended after a half hour with Company G driving the battered remnants of the NKPA platoon back down the hill Despite his wound, Bohn stayed with his company and reorganized it for the attack on Kosong. He also had the satisfaction of overseeing the evacuation of the two wounded survivors of McNeely's ill-fated patrol.

[42] This section is derived from: Annex How; Craig, 12 Jan 54; Fegan and Bohn, 17 Apr 54 (with comments by LtCol R. D. Taplett).

At 0800, the Brigade moved out in a route column, with 3/5 as the advance guard and Company G in the role of advance party. Bohn's point consisted of Second Lieutenant John D. Counselman's 3d Platoon, whose leading element, under Corporal Raymond Giaquinto, was on the MSR with flank guards slightly withheld on each side.

The Brigade column moved swiftly. About a mile beyond the line of departure, Giaquinto braked his roadbound unit in the face of doubtful ground ahead. Simultaneously, the flank guards surged forward and wrapped around the suspected area. Then Giaquinto's force raced down the road, and the 3 prongs of the point converged on an enemy machine-gun emplacement, killing the 5 occupants before they could fire a shot.

With Bohn calling the shots and Giaquinto setting the pace, the point swept aside three more enemy positions along the route. The effective combination of limited frontal attacks and envelopments brought the head of the column to the bridge north of Kosong at 1000. Here Company H passed through on the road and pushed into the town.

Using 1 rifle platoon and 2 tanks, Fegan easily cleared northern Kosong of light resistance. Then he gradually wheeled his force to the right, tracing the road to Sachon. His other two platoons continued southward with the mission of seizing a high hill below Sunam-dong.

General Craig reached Kosong by jeep just as Taplett was setting up his CP in a schoolyard north of the town. A small group of enemy snipers suddenly opened up from positions in and around the schoolhouse, and the Brigade commander observed sniper teams of 3/5's headquarters spring into action and destroy the North Koreans.

Shortly after Fegan entered Kosong, Bohn swung his company to the southwest from above the town, drove through the western suburbs and launched an attack against Hill 88 below the Sachon road. Approaching the hill, Company G sustained a few casualties while eliminating a stubborn Communist pocket in the low ground on its right flank.

MAG-33 preceded the attack on Hill 88 with a thundering air strike on 100 enemy entrenched along the crest. This attack coupled with a thorough shelling by 1/11, shattered the Reds' will to fight, and Company G found only evidence of a hasty flight when it reached the summit at 1330.

General Craig ordered Taplett to cancel all further missions around the captured town and attack toward Sachon immediately. Company G was quickly recalled from Hill 88; the high ground above Sunam-dong was ignored, and Fegan assembled his unit at the western edge of Kosong preparatory to leading the attack.

Just as Company H was reforming, a jeep ambulance driven by Corpsman William H. Anderson raced into the area to pick up casualties from Bohn's earlier skirmish below Hill 88. Passing through Fegan's troops, the vehicle failed to make the turn southward and sped toward Sachon. Two enemy antitank guns lying in wait west of Kosong blasted the jeep as it rounded a bend, killing Anderson and spilling two passengers out of the wrecked vehicle.

Fegan led two M–26 tanks to the bend, and Technical Sergeant Johnnie C. Cottrell quickly destroyed the North Korean position. Three rounds from his 90-mm. gun wiped out the last NKPA opposition in the area, and the 3d Battalion moved out for the drive on Sachon.

CHAPTER VIII

Fight on Two Fronts

The Kosong Turkey Shoot—The Changchon Ambush—Marines Ordered to New Sector—Attack of 3/5 to the Rear—Enemy Dawn Attack at Changchon—Breaking Off Action

MARINE AIR AND artillery had a field day on 11 August 1950 that the rifle companies will never forget. The occasion was known as "the Kosong Turkey Shoot," and it was a victory won entirely by supporting arms.

It happened just as 3/5 was about to enter Kosong. As a preliminary, 1/11 was called upon just before noon for preparatory fires. Shells from the 105's landed in the town, sending up geysers of rubble in the bright sunlight. Then, suddenly, the Marine artillery flushed out a column of enemy vehicles making a frantic dash for safety.

This flight explains the light resistance which the Marine infantry met in Kosong. But the enemy could hardly have chosen a less propitious moment, for he had merely escaped from the frying pan into the fire. Overhead, to his sorrow, was a division of VMF-323 planes from the *Badoeng Strait,* which the forward TACP had sent on a search and attack mission just beyond the town.[1] Major Lund and his pilots were thus presented with a fabulous target of opportunity—an estimated 100 vehicles of the NKPA 83d Motorcycle Regiment, including jeeps, motorcycles and troop-carrying trucks.[2]

The Kosong Turkey Shoot

The Corsairs came screaming down in low-level strafing runs the entire length of the column for the purpose of bringing it to a halt. Vehicles

[1] VMF-323 SAR, 3 Aug-6 Sep 50.

[2] Estimates as to the number of vehicles vary widely. Apparently no exact count was ever made.

crashed into one another or piled up in the ditch while enemy troops scrambled out for cover. The Soviet-made jeeps and motorcycles were now sitting ducks for F4U's which worked over individual targets with rocket or 20-mm. fire. After the Marine planes had set about 40 vehicles on fire, they were relieved by another flight of VMF-323 machines and Air Force F-51's which added the finishing touches to the picture of destruction.[3]

Under the circumstances the enemy put up a creditable fight. Lund and his low-flying pilots encountered fierce small arms and automatic weapons fire. Two of the four Corsairs in the first flight were badly damaged and had to try for emergency landings. Lieutenant Doyle Cole ditched into the bay just as General Craig was making a tour of inspection by helicopter; and the Brigade commander operated the hoist which pulled the dripping flier up to safety.

Captain Vivian Moses was not so fortunate. While putting his crippled plane down in enemy territory, he was thrown unconscious from the cockpit and drowned in a rice paddy a few minutes before a VMO-6 helicopter arrived. Only the day before, this gallant Marine pilot had been rescued by helicopter, after being shot down behind the NKPA lines, and flown back unhurt to his carrier. Despite this experience, Captain Moses volunteered for duty on 11 August, when he became the first death casualty of MAG-33.

Several hours later, after securing Kosong and resuming the attack toward Sachon, the Marine ground forces caught up with the scene of chaos left by the F4U's. Among the twisted and charred vehicles were some that the enemy had abandoned in perfect condition. Tolerant NCO's relaxed discipline for a moment while their men tried out the motorcycles with sidecars and the sleek, black Soviet jeeps, most of which had gone into the attack practically new. Almost identical in design to American jeeps, these vehicles were found to be powered by familiar Ford-type engines—a throwback to United States Lend Lease to Russia in World War II.

Generals Craig and Cushman surveyed the wreckage from a helicopter next day. This strike, however, was only one of the more dramatic examples of the Brigade air-ground team in action. MAG-33 aircraft were constantly orbiting on station over the front line as the ground forces advanced. Flown by infantry-trained pilots briefed on the local ground

---

[3] Ernest Giusti, "Marine Air Over the Pusan Perimeter," *Marine Corps Gazette,* 36, No. 5:20–21 (May 52).

situation, the Corsairs were available for employment on short notice. It was a simple and flexible system; and the fact that VMF–214 and VMF–323 were based on the two carriers meant that they could arrive on station with more fuel and ordnance for strikes as compared to Japan-based squadrons.[4]

Overall control of tactical air operations in Korea was exercised by the Fifth Air Force. Marine aviation units, as components of an integrated Fleet Marine Force, operated in support of the Brigade as their highest priority, and in support of other UN forces as a lower priority. After checking in with Fifth AF TACC at the Joint Operations Center (JOC), Marine aviation units came under Marine operational control when supporting Brigade ground forces. When providing tactical air support for other UN forces, Marine air units operated under the Air Force-Army system for tactical air support.

The Brigade control organization included 3 battalion TACP's and 1 regimental TACP, each consisting of an officer and 6 enlisted men, and each equipped with a radio jeep, portable radios and remoting equipment. MAG–33 provided a Brigade control agency consisting of the Air Support Section of MTACS–2. Other Brigade units associated with control of aircraft were:

(1) The Air Section of the Brigade Staff, consisting of the Brigade Air officer and six enlisted men responsible for planning as well as tactical control and coordination of supporting aircraft;

(2) The Brigade observation section, consisting of the tactical air observer, three gunnery observers, and the OY and rotary-wing aircraft of VMO–6.

Carrier-based Marine aviation units maintained a TAC and one or more flights of aircraft on station during daylight hours. Night heckler and intruder missions of VMF(N)–513 from Itazuke reported to the Fifth AF TACC and were routed by that agency to the Air Support Section (MTACS–2) with the Brigade. During the early Brigade operations, with the Air Force TACC located at Taegu, delays of incoming flights reporting to JOC were caused by overloaded communications nets. An improvement resulted when such flights by-passed JOC and reported directly to the Air Support Section of Brigade. And when JOC moved back to Pusan, improved communications resulted in incoming flights reporting first to JOC again.

---

[4] This summary of tactical air operations is derived from MCBS, I–IV–B, 9–14; Maj George J. King, interv with author, n. d.

The Brigade control agency (Air Support Section) made use of the following communications for the control of tactical air operations:

(1) TAR net connecting battalion TACP's, the regimental TACP, and the Air Support Section, and monitored by the Brigade Air Section. This was an HF net.

(2) TAD net connecting above-named agencies as well as TAC flights of support aircraft and on occasion the TAO. This was a VHF net of four frequencies used to brief and control aircraft reporting for support missions.

(3) TAO net connecting observation aircraft, the Brigade CP (Air Section) and the Air Support Section. This was an HF net.

(4) An administrative (HF) net connecting the Air Support Section and the carriers *Sicily* and *Badoeng Strait.*

The workings of the control organization of the Brigade air-ground team in the Pusan Perimeter have been described as follows in the survey of the Marine Corps Board Study:

"Battalion TACP's made requests for air support missions direct by TAR net to the Air Support Section. The regimental TACP and Brigade Air Section monitored this net. The Brigade control agency having received a request for a mission, contacted the TAC and the Flight Leader (FL) of the aircraft orbiting on station awaiting a mission. The TAC and the FL were then directed to the vicinity of the TACP from whom the request had originated.

"The TACP controlled the execution of the mission in accordance with the wishes of the battalion commander. The TACP gave the location of the target to the TAC. The latter designated the target to the FL and his flight of supporting aircraft. The unit being supported marked its front lines. The TAC directed the attacking aircraft in making attacks on the target. His directions related to the technique of attacking specific targets with aircraft. Control of the attack was exercised by the ground unit being supported.

"In many instances the TAC or the TAO would locate targets not yet located by ground units. This was often done in response to a request from ground units. Both the TAC and TAO located targets beyond the vision of ground units, and both were capable of, and did, designate these targets to flights of supporting aircraft and directed attacks on such targets, when requested to do so by ground units. Conditions favored delegating control to forward TACP's beyond convenient VHF range between them and the Brigade (Air Support Section). Brigade attack formations frequently consisted of battalions in column. The forward battalion was free to employ air support at a moment's notice."

This was the situation on the afternoon of 11 August 1950 as the 3d Battalion of the 5th Marines attacked toward Sachon, followed by 2/5 in trace. Overhead a flight of VMF-323 Corsairs orbited on station, and

OY observers reported the enemy to be pulling back rapidly toward Sachon.

How Company led the Marine attack, with lead tanks employing reconnaissance by fire. At 1800, after the column had covered several miles, a lone enemy machinegun in a valley on the left held up the advance by wounding three Marines. By the time the tanks silenced the weapon with .50-caliber fire, it was decided to halt. Taplett deployed his battalion on two hills north of the road, and the infantrymen settled down for a quiet night.

The gravel crunchers could thank air and other supporting arms for an impressive demonstration of power that day. There was even the suggestion of an amphibious operation in the Brigade advance, for an LST followed the column and anchored near the fishing village of Tanghong-ni after the securing of Kosong.

This was LST QO119, a supply ship manned by Team No. 1 of Major William L. Batchelor's Company A, 1st Shore Party Battalion. Team No. 2 set up forward dumps along the MSR as the infantry advanced, while No. 3 unloaded supplies and equipment at the Masan railhead. Shore Party personnel also assisted in salvage operations, which were conducted mainly at Changwon.[5]

LST QO119 was not only the workhorse of normal Shore Party missions; it served also as an improvised hospital ship. For the Medical Section and Company C, 1st Medical Battalion, had an extra responsibility these sweltering days in caring for victims of heat prostration as well as the wounded. Thus it may have set some sort of a record when casualties were evacuated at one time by land, sea and air—motor ambulance, LST and helicopter.

The Changchon Ambush

At sundown on 11 August, as Taplett's battalion dug in for the night on the road to Sachon, the enemy seemed to be disorganized if not actually demoralized. For the first time since the invasion began, a sustained Eighth Army counterattack had not only stopped the Red Korean steamroller but sent it into reverse.

With the Marines a day's march from Sachon, the Army 5th RCT was running a dead heat on the shorter Chinju route to the north, where

---

[5] Annex Mike to Brig SAR.

opposition had been light the last 2 days. It might even have appeared on the evening of the 11th that the combined operation had turned into a friendly rivalry between two outfits racing toward their final objective by parallel roads. But any such assumption would have been premature, as General Craig and his staff well realized. They looked for further resistance and were not disillusioned. Within the next 48 hours, in fact, Craig's men were destined to carry out one of the most astonishing operations in the history of the Marine Corps—simultaneous BLT attacks in opposite directions on two fronts 25 miles apart.

There was no hint of any such development at 0630 on the morning of 12 August, when the 1st Battalion of the 5th Marines passed through the 3d Battalion with a mission of seizing Sachon. If anything, the front was too quiet to suit veteran NCO's, who suspected the enemy of being up to no good. The column moved out behind a 15-man detachment of Recon Company acting as the point under the command of Captain Kenneth J. Houghton. Next came Baker Company with the 1st, 2d, and 3d Platoons in that order. Two Marine tanks were sandwiched in between the 1st and 2d Platoons, and three more M-26's brought up the rear of Captain Tobin's company, followed by the main body of the battalion.

No opposition awaited the column. This unnatural calm continued for 4½ hours as the Marines advanced about 11 miles. At noon, with Sachon only 4 miles away, Houghton and the point rounded a bend into the thatched-hut hamlet of Changchon. The first enemy soldiers of the day were sighted when two skulking figures took cover. Several Marines opened fire, and in reply the hills on both sides of the road erupted into flame.[6]

The enemy had obviously planned to allow the entire column to come within range. But the trap was sprung prematurely as NKPA machineguns blazed away from the high ground in front and on both flanks. Captain Tobin immediately sent the 1st Platoon to the aid of the point. First Lieutenant Hugh C. Schryver led his men forward along the roadside ditches, and at the cost of three casualties they reinforced the thin line of Recon troops returning the enemy's fire.

Next, the company commander ordered First Lieutenant David S. Taylor's 2d Platoon to move up behind three Marine tanks. The M-26's were unable to maneuver off the road because of the danger of bogging

[6] This section is derived from: Brig SAR, 5th Marines, 1st Bn rpt; Maj John L. Tobin, ltr to author, 26 Apr 54 (Tobin, 26 Apr 54); Maj John R. Stevens, ltr to author, 11 Jan 54; and T/Sgt F. J. Lischeski, ltr to author, 14 Jan 54.

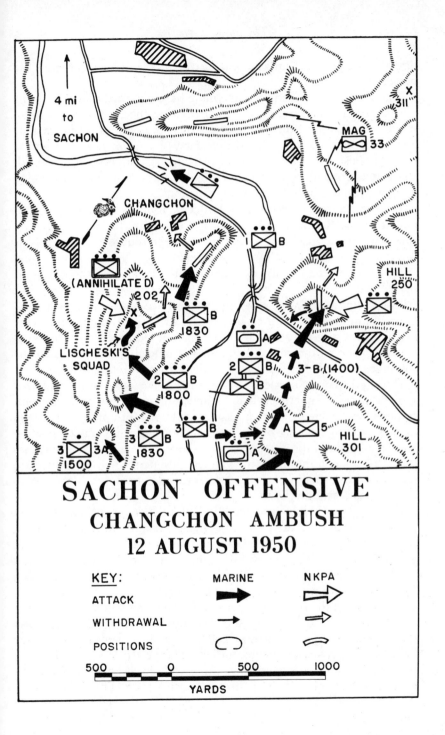

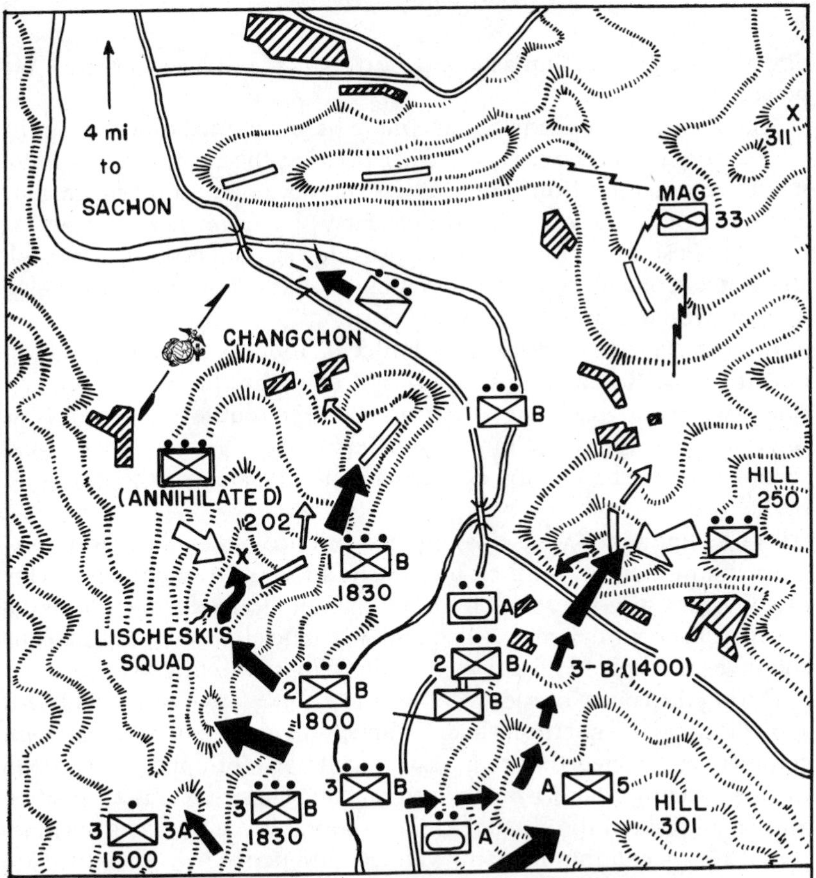

SACHON OFFENSIVE

CHANGCHON AMBUSH

12 AUGUST 1950

KEY:

	MARINE	NKPA
ATTACK		
WITHDRAWAL		
POSITIONS		

500 0 500 1000

YARDS

down in rice paddies, but as mobile fortresses they added to Marine fire power.

Tobin's whole company became more or less pinned down when the 3d Platoon and headquarters, farther back on the road, received automatic weapons fire from Hill 250 on the right. Newton immediately requested the battalion air controller, First Lieutenant James W. Smith, to call for a strike in this area. This was the only supporting arm available at the moment, since the mortar and artillery crews were just setting up their weapons in hastily selected positions.

After the Corsairs worked over Hill 250, Tobin ordered Second Lieutenant David R. Cowling's 3d Platoon to attack the high ground. A rifle platoon and machinegun section had been sent forward from Able Company by the battalion commander, and Newton gave these reinforcements the mission of seizing Hill 301, also on the right side of the road.

As Cowling's men were crossing the open rice paddy, the Marine tank guns and mortars added their fires to the air strike. But enough enemy machineguns survived to catch the 3d Platoon in a crossfire which forced it to fall back with 1 man killed and 4 wounded. The Able Company contingent occupied Hill 301 meanwhile without meeting any resistance.

During the course of these actions, the FAC reported to Newton that 2 of the Corsairs overhead had 5 minutes of time left. The battalion commander directed that they search for targets of opportunity along the road leading from Changchon to Sachon. The result was a repetition on a small scale of the Kosong turkey shoot, for the Marine planes surprised a little column of enemy vehicles and personnel. After the Corsairs unloaded their remaining ordnance, the road was strewn with twisted and burning vehicles.

The 3d Platoon fell back on Hill 301 as Newton ordered Captain John R. Stevens to secure the nearby high ground on the right side of the road with the rest of his Able Company troops. This left Hill 250 as the center of enemy resistance on the right. A total of 113 Marine mortar rounds were delivered on these positions, followed by a second air strike. The concentration of fire finally silenced the enemy's remaining machineguns, and the Baker Company right flank was secured.

The other two Baker Company platoons and Houghton's men had their hands full meanwhile on the left flank. They kept up a brisk fire fight from the roadside ditches until the Marine artillery took charge of the situation. One enemy position after another was knocked out in this quarter as Newton called for three more air strikes. These preparatory fires enabled the 1st and 2d Platoons to attack on the left after a laborious crossing of an intervening rice paddy.

The Marines proceeded to clean up the remaining NKPA positions methodically. A climax was reached when Lieutenant Taylor spotted an enemy group approaching the crest of Hill 202 from the reverse slope. He sent Technical Sergeant F. J. Lischeski with a squad to prepare a welcome. The veteran NCO coolly formed a line along the ridge and directed his men to wait until the enemy came within 75 feet before opening fire.

It would be hard to find a more striking example of Marine infantry firepower. Of the 39 men in the NKPA group, all were killed outright in a matter of seconds except a single officer. This survivor was so badly wounded that he died on the way to the regimental CP.

The fight had lasted all afternoon, and darkness fell before Company B could complete its movement to the high ground on the left side of the road and set up a perimeter of defense. It was estimated that an enemy company was operating in the area, covering the retreat of sorely battered elements of the NKPA 6th Infantry Division and 83d Motorcycle Regiment.

Marine losses were 3 killed and 13 wounded. After the securing of the high ground to the right, casualties were evacuated by road on the lee side of slowly moving tanks which provided shelter from enemy fire on the left.

Marines Ordered to New Sector

The Marines of 1/5 anticipated that the next day's advance would take them to Sachon. At midnight on 12 August, however, Lieutenant Colonel Newton received orders from the regimental commander to form the battalion on the road at 0630 in preparation for a lift by trucks to another sector, where the Marines were to reinforce Army units.

While Newton's men were fighting at Changchon, the Brigade commander had come up against a most unusual command situation. It began late on the morning of the 12th, when General Craig received orders from CG Task Force Kean, directing him to move a reinforced Marine rifle battalion back to Chindong-ni. General Kean emphasized that the shift be made without delay. Infiltrating enemy forces had penetrated far back in the rear to overrun positions of Battery C, 555th ("Triple Nickel") Field Artillery Battalion and Headquarters and Able Batteries, 90th Field Artillery Battalion, supporting the 25th Division.

The MSR being endangered, Marine reinforcements were urgently needed for a counterattack.[7]

At 0800 that morning Craig had set up his CP at Kosong. It was his custom to keep a terse and factual record of events from day to day, and the following chronological account is derived from entries in the Brigade commander's field notebook:

"1130—Received telephonic orders from CG 25th Div. stating that enemy was attacking in force across our MSR near Chindong-ni. He directed that I send one reinforced battalion to rear at once to give assistance to 24th Infantry engaged in that area and to recapture artillery pieces.

"1200—Proceeded by helicopter to CP 5th Marines to give necessary instructions. Made two landings en route to gather trucks for troop lift.

"1300—The reinforced 3d Bn., 5th Marines, now on way to Chindong-ni area.

"1330—Sent my G-3, LtCol Stewart, and LtCol Taplett, CO of 3/5, by helicopter to bridge indicated by CG 25th Div. to reconnoiter and formulate plans prior to arrival of battalion. Marines to operate directly under 25th Division for this action.

"1400—We are out on a limb with only two battalions left and Sachon still to take. Went to leading elements to check. They were engaged in a heavy fire fight at an attempted ambush position. Air brought to bear and helped, plus artillery. Enemy positions taken by 1/5, which dug in on high ground while 2/5 was disposed to protect rest of Brigade column.

"1730—Returned to Brigade CP at Kosong and received orders to proceed via helicopter to Masan to confer with CG 25th Division.

"1815—On flight to Masan I detoured to Chindong-ni area to make sure by air observation that 3/5 had arrived and apparently was not having any trouble.

"1830—Arrived Masan and was directed by General Kean to commence a tactical withdrawal from Sachon.

"1945—Returned by helicopter to my Kosong CP in early darkness and issued necessary orders."

The preparations for withdrawal lowered the spirits of Marines who believed that they had broken the back of enemy resistance in the Sachon area. This reaction may even be noted in the first paragraph of the Brigade withdrawal order:

"1. General Situation. Following Brigade rapid advance from Chindong-ni to Sachon in which this Brigade attacked, overcame, and pursued the enemy, the 25th Infantry Division has directed the withdrawal of this Brigade in order to hold a defensive position and mop up enemy resistance in the zone of action of elements of the 25th Division."

[7] This section is derived from: Craig, 18 May 5 and 12 Jan 54; Murray, 14 Jan 54; and Brig SAR, 5th Marines, 1st Bn and 3d Bn rpts.

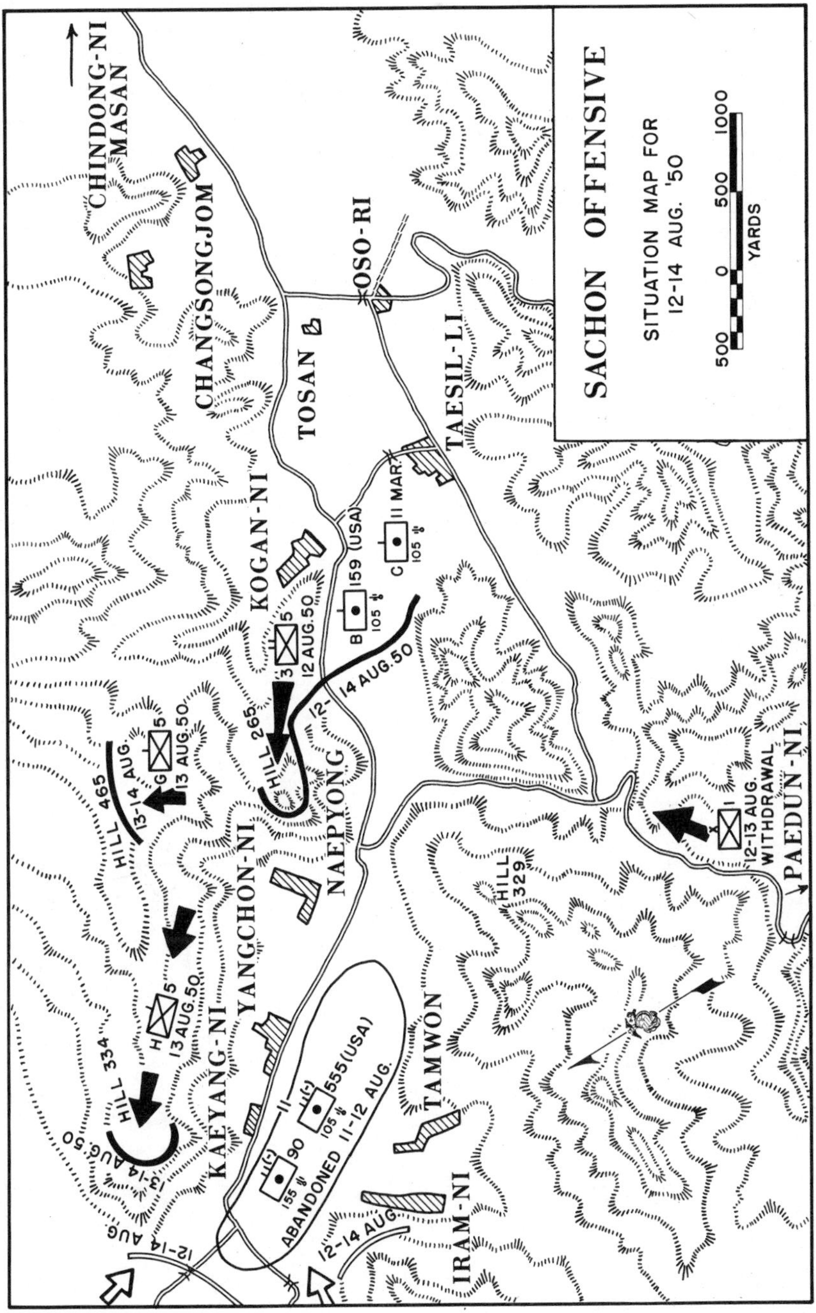

305713 O-F-55——11

It would later be known that the basic reason for the Brigade withdrawal was a decision by the Eighth Army command and staff. The enemy had crossed the river Naktong, the last natural barrier of the Pusan Perimeter, and this emergency had caused the Marines to be pulled back in readiness for a counterattack in the Naktong bulge.

Attack of 3/5 to the Rear

The foregoing chronology makes it evident that General Craig could never have handled this situation in an afternoon without helicopter transportation. Jeeps could not have reached so many destinations over narrow, twisting roads choked with traffic; and fixed-wing planes, even the adaptable OY's, could not have landed wherever the Brigade commander willed. Marine helicopters set a good many precedents in Korea, and the events of 12 August 1950 established the usefulness of these versatile machines for command and staff flights.

Early that afternoon, as Craig had directed, Stewart and Taplett flew back to the Chindong-ni area for reconnaissance and planning prior to the arrival of 3/5. The Brigade commander had been able to give them very little initial information. About 2,000 to 2,500 enemy had infiltrated to the vicinity, according to Army estimates. The two Marine officers were instructed to fly to a bridge over a dry stream bed, where they would be met and briefed by a 25th Division liaison officer awaiting them in a jeep with a red air panel on the hood.[8]

Stewart and Taplett found the bridge, though no jeep was in sight. After landing in the stream bed, they discovered a camouflaged Army light tank; but the officers of the armored company could not offer any enlightenment.

A number of wire lines lay in the roadside ditch, and the Marine officers checked them, one by one. At length, by a process of trial and error, they found a line leading to the 25th Division CP and talked to the G-3. He instructed them to "look the situation over" and decide upon a course of action to eliminate enemy activity in the area and provide security for the remaining artillery unit—a battery of the 159th Field Artillery Battalion which had been attached to the 555th. Then the Marine officers were to report to General Barth, ADC of the 25th Division, upon his arrival in the area to take the overall command.

---

[8] This section is derived from LtCol Robert D. Taplett's detailed statement to Marine Corps Evaluation Board, n. d.

Ever since the jump-off of 7 August, the operations of Task Force Kean had been distinguished for informality. Oral orders were the rule rather than exception, with unusual latitude of decision being permitted to officers in the field. After their telephone conversation, Stewart and Taplett made a helicopter reconnaissance of the area, followed by a flight back over the MSR to locate 3/5. Upon their return, they encountered Colonel John Daly, USA, CO of the 555th Field Artillery Battalion. Battery C of that unit, he informed them, had been surprised the night before, along with two batteries of the 90th, and completely overrun about 3,000 yards up the stream bed. They were destroyed as a fighting force, though scattered survivors and wounded men remained in the area. Daly briefed the Marine officers as to the location of enemy forces; and they decided to seize two key ridges commanding the MSR, which ran parallel to the stream bed. The troops of 3/5 were just then piling out of the trucks at the debarkation point, and Taplett ordered them to attack without waiting for Barth, since it would soon be dark.

These Marines, contrary to standing operating procedure, had turned their backs on the roar of battle at Changchon early that afternoon and ridden away in the opposite direction. Then, to complete the mystery, they traveled 25 miles to the rear to assault a ridge which was supposedly secured. How Company jumped off with George following in trace. Colonel Daly provided a 15-minute artillery preparation, though he had no orders, and Taplett's FAC managed to summon a flight of Corsairs with partial loads aboard, including napalm. No one had any idea of the enemy's strength, and after receiving some fire from the ridge, Captain Fegan picked the locations for an air strike. How Company moved in rapidly afterwards against such light resistance that the Marines seized the first position without a single casualty. Only one casualty was inflicted upon the enemy, who apparently had put up a rearguard fight while withdrawing.

At 1900, when General Barth arrived, he asked when the Marine battalion would be ready to attack. Taplett replied that he already had one company on the first objective, and the 25th Division ADC congratulated the Marines on their promptness. He approved Taplett's course of action and gave his sanction for the seizure of the rest of the dominating high ground the following morning.

Again the Marines received the most cordial cooperation from the Army. General Barth ordered several light tanks and three M–44 armored personnel carriers to support the attack at 0700 on 13 August. The same Army artillery battery was assigned to the operation, and

Battery C of the 11th Marines took part after arriving the night before. As it proved, the infantry needed little assistance to seize the remaining objectives against negligible resistance. By 1000 the Marine rifle companies were in full possession of the two commanding ridgelines. No casualties were suffered or inflicted.

Despite the lack of opposition, the enemy had not pulled out of the area. When Lieutenant Colonel Murray made a helicopter flight to drop a message to survivors of the 555th, his helicopter was ambushed in a defile by NKPA marksmen concealed on both sides. Only the pilot's skillful maneuvering got them out safely, and they were unable to complete their mission.

A plan for the Marines to advance to the west across the valley floor while the Army 5th RCT attacked rearward to meet them was considered by the 25th Division. Taplett's battalion would have been accompanied by 2/5, then on the way to the Chindong-ni area. But this scheme of maneuver was canceled, and the 2d Battalion of the 5th RCT relieved 3/5 on 14 August. By that time, as will be related later, other elements of the Brigade were on the way to an assembly area at Miryang in preparation for an operation in another sector.

At least the attack by 3/5 enabled elements of the 25th Division to rescue survivors of the artillery batteries who straggled back. Both Taplett and Stewart believed that enemy numbers in the area had been much smaller than the original Army estimate of 2,000 to 2,500 men. The 3/5 commander wanted to complete his mission by attacking to recover the howitzers and other lost equipment while the opportunity still existed. But he was unable to accomplish this aim because of orders for Brigade withdrawal, and the artillery pieces were never recaptured. Air strikes were called to destroy them after the relief of the Marine battalion, and the area itself was abandoned a few days later when 25th Division units fell back before renewed NKPA attacks.

Enemy Dawn Attack at Changchon

On the other Marine front, 25 miles distant, 1/5 had a return engagement before dawn on 13 August with the enemy in the Changchon area. Company commanders had received orders the night before to alert their units at 0400 for the withdrawal. General Craig's Op Order 10–50 was a complete and well planned field order, despite the need for haste; but the enemy interrupted with a surprise attack launched from concealed positions occupied under cover of darkness.[9]

Baker Company's defense setup for the night on Hill 202 consisted of the 3d, 1st, and 2d Platoons tied in from left to right in that order. The action began at 0450 with enemy automatic weapons fire. Marine 60-mm. mortar illuminating shells revealed an NKPA infiltration on the right in the area of the 2d Platoon.

This effort soon proved to be a diversionary attack for the purpose of masking the main blow. At 0455 3 enemy flares went up, 2 red and 1 green. They were the signal for an assault on the left flank at the other end of the Baker Company position. The enemy, as a wounded Marine NCO put it afterwards, was "right on top of the 3d Platoon in a few seconds" with grenades and burp guns.[10]

This was one of the occasions when the Marines were painfully reminded that the NKPA 6th Division had been made up originally of veterans of the Chinese civil war, conditioned by experience for the rigors of night fighting. Marine security had not been at fault, yet the enemy had managed to creep forward in uncanny silence to positions within grenade-throwing distance.

In an instant the Marine position was overrun, with the machinegun section being wiped out except for two men. Communication troubles added to the confusion. Platoon radios had been rendered inoperative by mud and water while crossing rice paddies, and telephone wires were believed to have been cut. Two runners were killed during Tobin's efforts to maintain contact with the hard pressed troops on the left flank. A third runner got through with orders for the remnants of the platoon to fall back within the perimeter of the adjacent 1st Platoon.

The troubles of Baker Company were compounded at this stage when the enemy turned two of the Marines' own machineguns against them.

During the next hour the fight became a slugging match. When the first gray light of dawn permitted some visibility, Baker Company 3.5″ rocket launchers knocked out the two Marine machineguns being fired by the enemy. The left flank was holding well when the 60-mm. mortars ran out of ammunition. To make matters worse, the artillery FO's radio took destructive hits from machinegun fire just as the enemy changed the direction of his attack. Now his main effort was being channeled up the draw between the 1st and 2d Platoons for the obvious purpose of

[9] Craig, 12 Jan 54.
[10] Tobin, of 26 Apr 54.

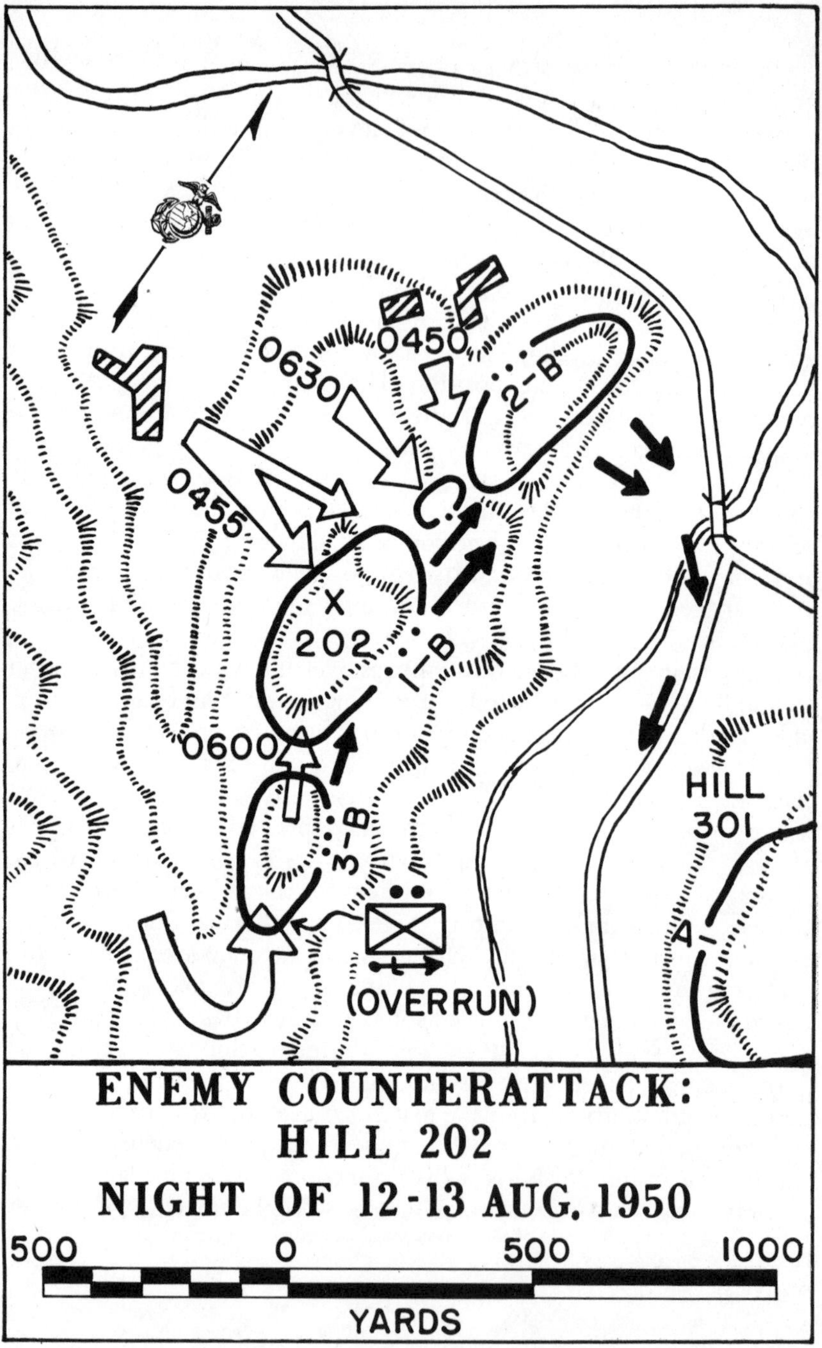

ENEMY COUNTERATTACK:
HILL 202
NIGHT OF 12-13 AUG. 1950

500 0 500 1000
YARDS

splitting the company and beating it in detail. The attackers had been bled white by casualties, however, and Tobin's men had little difficulty in beating off the new assault.

Breaking Off Action

Battalion orders were received through Able Company to disengage at 0630 and pull down from the high ground to the trucking point at Newton's CP. Tobin was now depending on Company A radios for 4.2″ and 81-mm. mortar support which slowed up enemy efforts. As his first move toward breaking off action, he ordered his 3d and 1st Platoons to withdraw into the perimeter of the 2d.[11]

By this time the enemy had fallen back toward the lower levels of Hill 202. Small arms fire had slackened but the Marines still received mortar bursts.

Tobin ordered his executive officer, Captain Francis I. Fenton, to take the wounded across the rice paddies to the road with the 3d Platoon and Headquarters troops. The company commander remained on the hill to cover this movement with the other two platoons. After Fenton got well underway, Tobin ordered the 2d Platoon down to the road. Then, a squad at a time, the remaining Marines disengaged; and the Baker Company commander came off Hill 202 with the last squad at 0815. The entire movement had been accomplished with precision, and a final air strike kept the enemy quiet at the climax.

Considering the fury of the fighting on Hill 202, a Marine casualty list of 12 KIA, 18 WIA, and 8 MIA was not as large as might have been expected. The idea of men missing in action is always disturbing to Marine officers, but it was considered a moral certainty that the eight casualties of this type were killed when the enemy overran the machinegun section on the Baker Company left flank.[12] Before leaving Hill 202, Captain Tobin asked permission to lead an attack for the purpose of recovering the bodies. He believed that he could retake the lost ground in an hour, but his request could not be granted at a time when the battalion was belated in carrying out Brigade withdrawal orders.[13]

---

[11] *Ibid.*

[12] Seven of these casualties were transferred from the MIA to the KIA column in September 1950 after the recovery of their bodies, following enemy withdrawal from the area. The eighth continued to be listed as MIA until November 1953, when the man was assumed to be dead.

[13] *Ibid.*

It fell to the engineers and armor to cover the rear after the infantry pulled out. Midway between Sachon and Kosong, the MSR is joined by a road from Samchonpo, a minor seaport on the tip of the peninsula. In order to block this approach to the Brigade's southern flank, General Craig ordered the engineers to mine the road. First Lieutenant Nicholas A. Canzona was assigned to the task with a detachment of his 1st Platoon of Able Company, 1st Engineer Battalion. After laying an extensive field, this officer discovered to his embarrassment that he had erred in arming nearly half of the mines with wrong fuses, so that they were harmless. Apparently the moral effect was enough, however, to keep the enemy at a distance.

Lieutenant Hetrick's 3d Platoon of the engineer company brought up the Brigade rear on the morning of 13 August to crater roads, lay antitank minefields and destroy bridges and culverts. Personnel left behind for such missions had the privilege of riding the rearmost tank to catch up with the column.[14] Thus the withdrawal proceeded systematically and was completed without enemy interference.

---

[14] Annex Jig to Brig SAR.

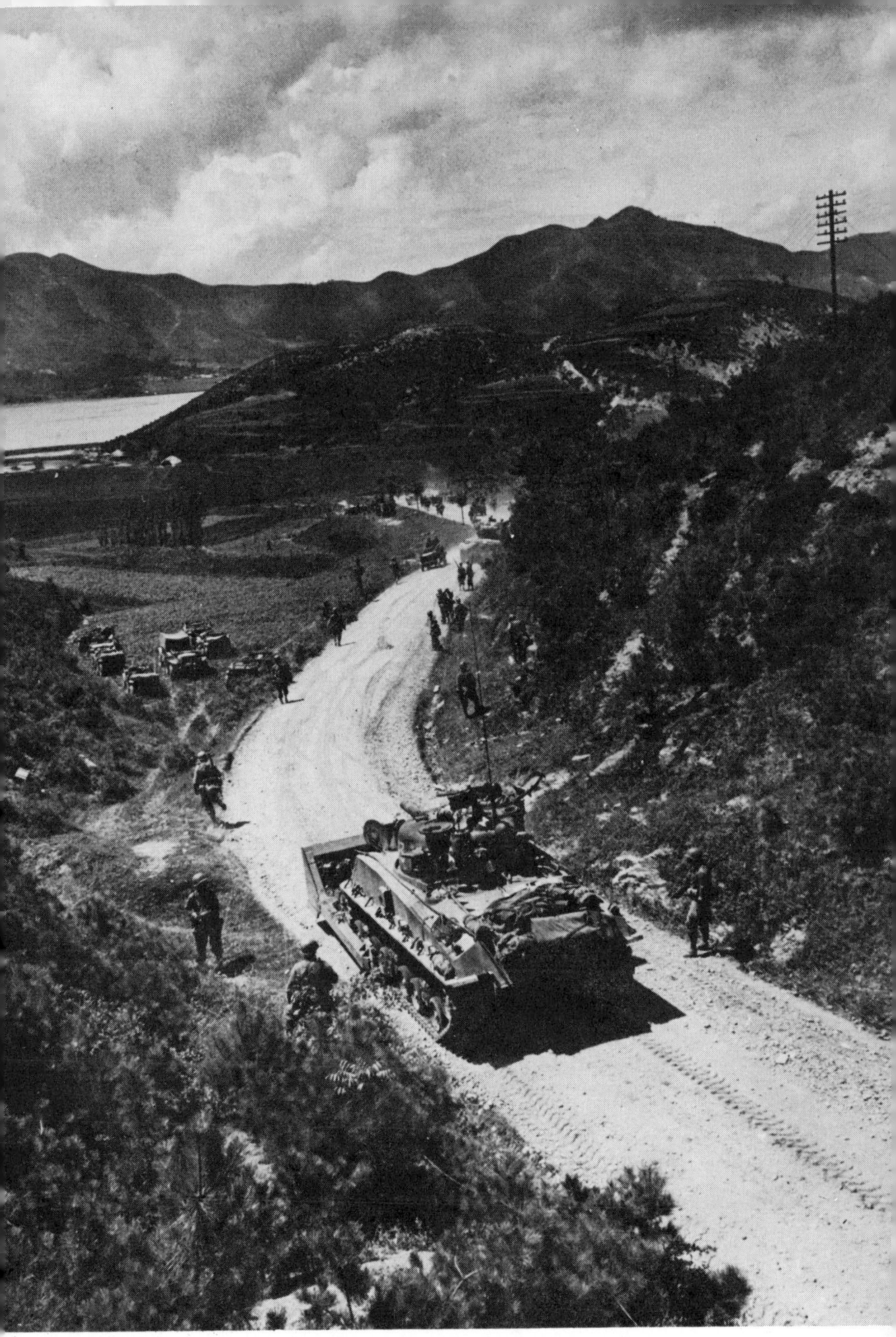

The Iron Cavalry—Brigade infantry and tank supporting each other during advance of Marines to Sachon (Life Magazine Photo).

Guests of the Brigade—Above, Lieutenant General Lemuel C. Shepherd, Jr. (center) is shown captured NKPA motorcycle by Brigadier General Craig (left) and First Lieutenant N. G. Rhodes (right); below, left to right, General Craig introduces ROK President Syngman Rhee to Second Lieutenant F. W. Muetzel and Technical Sergeant E. L. DeFazio, both wounded three times (Marine Corps Photo).

Marine Chiefs—Above, left to right, Major General Field Harris, CG of the 1st Marine Aircraft Wing; Major General Oliver P. Smith, CG of the 1st Marine Division, and Brigadier General Thomas J. Cushman, commanding MAG–33, meet at a conference in Tokyo; and, below, left to right, Congressman Hugh D. Scott, Jr., of Pennsylvania and Henry J. Latham, New York are shown captured gun by Brigadier General Edward A. Craig while visiting the Naktong front (Marine Corps Photo).

Naktong Fights—Above, Lieutenant Colonel Arthur A. Chidester, Brigade G–4, watches while tank 90-mm. gun fires across Observation Hill to knock out enemy machinegun on Obong-ni Ridge; and, below, Marine infantry advancing in second battle of the Naktong as Marine air and artillery hit the enemy up ahead (Marine Corps Photo).

Fight for a Foothold—Above, Marines advancing in first battle of the Naktong pass casualties on way to the rear; and, below, Private First Class Eugene A. Obregon (left) of Los Angeles and Private First Class Ralph J. Summers, of Tehama, Calif., in a Marine machinegun position (Marine Corps Photo).

Graveyard of Enemy Tanks—Three dead T-34's at the bend where the road skirts Hill 125, with Obong-ni Ridge looming up ahead. Bodies of three Marines show in the foreground (Marine Corps Photo).

Naktong Casualties- Above, wounded Marine, with right leg bandaged, passes M–26 tank on his way to the rear; and, below, a stretcher casualty being evacuated through rice paddy, with South Korean laborer bringing up the rear (Marine Corps Photo).

Burning Enemy Tank—Marines advancing past Hill 117 (background) along MSR west of Yongsan are giving a wide berth to the dying T–34 in anticipation of exploding ammunition (Marine Corps Photo).

Combat Leadership—Marine platoon leader calls for another rush on enemy hill position in second battle of the Naktong (Marine Corps Photo).

Interlude at the Bean Patch—Above, Marine truck column on way to Masan area after first battle of the Naktong; and, below, Brigade riflemen renew their acquaintance with hot food at the Bean Patch (Marine Corps Photo).

The Quick and the Dead—Marine tank, advancing along MSR at second Naktong, passes burning hull of enemy T–34 (Life Magazine Photo).

Readying for a Strike—*Effectiveness of Marine air attacks depends not only on Corsair pilots but also on crewmen such as Staff Sergeant Carl W. Peters (left) and Sergeant Melvin R. Bataway, of VMF–214, shown while arming rockets on the flight deck of the U. S. S.* Sicily *in preparation for a strike in Korea (U. S. Navy Photo).*

Enemy Mortar Fire—Marines hit the deck as NKPA mortar fire reaches out for them while advancing in the second battle of the Naktong (Marine Corps Photo).

Between Attacks—Above, tired Marines take a short break during first battle of Naktong, with body of NKPA soldier in foreground; and, below, Marine walking wounded are helped back to the rear (Marine Corps Photo).

Supporting Arms—Above, headquarters officers keep careful tab on Marine advances in order to co-ordinate fires of supporting weapons; and, below, the 105-mm. howitzers of 1/11 cleaned up, packed and ready for embarkation at Pusan (Marine Corps Photo).

Objective Secured—Marine patrol moves out from Hill 311, overlooking the river Naktong, after Brigade troops take their final objective in the first battle of the Naktong (Marine Corps Photo).

CHAPTER IX

The Battle of the Naktong

Task Force Hill Organized—Planning the Next Operation—Reconnaissance of Terrain—Air and Artillery Preparation—Company D on Objective—Attack of Company E

THE MOVEMENT OF the Brigade to Miryang was completed by rail, LST and shuttling trucks on 15 August. For the infantry, it meant the first hot meal in Korea, and the bivouac area seemed a cool, green paradise as compared to the sun-scorched hills the men had been climbing under fire this past week. A grove of stately trees provided shade; and thanks to the frugality of peasants who picked up every twig, the grass and moss were like a well-swept carpet. There the troops of the Brigade slept under the stars that night and swam in the nearby Miryang river. It was a veritable reunion for Leathernecks who swapped tales of experiences in the recent combats.

Being Marines, they realized of course that this was merely an interlude between operations. The Brigade had passed under operational control of the 24th Infantry Division upon arrival in the Miryang area. And on the 15th General Craig reported to General Church's CP to be briefed on the situation in the Naktong Bulge, where the next assault would be launched.

The ability of the Russians to cross the widest rivers in World War II, using only determination and field expedients, constantly amazed *Wehrmacht* generals with much better equipment.[1] This know-how seemed to have been passed on to the NKPA, judging by the crossings of the Han and Kum Rivers early in the Korean conflict. On 6 August 1950, the Red Koreans gave a repeat performance when they forced a 1,000-man bridgehead across the Naktong river, thus breaching the last natural barrier protecting the lifeline from Pusan to Taegu.

---

[1] U. S. Dept of the Army, *Russian Combat Methods in World War II*, DA Pamphlet No. 20–230.

The 24th Infantry Division was unsuccessful in its immediate attempts to dislodge the enemy.[2] Wading through chest-deep water by night, pulling crude rafts loaded with vehicles, heavy weapons and supplies, the North Koreans placed an entire reinforced regiment on the east bank by 8 August. Termite tactics during the next 2 days broadened their foothold until the Naktong Bulge was overrun by most of the NKPA 4th Division.

Consisting of the 5th, 16th, and 18th Infantry Regiments and strongly supported by artillery and armor, the 4th Division was among the most distinguished of the major Communist units. With the 107th Tank Regiment attached at the outset of the invasion, it had breezed through Uijongbu before sharing in the capture of Seoul. On 5 July 1950, the 4th became the first NKPA outfit to tangle with the newly arrived United States Army forces. Task Force Smith delayed it a few hours near Osan, despite the Reds' great advantage in numbers and armor. Later, after capturing Nonsan and aiding in the reduction of Taejon, the unit was selected to spearhead the assault over the Naktong.

Task Force Hill Organized

In an effort to plug the hole in the Pusan Perimeter, General Walker attached the 9th Infantry (2d Infantry Division) commanded by Colonel John G. Hill, to the 24th Division. In turn, General Church placed Colonel Hill in control of all units in his southern zone and ordered a counterstroke against the Naktong Bulge.

Task Force Hill attacked on 11 August but lost its momentum in a confused situation which found the enemy attacking at the same time. Reinforced to a strength of three infantry regiments, Hill's provisional unit again struck out against the bridgehead on 14 and 15 August. After encountering a stone wall of resistance, the task force was ordered to cease the attack and defend the ground it occupied east of the enemy pocket.[3]

This was the situation as outlined to General Craig at the planning conference, and he was also briefed on the topography of the target area. The Naktong Bulge west of Yongsan results from a bend in the river resembling a stubby thumb pointing westward. Bounded on three sides

[2] Capt R. A. Gugeler, "Attack Along a Ridgeline," in *Combat Actions in Korea* (Washington; Combat Forces Press, 1954).

[3] *Ibid.*

by the stream, with its inland border formed by a long valley, the bulge is an isolated terrain feature—a fortress of mountains topped by Hill 311, the key height.

As the Yongsan road reaches the Bulge from the east, it turns southwest, winds around Hill 311, and stops at the tip of the "thumb" where a ferry links it to the road west of the river.

Guarding the eastern approach to the natural fortress are two hills astride the Yongsan road—Finger Ridge to the north and Hill 207 to the south. The former is set off on the east by a deep gully containing the village of Tugok. Eastward from Hill 207 and directly below Tugok is Obong-ni Ridge—so called because of a village by that name at its eastern base.

Not only had the NKPA 4th Division overrun the Naktong Bulge; it had pushed on along the road to Yongsan, seizing Hill 207, Tugok, and both Finger and Obong-ni Ridges. These latest gains and the Bulge itself were being consolidated by elements of all three regiments.

Although units were somewhat depleted, at least 6 infantry battalions occupied the area, supported by 4 mortar companies, over 100 machine-guns, and several artillery pieces. There were 4 or more T34 tanks within the bridgehead, and a signal and engineer company for overall support. As the spoils of earlier victories, particularly the one at Taejon, enemy arms were generously augmented by a number of American carbines and two 105-mm. howitzers.[4]

Planning the Next Operation

It was decided by General Church and General Craig at their conference of 15 August that the entire 24th Division, Reinforced, would assault the enemy bridgehead at 0800, 17 August, after strong air and artillery preparations. The 19th and 34th Infantry would converge on the Bulge from the northeast. In the center, the 9th RCT and the Marine Brigade would strike frontally astride the MSR, the former on the north of the road and the latter on the south. The 1st Battalion, 21st Infantry, was to hold blocking positions in the south to protect the left flank of the Brigade.[5]

On 15 August, front lines in the center of the zone were on Hill 125 and Observation Hill, both defended by the 9th RCT. A thousand yards

[4] Brig Op Plan 13–50; Brig Periodic IntelRpts Nos. 12–14; Annex How.

[5] *Ibid.;* and Brig Op Plan 13–50.

to the rear, the 34th Infantry occupied Cloverleaf Hill and adjacent high ground. Before the attack, the Brigade was to relieve the 34th on position so that the Army unit could move to the north for its assigned mission. Then, at H-hour, the Marines would jump off from Observation Hill and seize Obong-ni Ridge—Objective One. Simultaneously, the 9th RCT would drive forward through Tugok and take Finger Ridge, from which it was to support the Brigade's advance. The 1st Battalion, 11th Marines, would be under operational control of the 24th Division artillery commander, and priority for all supporting fires would go to the Marines.[6]

During the planning, General Church emphasized that Cloverleaf Hill must remain occupied and defended until Brigade Objective One was seized. He considered this hill of utmost importance in blocking the MSR to the 24th Division CP and Miryang. This collateral responsibility would tie up a number of Brigade troops and have strong influence on the tactics used against Obong-ni Ridge.[7]

Before the conference closed, Church promised Craig that 145 Army trucks would be available the next day to transport the Marines from their Miryang bivouac to an assembly area near the line of departure.[8]

At 1900, 15 August, Craig briefed his staff and unit commanders. The next morning the Brigade commander flew by helicopter to Church's CP and received the actual attack order, which was identical with the planning of the previous day.[9]

Later on the 16th, Craig drove to the front to reconnoiter the area marked for the Brigade jump-off. He visited the 9th RCT command post where Colonel Hill informed him that the Army unit was in good condition as it stood by for the great attack.[10]

Reconnaissance of Terrain

After Craig's reconnaissance, Lieutenant Colonel Murray arrived at the front to discuss the tactical plan with the 9th RCT Commander. Although Colonel Hill spoke confidently of his outfit's readiness for the attack, Murray observed that the ranks of soldiers on Observation Hill

---

[6] Brig Op Plan 13–60.
[7] Craig, 4 Mar 54.
[8] *Ibid.;* and Brig SAR, basic rpt.
[9] Craig, 4 Mar 54.
[10] *Ibid.*

and Hill 125 were thin and the men obviously wearied by the fighting of the previous 5 days.[11]

With this impression in mind, the 5th Marines commander studied the terrain soon to be his regiment's battleground. Between Observation Hill and Obong-ni Ridge, a 300-yard rice paddy was flanked to the north of the road by the 9th RCT positions on Hill 125. Across the MSR from the northern tip of Obong-ni Ridge was the congested village of Tugok. West of the hamlet and northwest of Brigade Objective One was long, low Finger Ridge, target of Hill's RCT.[12]

Murray quickly concluded from the terrain that both regiments should not attack together and become exposed simultaneously in the low ground ahead. Since Obong-ni Ridge was closer than the Army objective and dominated both Tugok and Finger Ridge, Murray suggested that the 5th Marines jump off alone at 0800, 17 August. If the 9th RCT would support him by fire from Hill 125, he would take Obong-ni Ridge and return the courtesy while the Army unit cleared Tugok and seized its objective. And though offering his plan on a tactical basis, Murray also took into consideration the condition and numbers of Hill's troops.[13]

The 9th RCT commander agreed, and the responsibility of delivering the first punch lay with the 5th Marines.[14]

Time and chance were against the Brigade throughout 16 August and the following morning. Banking on the use of 145 Army trucks, Craig and Murray hoped to move quickly on the 16th, in order to have one infantry battalion take over Observation Hill and the other two available for the attack on the 17th. Unfortunately, only 43 trucks were actually provided, with the result that time schedules were thrown off and troops forced to march long distances the night before the attack.[15]

At 1900, 16 August, Lieutenant Colonel Taplett's 3d Battalion entrucked at Miryang and rode to the 5th Marines CP about 3,000 yards behind the front. Dismounting, 3/5 marched to Cloverleaf Hill and relieved the 34th Infantry on position. Control of the area south of the MSR passed to Taplett at 0445, 17 August.[16]

---

[11] 24th InfDiv Op Instr No. 26 for this period showed the 9th RCT(–) at 47 percent strength and 44 percent estimated combat efficiency. Morale for the consistently hard-hit 24th Division was gauged "Fair."

[12] *Ibid.*

[13] *Ibid.*

[14] *Ibid.*

[15] Brig SAR, basic rpt; Annex How; and Craig, 4 Mar 54.

[16] Annex How.

The 2d Battalion proceeded on foot to its assembly area near Cloverleaf Hill at 0130 on the 17th, and Lieutenant Colonel Roise's men got little sleep as they prepared for the jump-off a few hours later. Owing to the shortage of trucks, the 1st Battalion arrived at the forward assembly area several hours later than planned.[17]

Overloaded trucks had shuttled Lieutenant Colonel Wood's artillery battalion forward on 16 August. Although registration fires were completed by evening, the haste of the displacement and the doubtful information at the front left much to be desired from the standpoint of accuracy.[18]

While Obong-ni Ridge was known to be heavily defended, it was generally thought that Hill 207—Brigade Objective Two—would be the hard nut to crack. And the potential of Objective Three, towering Hill 311, was by no means minimized in preattack estimates.[19] Later events proved these assumptions to be the reverse of reality, but Marine planners could do no better with the meager intelligence then available.

The regimental commander and General Craig concluded that a frontal assault on Obong-ni Ridge with a column of battalions was the only answer to the problems posed by the terrain and situation.

Since the Brigade commander had been specifically charged with the security of the MSR, it was necessary that 3/5 remain in position on Cloverleaf Hill until Objective One was taken. Taplett's battalion had a second responsibility in guarding the Brigade's left (south) flank, because Craig considered the 1st Battalion, 21st Infantry, too far out to provide the required close-in protection.[20]

The Brigade commander, unaware of Murray's arrangement with Colonel Hill, could not have envisioned an approach to the enemy's left through the 9th RCT zone. He expected the Army unit to advance side by side with the Brigade and give supporting fire as directed by General Church. On the other hand, an envelopment of the enemy's right seemed out of the question. Using the southern approach to Obong-ni Ridge would have created a gap of several thousands yards in the center of the critical area, and the low, barren marshland to the left would have impeded the movement of tanks and the employment of the 5th Marines' integral supporting arms.[21]

---

[17] *Ibid.*

[18] Annex Item to Brig SAR; and Craig, 4 Mar 54.

[19] Stewart, 15 Jan 54; Murray, 15 Feb 54.

[20] Craig, 4 Mar 54.

[21] *Ibid.*

Lieutenant Colonel Murray's reasoning closely paralleled that of his superior. He did not visualize an envelopment from the north because he expected a comparable effect from supporting fire by the 9th RCT. An attempt to flank the North Korean right would have placed the attacking unit far from the power consolidated along the MSR. The enemy situation in the hills and swamps to the south was unknown, and the Marine regimental commander did not relish the thought of one or two of his battalions becoming isolated in that remote area. Then too, the southern peaks on Obong-ni Ridge were considerably higher and more rugged than those nearer the MSR. So it seemed logical to Murray to retain depth and strength by striking frontally, quickly gaining a foothold on the lower, northern reaches of the ridge, then exploiting the penetration rapidly and vigorously.[22]

When asked about his tactical plan by General Craig, he stated that the 5th Marines would attack in a column of battalions, 2/5 seizing Objective One, 1/5 passing through to take Hill 207, and 3/5 completing the reduction of the bulge by following with an assault on Objective Three.[23]

The Brigade commander voiced his concurrence, and the plan was put in motion.[24]

Air and Artillery Preparation

Obong-ni Ridge sprawled across the Marine front like some huge prehistoric reptile. Its blunt head overlooked the MSR below Tugok, and the elongated body stretched to the southeast more than 2,000 yards before losing its identity in a complex of swamps and irregular hill formations. The high, narrow spine was marked by a series of peaks, beginning with Hill 102 at the neck, followed by 109, 117, 143, 147, and 153. There were still other peaks to the southeast, but so small and irregular as to be almost indistinguishable.

A procession of steep spurs, separated from one another by pronounced gullies, ran down from the numbered peaks to the rice paddies far below. At the top of a gully extending down from the saddle between Hills 109 and 117 was a fault caused by erosion of the red clay and shale. Gaping like an ugly wound, the raw blemish inspired one of the ridge's first names—"Red Slash Hill." It was also dubbed "No

[22] Murray, 15 Feb 54.
[23] *Ibid.;* and Annex How.
[24] Murray, 15 Feb 54.

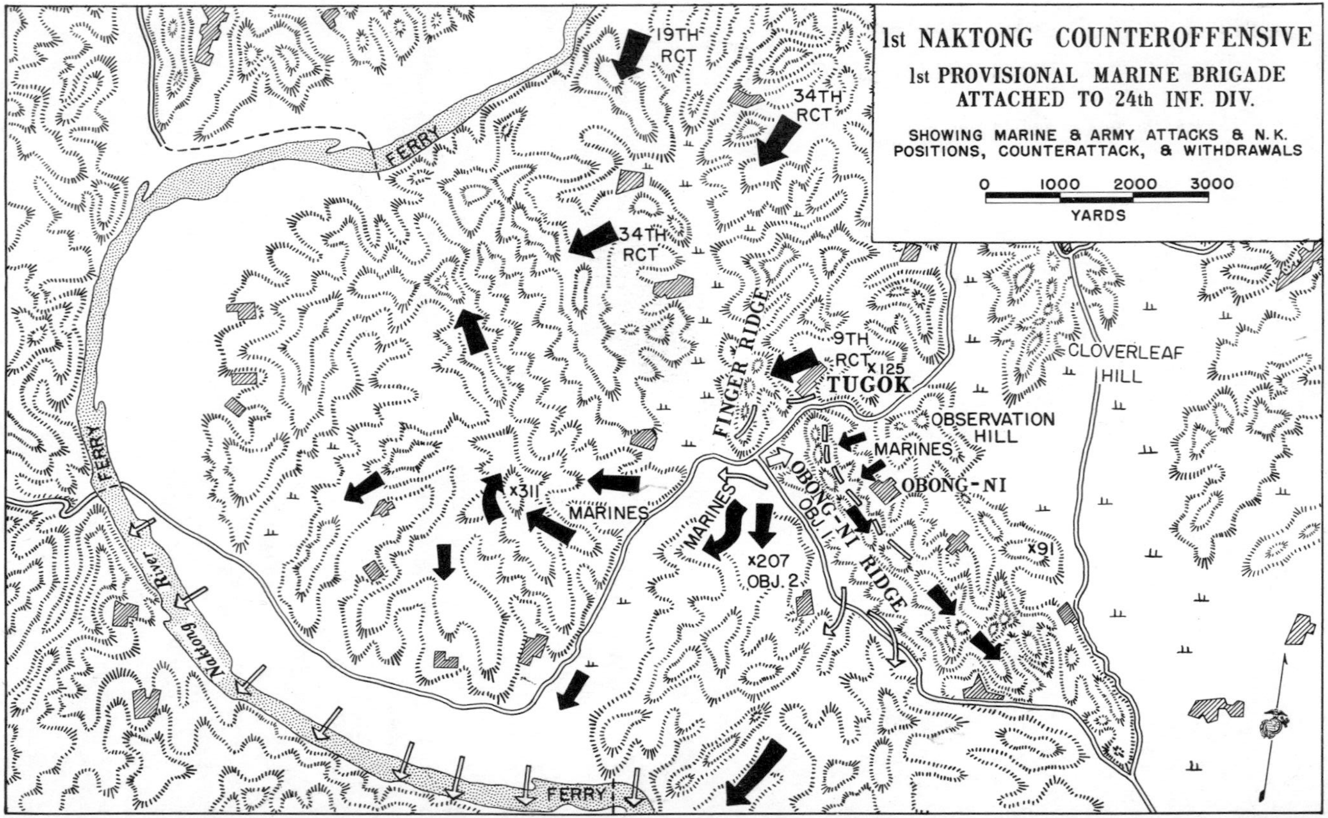
1st NAKTONG COUNTEROFFENSIVE
1st PROVISIONAL MARINE BRIGADE ATTACHED TO 24th INF. DIV.
SHOWING MARINE & ARMY ATTACKS & N.K. POSITIONS, COUNTERATTACK, & WITHDRAWALS
0 1000 2000 3000
YARDS
19TH RCT
34TH RCT
34TH RCT
9TH RCT
x125
TUGOK
FINGER RIDGE
CLOVERLEAF HILL
OBSERVATION HILL
MARINES
OBONG-NI
OBONG-NI RIDGE
OBJ. 1
MARINES
x207
OBJ. 2
x91
x311
MARINES
FERRY
FERRY
FERRY
Naktong River

Name Ridge" by some of the newspaper correspondents.

Marine air and artillery were to pound the ridge on 17 August from 0725 to H-hour, 0800, after which MAG-33 would strafe the hill to cover the advancing infantrymen.[25] Brigade artillery fired its preparation as planned; but due either to the hasty registration of the previous day or to error on the part of observers, the shelling was not effective against the enemy on Objective One. It was so inacurrate, in fact, that many officers of 2/5 thought there had been no preparation at all.[26] To make matters worse, air attacks scheduled to begin at 0725 did not materialize until 0740; and the 18 Corsairs assigned to the job had time for only one strike before H-hour.[27]

The two rifle companies of the 2d Battalion jumped off abreast at 0800. On the right was Captain Zimmer's Company D, emerging into the open from the road cut between Hill 125 and Observation Hill.[28]

Zimmer ordered the 2d Platoon into reserve on the southern spur of Hill 125 and established his OP there. The 3d Platoon, commanded by Second Lieutenant Michael J. Shinka, stepped from the road bend below the spur into the rice paddy. Advancing behind this unit were the 1st Platoon and a rocket section, the latter stopping in positions along the road bend to protect the MSR.

Halfway across the rice paddy, Staff Sergeant T. Albert Crowson led his 1st Platoon to the right from behind the 3d, and both units approached the base of the ridge on line. On Shinka's left was the 2d Platoon of Company E. An eerie silence pervaded the front while the assault platoons crossed the wide open area unmolested.

Providing covering fire from its positions on Hill 125, Technical Sergeant Sidney S. Dickerson's 2d Platoon was hit by long-range machinegun bursts from Hills 117 and 143 on Obong-ni. Company D's first two casualties were taken.

Company D on Objective

While General Craig watched from the road cut, and Lieutenant Colonel Roise from his OP on Observation Hill, Company D's assault

---

[25] Brig Op Plan 13–50.

[26] Annexes How and Item to Brig SAR; Maj A. M. Zimmer, ltr to author, 6 May 54 (Zimmer, 6 May 54); and W. E. Sweeney, ltr to author, 22 May 54 (Sweeney, 22 May 54).

[27] Annexes Easy and How to Brig SAR; and Brig Op Plan 13–50.

[28] Co D Action is derived from: Annex How; Zimmer, 6 May 54; and Capt M. J. Shinka, ltr to author, 7 Jun 54.

305713 O-F-55——13

platoons began to ascend the objective. Gradually turning its back on the village of Tugok, Crowson's unit traced the draw on the right of the spur leading to Hill 102, while Shinka led his 3d Platoon up the gully on the left. The infantrymen were almost halfway up the slope when a battalion of the NKPA 18th Regiment opened fire with dozens of machineguns.

Despite the hail of lead, Shinka and Crowson edged their units upwards. The fire from Hills 117 and 143 finally became so intense, however, that the 3d Platoon was momentarily unable to emerge from its gully. Almost simultaneously, enemy machineguns poured it into the 1st Platoon, pinning that unit down and inflicting heavy casualties.

Again pushing upward despite mounting casualties, the 3d Platoon attempted to assault Hill 109 about 1000. Communist automatic weapons and a shower of hand grenades from the crest sent the thin skirmish line of Marines reeling back down the barren slope.

As the 3d Platoon came under increasing machinegun and mortar fire from Hills 117 and 143, Zimmer decided to commit his reserve. Realizing the apparent futility of pressing the attack up the 3d Platoon's gully, he ordered Dickerson to attempt an assault through the draw in which the 1st Platoon was pinned down.

The 2d Platoon crossed the rice paddy, following the route used earlier by the 3d. Reaching the draw in which the latter was regrouping after its abortive assault, Dickerson led his men over Hill 102's spur, attempting to gain the avenue of approach being used by Crowson's unit. In the process he came under heavy automatic weapons fire from both flanks—Hills 117 and 143 on the left, and the hillside north of Tugok across the MSR.

At this time the company commander spotted North Korean positions above the village and realized why his pinned-down 1st Platoon was taking so many casualties. From their vantage point in the 9th RCT zone, the Communists were firing on the flank and rear of the Marines along the northwest approaches of Objective One.

Zimmer requested that 2/5 lay supporting fires on Tugok. When he got no response, his forward observer, Lieutenant Wirth, transferred the mission to 1/11. But the 105's had scarcely begun firing when they were cut off because the impact area was in the 9th RCT's zone. The company commander turned his own 60-mm. mortars on the enemy machineguns, only to discover that the target lay beyond effective range.

Zimmer had more success with supporting arms when the enemy posed another threat. Practically all the machinegun fire had been coming from the north and south of Hills 102 and 109, while the enemy on these summits relied on rifles and vast numbers of hand grenades. Then, apparently shaken by the 3d Platoon's tenacity, the Communists tried to wheel a heavy machinegun into position on the saddle between the northernmost peaks. Twice the mounted weapon was hauled up, and twice pulled back under heavy Marine fire. By this time Zimmer had requested battalion to use a 75-mm. recoilless rifle on the target. When the persistent North Koreans wheeled the machinegun onto the saddle a third time, one round from a Marine 75 obliterated gun and crew.

With only 15 men left in his platoon, Shinka prepared for a second assault on Hill 109. Following an air strike at 1100, the Marines stormed the high ground and overran enemy positions on the crest. Only a squad of North Koreans could show similar determination on the reverse slope, but the enemy's small-scale counterattack was stopped cold by Company D's riflemen.

One of the few Marines who reached Obong-ni's summit during 2/5's attack and lived to tell the story, Shinka later related the events following his seizure of Hill 109:

"Fire from Hill 143 was gaining in intensity, and they had observation over our position. Fire was also coming from the hill to our front [Hill 207]. I reported the situation to Captain Zimmer. A short time later phosphorus shells were exploding in Hill 143. This slowed the fire but it never did stop.

"My resupply of ammo did not arrive. Running short of ammo and taking casualties, with the shallow enemy slit trenches for cover, I decided to fall back until some of the fire on my left flank could be silenced. I gave the word to withdraw and take all wounded and weapons. About three-quarters of the way down, I had the men set up where cover was available. I had six men who were able to fight.

"I decided to go forward to find out if we left any of our wounded. As I crawled along our former position (on the crest of Hill 109), I came across a wounded Marine between two dead. As I grabbed him under the arms and pulled him from the foxhole, a bullet shattered my chin. Blood ran into my throat and I couldn't breath. I tossed a grenade at a gook crawling up the slope, didn't wait for it to explode, turned and reached under the Marine's arms and dragged him as far as the military crest.

"Another bullet hit my right arm, and the force spun me around. I rolled down the hill for a considerable distance before I could stop myself.

"I walked into my lines and had a battle dressing tied on my face and arm. I learned that the ammo was up and that a relief was contemplated; and then I walked back to 2/5's aid station where they placed me on a jeep and took me to regimental aid."

Lieutenant Shinka was later awarded the Bronze Star for this action.

Attack of Company E

At 0800 Lieutenant Sweeney had ordered his 1st and 2d Platoons of Easy Company into the attack from their line of departure on the southern portion of Observation Hill. Although the boundary separating the zones of Companies E and D extended from the left of Hill 109 and down through the red slash, Sweeney centered his advance on the village of Obong-ni, directly below Hills 143 and 147.[29]

The leading platoons encountered nothing more than scattered shots crossing the rice paddy. Before they could gain a foothold on the slope of the objective, however, heavy fire from the village ripped into the skirmish line.

In the center, Second Lieutenant Nickolas A. Arkadis led his 1st Platoon through the hail of bullets and drove through the village to the slopes of the ridge. On the right the 2d Platoon faltered and lost its momentum. Then a number of North Korean machineguns poured in flanking fire from Hills 147 and 153.

Sweeney, from his OP on the southern slope of Observation Hill, tried to get an artillery mission on the two dominating peaks, but his forward observer was unable to contact the rear. Nor could the 4.2 mortar observer be located.

Faced with the necessity of giving his assault elements some protection, the company commander committed 2d Lieutenant Rodger E. Eddy's 3d Platoon, sending it to the spur on the left of the village. Working its way up the nose which led to Hills 147 and 153, Eddy's unit was able to concentrate its fire on the enemy-held peaks and relieve pressure on the other two platoons.

With enemy fire gradually increasing from new positions on the lower slopes of the ridge to the south of the village, Sweeney ordered the mortar section and all of his headquarters personnel into the valley to block the southern approach through the rice paddy. Leaving this flank guard in command of his executive officer, First Lieutenant Paul R. Uffelman, the company commander rushed to the base of the objective. Every single man in his unit was now committed.

Sweeney found the 2d Platoon leaderless and disorganized. The 1st had fought its way well up the slope, aided by excellent supporting fire from 2/5's 81-mm. mortars. As that dogged group of Marines neared the crest, it was stopped when a friendly artillery barrage fell short,

[29] This section is derived from: Annex How; and Sweeney, 22 May 54.

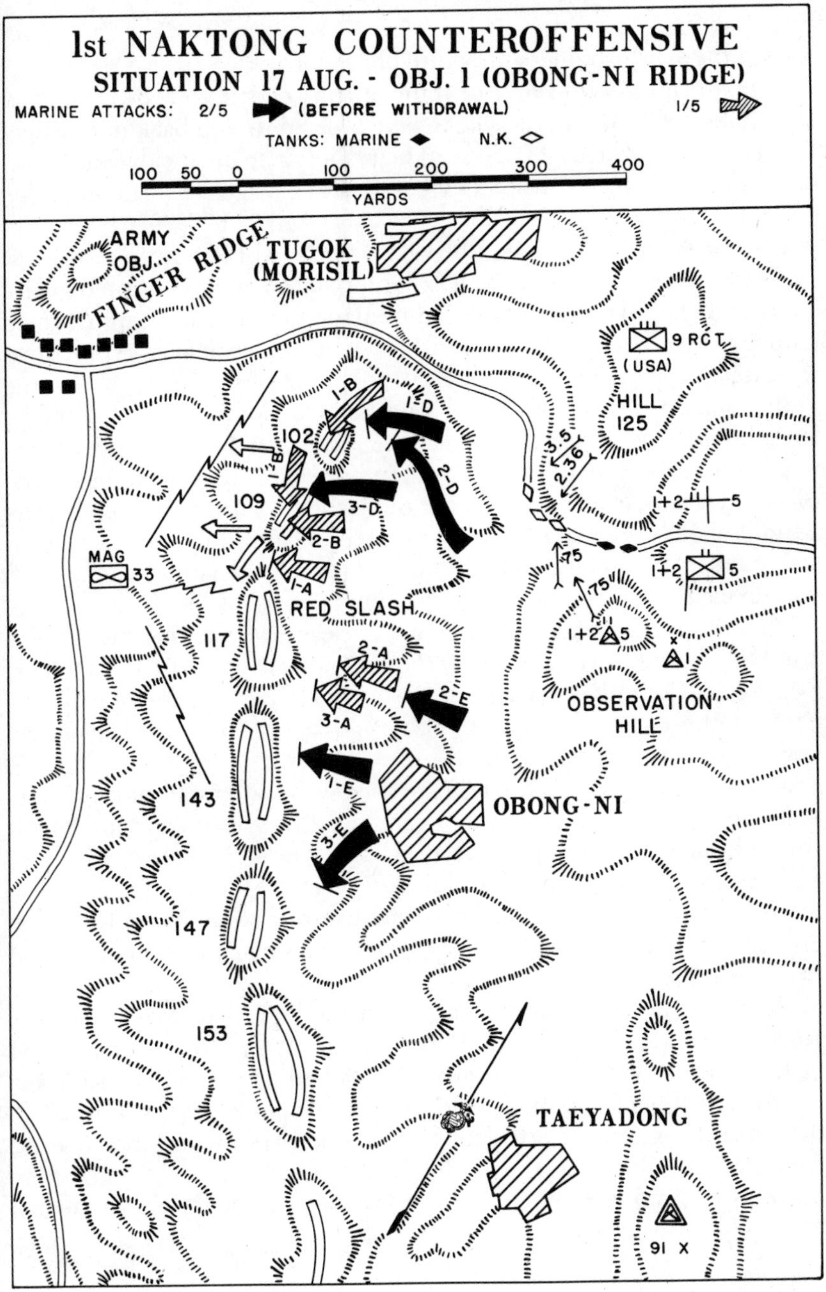

1st NAKTONG COUNTEROFFENSIVE
SITUATION 17 AUG. - OBJ. 1 (OBONG-NI RIDGE)
MARINE ATTACKS: 2/5 (BEFORE WITHDRAWAL)
1/5
TANKS: MARINE
N.K.
100 50 0 100 200 300 400
YARDS
ARMY OBJ.
FINGER RIDGE
TUGOK (MORISIL)
9 RCT (USA)
HILL 125
1-B
1-D
102
2-D
3.5
2.36
109
3-D
2-B
1-A
1+2 5
75
MAG 33
RED SLASH
117
2-A
2-E
3-A
OBSERVATION HILL
143
1-E
OBONG-NI
3-E
147
153
TAEYADONG
91 X

searing the skirmish line with white phosphorus.

Late morning found part of the company closing on the crest; but shortly before 1130, the attackers were ordered to pull back in preparation for an air strike by MAG-33. The planes came in quickly, and some of Company E's men, within 25 yards of the summit, were caught in the strafing.

During the hammering by the Corsairs, the 3d Platoon slipped back 100 yards, leaving the critical left flank open to enemy-infested peaks 147 and 153. This time the hail of enfilade fire from Communist machineguns caught the remnant of Easy Company rifleman exposed on the higher slopes, and the Marine advance crumbled.

By noon on 17 August, the 2d Battalion, 5th Marines was wobbling. In 4 hours of fighting it had lost 23 dead and 119 wounded, practically all of the casualties being taken by the 2 rifle companies. Every officer in the Brigade could lament the lack of a third company in each battalion; for just when 2/5's assault needed the added punch of a reserve unit, the outcome of battle had to rest on the failing strength of six depleted rifle platoons. The ridge could not be taken.

This was unfortunate, since there was clear evidence that the NKPA 4th Division was weakening. Although not apparent to the men of Companies D and E, their repeated attempts to carry the ridge had torn gaps in the enemy's defenses. Bodies, weapons and wreckage were strewn along the entire northern crest.[30]

Marine air and artillery, having settled down after a fumbling start, not only blasted the North Korean lines, but also wrought havoc throughout the entire bridgehead. A large number of enemy mortars and field pieces were knocked out, troop concentrations cut down or scattered while trying to reinforce the front lines, and supply points obliterated. There were definite signs of increasing confusion in the enemy's rear.[31]

General Craig had become alarmed at the lack of activity in the 9th RCT's zone, resulting in the enemy being left free to pound the Brigade's right flank from the Tugok area. When he inquired concerning the Army's supposed failure to advance on schedule, he first learned of the prebattle agreement reached by Murray and Hill. It was then that he requested the village be taken under fire.

Deeply concerned himself over the situation on the right, particularly

---

[30] LtGen E. A. Craig, ltr to author, 17 Mar 54 (Craig, 17 Mar 54); Annex Easy to Brig SAR.

[31] *Ibid.*

since no supporting fire at all had been received from the 9th RCT, Murray tried to contact Hill and request that he commit his regiment. Unable to get the message through immediately, he was forced to leave the matter dangling while directing the conduct of the battle.[32]

About 1300 the 5th Marines commander ordered the 1st Battalion to pass through the 2d and seize Obong-ni Ridge. While Newton moved his unit forward from its assembly area, MAG-33, 1/11 and Able Company tanks laid down devastating fires on the blackened objective.

---

[32] Murray, 15 Feb 54.

CHAPTER X

Obong-ni Ridge

Company B to the Attack—Advance of Company A—Defeat of Enemy Tanks—End of the First Day—Enemy Counterattack on Ridge—Obong-ni Ridge Secured—Supporting Arms Clear the Bulge

SHORTLY AFTER 1330, WHILE reporting his situation to the battalion commander, Captain Zimmer was wounded by enemy machinegun fire which ripped into his OP and caused several other casualties. Crawling to the company CP on the reverse slope of the spur, he turned his command over to Lieutenant Hanifin, who went forward. Zimmer then joined the steady stream of casualties returning through the road cut to the battalion aid station.[1]

On the way, he met Captain Tobin leading Company B forward for the attack, and paused long enough to warn him about the enemy guns in Tugok.

Company D, its part in the battle having come to an end, prepared to withdraw to positions on Observation Hill. The long list of wounded for 17 August included the names of Dickerson and Wirth.[2]

Newton established his OP near that of Roise on Observation Hill. The 1st Battalion CP and aid station were set up with those of 2/5 immediately behind the road cut, while farther back Major John W. Russell placed 1/5's Weapons Company in position.

Company B to the Attack

Tobin deployed his 3d Platoon and machineguns on the forward slopes of Observation Hill to support Company B's attack. The 1st and 2d

[1] This section is derived from: Brig SAR; Zimmer, 6 May 54; and Maj F. I. Fenton, Jr., ltr to author, 8 May 54 (Fenton, 8 May 54).

[2] Lt Wirth was actually attached from 1/11.

Platoons, the latter on the left, crossed the rice paddy and at 1500 passed through Company D on the slopes of the objective. Lieutenant Schryver led his 1st Platoon toward Hill 102 along the same avenue used by Crowson before him, while Lieutenant Taylor moved the 2d Platoon up the gully leading to the saddle between 102 and 109.

On Observation Hill Captain Tobin noted the rapidity of the advance and called his executive officer, Captain Fenton, preparatory to joining the two assault units. While briefing his assistant at the road bend, he was felled by a burst of machinegun fire. Fenton directed the evacuation of the seriously wounded officer, then took command of the company and joined the attackers on the ridge.

By this time both assault platoons had been pinned down, the 1st about two-thirds of the way up the slope, the 2d only half that distance. The latter was taking heavy casualties from Communist guns on Hills 109, 117, and 143, Taylor himself sustaining a mortal wound.

Fenton and his gunnery sergeant, Master Sergeant Edward A. Wright, were stalled with the 2d Platoon. Since Schryver's unit was also held up, the company commander radioed Observation Hill and committed his 3d Platoon.

Schryver realized that the main obstacle to his advance was the fire hitting his flank from Tugok, and he requested a fire mission from 1/5's Weapons Company. As 81-mm. mortar shells rained down on the village, the 1st Platoon worked westward to the spur above the MSR and outflanked the NKPA 18th Regiment. A quick assault carried Hill 102 at 1710.

With Schryver's men driving down from the south and Company B's machineguns pouring fire on peaks 117 and 143, the 2d Platoon barreled its way up the draw and seized Hill 109 at 1725.

Advance of Company A

Leaving the line of departure from the southern reaches of Observation Hill, the 1st and 2d Platoons of Company A crossed the rice paddy while Marine air and artillery savagely blasted the forward and reverse slopes of the objective. The two assault units, each with a machinegun section attached, passed through Company E at 1500 and scrambled up the scarred hillside.[3]

---

[3] This section is derived from: Annex How; Maj J. R. Stevens and Capt G. C. Fox, interv with author, 24 Feb 54 (Stevens and Fox, 24 Feb 54); and 1st Lt Francis W. Muetzel, USMC Ret., interv with author, 5–6 Jan 54 (Muetzel, 5–6 Jan 54).

Sweeney's battle-worn company withdrew, carrying its dead and wounded back to Observation Hill. The list of casualties included Lieutenant Arkadis, wounded while spearheading the unit's advance.

As Company A's assault wave passed the halfway point of ascent, it met only sniping fire from the crest and forward slopes of Obong-ni Ridge. But any delusions that the enemy had quit were soon shattered when the summit suddenly came alive with Communist machineguns.

Intense fire poured down on the attackers, and Marines pitched forward to roll limply down the hillside. First Lieutenant Robert C. Sebilian, leading the 1st Platoon up the draw between Hills 109 and 117, ignored the storm of steel and urged his men forward. Standing fully exposed while pointing out enemy positions to his NCO's, the young officer was struck by an explosive bullet which shattered his leg. Technical Sergeant Orval F. McMullen took command and resolutely pressed the attack.

The 1st Platoon reached the saddle above the draw just as Company B was taking Hill 109. When McMullen tried to advance southward to 117, he and his men were pinned down by a solid sheet of Communist fire.

On the left, North Korean guns had already cut Second Lieutenant Thomas H. Johnston's 2d Platoon in half. The pint-sized platoon leader proved to be a giant in courage. He pushed doggedly up the draw between Hills 117 and 143, but casualties bled his skirmish line white and finally brought it to a stop.

Marines watching the battle from Observation Hill saw Company A's attack bog down, despite the ceaseless pounding of Hills 117 and 143 by Brigade supporting arms. Startled, the observers noted a lone figure who bolted forward from the 2d Platoon's draw and stubbornly scrambled up the hill. It was Johnston attempting a single-handed assault on the core of enemy resistance.

The astonished onlookers saw him reach the saddle north of Hill 143. That he survived to this point was remarkable enough, yet he continued to push forward. Then, at the base of the blazing peak, the little figure sagged to the ground and lay motionless.

Technical Sergeant Frank J. Lawson immediately took over the platoon, displaying outstanding leadership in his attempt to continue the attack. Communist guns and grenades prevailed, however, and again the line of infantrymen stalled. The 2d Platoon now consisted of a squad.

Captain Stevens radioed Lieutenant Colonel Newton from his OP and requested permission to commit his 3d Platoon, then deployed on Observation Hill as battalion reserve. The request granted, First Lieutenant

George C. Fox led the platoon forward into the rice paddy just as a heavy mortar barrage fell in the area. One of Fox's men was killed outright.

Moving quickly to Obong-ni Ridge and ascending the slope, the 3d Platoon was joined by Lawson and the remnants of Johnston's outfit. The skirmish line passed the critical halfway point, and again enemy machineguns and grenades opened up.

Twice Fox attempted to develop an assault, failing both times to get his platoon through the curtain of fire above the gully. While Technical Sergeant Stanley G. Millar was reorganizing the skirmish line, the platoon leader and Private First Class Benjamin C. Simpson of the 2d Platoon made an attempt to reach Johnston.

The pair climbed to a point above the gully from which Simpson could see the fallen officer. Assured now that Johnston was dead, and unable to recover the body because of interlocking machinegun fire across the area, Fox and the rifleman slid down the draw to the 3d Platoon lines.

By this time Stevens had moved to the base of Obong-ni Ridge, but he had lost radio contact with the three units high on the hillside. He could see the combined 2d and 3d Platoons; but the 1st was out of sight, leaving the company commander unaware of a limited success that could have been exploited.

Defeat of Enemy Tanks

Shortly after 2/5's jump-off on 17 August, the M–26's of the 3d Platoon, Able Company Tanks, moved forward of the road cut and supported the advance by 90-mm. and machinegun fire. The Marine armor, led by Second Lieutenant Granville G. Sweet, concentrated on heavy NKPA weapons along the crest of Objective One and knocked out at least 12 antitank guns and several automatic weapons. In return, 1 M–26 withstood 3 direct hits by enemy mortars, and the 4 vehicles combined were struck by a total of 23 antitank projectiles. Neither tanks nor crews were bothered appreciably, and only one man was slightly wounded.[4]

After the 1st Battalion had passed through 2/5, a section of tanks moved forward on the road and blasted several North Korean positions

[4] This section is derived from: Annex How; Stevens and Fox, 24 Feb 54; Capt Almarion S. Bailey, interv with author, 17 Dec 53; T/Sgt C. R. Fullerton, ltr to Opns Research Office, Johns Hopkins University (cover ltr: OIC RS Cleveland, ser. 527–53, 31 Dec 53).

in Tugok. When Company B seized the northern tip of the objective, Sweet led all his vehicles back to the tank CP, 1,000 yards east of Observation Hill.

At 2000, while still refueling and replenishing ammunition stocks, the tankmen learned that four enemy T-34's were approaching the Brigade lines on the MSR. The Marine armor was clanking toward the front within a matter of seconds. About 300 yards from the road cut, the tankmen had to jump from their vehicles to remove trucks blocking the MSR. Then, approaching the narrow defile, Sweet ordered his 1st Section to load with 90-mm. armor-piercing shells.

Company B, consolidating its positions on Hills 102 and 109, had first noticed the four NKPA tanks and a column of infantry moving toward its lines at 2000. Corsairs of MAG-33 screamed down immediately, destroying the fourth armored vehicle and dispersing the Red riflemen. The first three tanks came on alone, passed Finger and Obong-ni Ridges, and approached the road bend at Hill 125.

Preparing a reception for the T-34's were the 1st 75-mm. Recoilless Gun Platoon on Observation Hill, and the rocket section of 1/5's antitank assault platoon on Hill 125. As the first enemy tank reached the bend, it took a hit in the right track from a 3.5″ rocket. Shooting wildly, the black hulk continued until its left track and front armor were blasted by Second Lieutenant Paul R. Fields' 75's. The enemy vehicle burst into flame as it wobbled around the curve and came face to face with Technical Sergeant Cecil R. Fullerton's M-26.

Still aimlessly firing its 85-mm. rifle and machinegun, the T-34 took two quick hits from the Marine tank's 90-mm. gun and exploded. One North Korean got out of the burning vehicle but was cut down instantly by rifle fire. He crawled beneath the blazing wreckage and died.

The second T-34 charged toward the bend, taking a 3.5 rocket hit from Company A's assault squad. Weaving crazily around the curve, with its right track damaged, the cripple was struck in the gas tank by a rocket from 1/5's assault section before meeting the fury of Field's recoilless rifles. It lurched to a stop off the road behind the first tank, and the 85-mm. gun fired across the valley into the blue yonder.

By this time a second M-26 had squeezed next to that of Fullerton on the narrow firing line, and the two Marine tanks blasted the T-34 with six 90-mm. shells. Miraculously, the Communist vehicle kept on shooting, although its fire was directionless. Marine armor poured in seven more rounds, which ripped through the turret and exploded the hull.

Before the kill, one Red tankman opened the turret hatch in an effort to escape. A 2.36″ white phosphorus round, fired by a 1st Battalion rocket man, struck the open lid and richocheted into the turret. The enemy soldier was knocked back into the tank as the interior turned into a furnace.

The third T–34 raced around the road bend to a stop behind the blazing hulks of the first two. Marine tanks, recoilless rifles, and rockets ripped into it with a thundering salvo. The enemy tank shuddered, then erupted in a violent explosion and died.

Thus the Brigade shattered the myth of the T–34 in five flaming minutes. Not only Corsairs and M–26's, but also every antitank weapon organic to Marine infantry had scored an assist in defeating the Communist armor.

End of the First Day

Throughout 17 August the evacuation of dead and wounded had been a major concern of every Marine, from fire team leaders up to the Brigade commander. Men risked their lives dragging casualties off the blazing slopes of Obong-ni Ridge to relative safety at the base. Litter bearers plodded back and forth across the fire-swept rice paddy, and a steady stream of wounded passed through the 1st and 2d Battalion aid stations behind the road cut. Medical officers of the two battalions, Lieutenants (jg) Bentley G. Nelson and Chester L. Klein, worked tirelessly with their corpsmen.

In the rear, Lieutenant Commander Byron D. Casteel had to commandeer every ambulance in the area—including 16 Army vehicles—to evacuate wounded to and from his 5th Marines aid station. So acute was the shortage of hospital corpsmen that the Brigade's Malaria and Epidemic Control Unit was used to reinforce the regimental medical staff. Even so, the hospital tents were busy for a straight 18 hours.[5]

The small number of deaths from wounds attested to the speed and effectiveness of helicopter evacuations; for the pilots of VMO–6 were ferrying the more serious casualties from the regimental aid station to the Army's 8076 Surgical Hospital at Miryang, some 20 miles away.

While medics toiled to save lives, the spiritual needs of casualties were filled by the inspiring labor of the 5th Marines' naval chaplains, Lieutenant Commander Orlando Ingvolstad, Jr., Lieutenant William G. Tennant, and Lieutenant (jg) Bernard L. Hickey. A familiar figure at the

[5] Annexes Love and Tare to Brig SAR.

front, frequently exposed to enemy fire as he administered to fallen Marines, was Lieutenant Commander Otto E. Sporrer, beloved chaplain of 1/11.

Two serious obstacles to the various missions behind the front were the dud-infested area east of Observation Hill and a section of collapsed MSR in the river bed occupied by the 5th Marines CP. First Lieutenant Wayne E. Richards and his 2d Platoon, Able Company Engineers, spent most of 17 August at the tedious task of removing unexploded missiles from the forward assembly areas. The engineers' 1st Platoon had to tear down part of an unoccupied village for material to reinforce the sinking road over which the jeep ambulances and supply trucks were struggling.

As the sun dropped behind Obong-ni Ridge, activity on the MSR continued unabated, although the battle for Objective One had diminished to a crackle of rifle fire and occasional machinegun bursts.

Company A had been unable to take Hills 117 and 143, still bristling with enemy automatic weapons. At 2030, shortly after the smashing victory over North Korean armor, Captain Stevens contacted his 1st Platoon and learned that it was on the saddle between peaks 109 and 117. Although tied in on the right with Company B, the platoon was separated by a 100-yard gap from Stevens' other two platoons on the slopes to the left.[6]

The company commander called Fox, Lawson, and McMullen together near the base of the ridge to consult them on continuing the attack. All platoon leaders advised against it, since darkness was falling and their units needed rest, food, water, and ammunition. Moreover, the enemy's bold tank attack had convinced the infantry leaders that a larger counterstroke by the Communists was imminent, and they wanted time for preparation.[7]

Stevens informed Newton of the situation by radio, and the battalion commander ordered him to discontinue the attack and tie in with Fenton's unit for the night. It was already dark when the 2d and 3d Platoons shifted to the right from their positions below Hills 117 and 143.

Company B had been busily consolidating its high ground since the seizure of Hills 102 and 109 earlier in the evening. While Fenton's machineguns dueled with those of the Reds on 117, his 1st and 2d Platoons deployed defensively on the forward slopes of the two captured peaks, and the 3d went into reserve on the reverse slope.[8]

---

[6] Annex How; and Stevens and Fox, 24 Feb 54.

[7] *Ibid.*

[8] Annex How; and Fenton, 8 May 54.

Company A's front extended left from the southern part of Hill 109—where the 1st Platoon was linked to Fenton's unit—to the center of the saddle toward 117. There the line bent down in an arch, formed by the 2d Platoon, to the spur below the enemy-held peak. Able Company's left was actually perpendicular to the ridgeline, for Fox's 3d Platoon was deployed up and down Hill 117's spur.[9]

To complete the Brigade front, Headquarters Company of 1/5 was to have extended across the rice paddy from Observation Hill and tied in with Company A's left flank. Due to the casualties and workload of the headquarters troops, this connection was never made, with the result that Fox's platoon remained dangling.[10]

When General Craig returned to his CP near Yongsan on the night of 17 August, he was not unduly concerned about the tactical situation. Although the Brigade had been thinned by heavy casualties, Murray's disposition in depth across a narrow front gave the Marines the advantages of concentrated strength and firepower. If the enemy attempted his usual night envelopment, both 2/5 and 3/5 could strike back from their reserve positions on Observation and Cloverleaf Hills.[11]

Across the MSR, the 9th RCT had launched its attack earlier in the evening, clearing Tugok and seizing Finger Ridge against negligible resistance. By darkness, the 19th and 34th Regiments were also sitting on their objectives to the north, leaving the 4th NKPA Division clamped in a vice. To the southeast, the 1st Battalion, 21st Infantry, was holding its blocking position with no difficulty.[12]

Enemy Counterattack on Ridge

Late on 17 August, when the attack on Obong-ni Ridge ceased, General Craig sent a message to his subordinate commanders, directing them to ". . . consolidate positions for night, account for location of each individual and be prepared for counterattack; carefully prepare plan of fires for night to include plans for fires within and in rear of positions; wire in where possible in front line elements."[13]

Long after nightfall, the weary Marines of both front line companies were still digging foxholes and organizing their defenses. While this

---

[9] Brig SAR; and Stevens and Fox, 24 Feb 54.

[10] *Ibid.*

[11] Craig, 17 Mar 54; and Col R. L. Murray, 20 Mar 54.

[12] 24th InfDiv Op Instr No. 26.

[13] This section is derived from: Annex How; Stevens and Fox, 24 Feb 54; Muetzel, 5–6 Jan 54; and Fenton, 8 May 54.

work continued in spite of sporadic Communist fire from Hill 117, the South Korean laborers were transporting supplies to the ridgeline or carrying casualties back to the rear.

Captain Stevens established Company A's command post at the top of the draw leading to the saddle between Hills 109 and 117. His 60-mm. mortar section set up its weapons in the gully itself.

Shortly before 2200, the telltale whine and rattle of mortar shells cut through the darkness and the men of Able Company crouched in their holes. The explosions were followed by a shower of fire as white phosphorus enveloped the center of the company area. Almost every man in the gully was painfully wounded, leaving Stevens without a mortar section. The edge of the barrage hit the 3d Platoon's area, wounding Fox and several of his men. Two riflemen had to be evacuated, but the platoon leader and the others applied first aid and remained in the line.

After this brief flurry the front settled down to an ominous quiet interrupted only occasionally by North Korean guns to the south.

At 0230 on 18 August, the Marines of Company A heard enemy movement on Hill 117. Suddenly there was a hail of bullets from Communist machineguns on the peak, and hand grenades began to roll down into the Marine positions. A North Korean platoon made a few bounds from the high ground and landed almost literally on top of Stevens' depleted 2d Platoon.

Simultaneously, Company B's position on Hill 109 was struck hard by two platoons advancing up the draw to the west. Heedless of illuminating shells fired by 1/5's 81-mm. mortars, the enemy assaulted methodically by alternately throwing small groups of grenadiers and submachinegunners against Marine positions. The NKPA infantrymen were covered by a heavy volume of automatic weapons fire pouring down from Hill 117.

An enemy squad emerged from the gully west of the saddle between peaks 102 and 109, attempting to divert strength from Fenton's main defensive effort to the south. Failing in this effort, the group fell back to fire harassing shots.

Company A's 2d Platoon slugged it out with three times its own numbers for a full half hour. This stand was due largely to the courage and leadership of Lawson, who stuck to his guns and refused evacuation, though wounded three times. About 0300, with Marines on the right devoting more attention to the heavier attack against Hill 109, the exhausted survivors of the 2d Platoon were overrun and the Brigade line penetrated.

305713 O-F—55——14

For some unknown reason, enemy troops did not pour down the eastern slopes after the breakthrough. Only one squad drove through, and it split Company A in half by invading Stevens' CP, directly behind the 2d Platoon's lines. The company commander and his headquarters were slowly forced down the draw by the methodical grenade and submachinegun fire from above.

The remainder of the North Korean platoon which had hit Company A remained on the crest for a joint effort with the larger force striking Hill 109. Stevens' 1st Platoon, with its left flank now exposed on the saddle, gradually fell back and curled around the southern face of 109.

Although Company B's left front held firm against the two-platoon assault, a few Reds slipped by the Marine foxholes and charged into Fenton's CP on Hill 109. Rocket gunners, mortarmen and clerks responded to the challenge and quickly eliminated the attackers.

When Fenton became aware that the saddle south of Hill 109 had been taken, he tightened his left flank by drawing it in to his 3d Platoon's reverse slope positions. This portion of his defense now took the shape of a football, and successfully withstood pressure from the south.

By 0400 Stevens had temporarily lost control of Company A, although the situation looked worse than it actually was. While the company commander stabilized his center near the bottom of the draw, his executive officer, First Lieutenant Fred F. Eubanks, Jr., made single-handed forays up the gully. He was eventually aided in his private war by the company's machinegun officer, Second Lieutenant Francis W. Muetzel. After the breakthrough, the latter had been wounded and left for dead in his foxhole behind the 2d Platoon. Upon regaining consciousness, he made his way down the draw, fighting it out with enemy soldiers until he reached the Marine lines. Company A's 3d Platoon along the spur below Hill 117 enjoyed a seemingly illogical immunity during the counterattack. Although isolated after the penetration and deployed ideally from the enemy's point of view, Fox's men had only occasional brushes with Red infantrymen who displayed a remarkable lack of interest. After the platoon leader learned of the situation on his right, he redeployed into an elongated perimeter which included a few survivors of the 2d Platoon.

Lieutenant Colonel Newton, when notified of Company A's withdrawal on the left front, called down such a tremendous volume of artillery fire on enemy approaches that 1/11 asked him to conserve a few shells for the Brigade attack scheduled for 0700. The battalion commander replied that the Brigade would be fighting to retake Objective

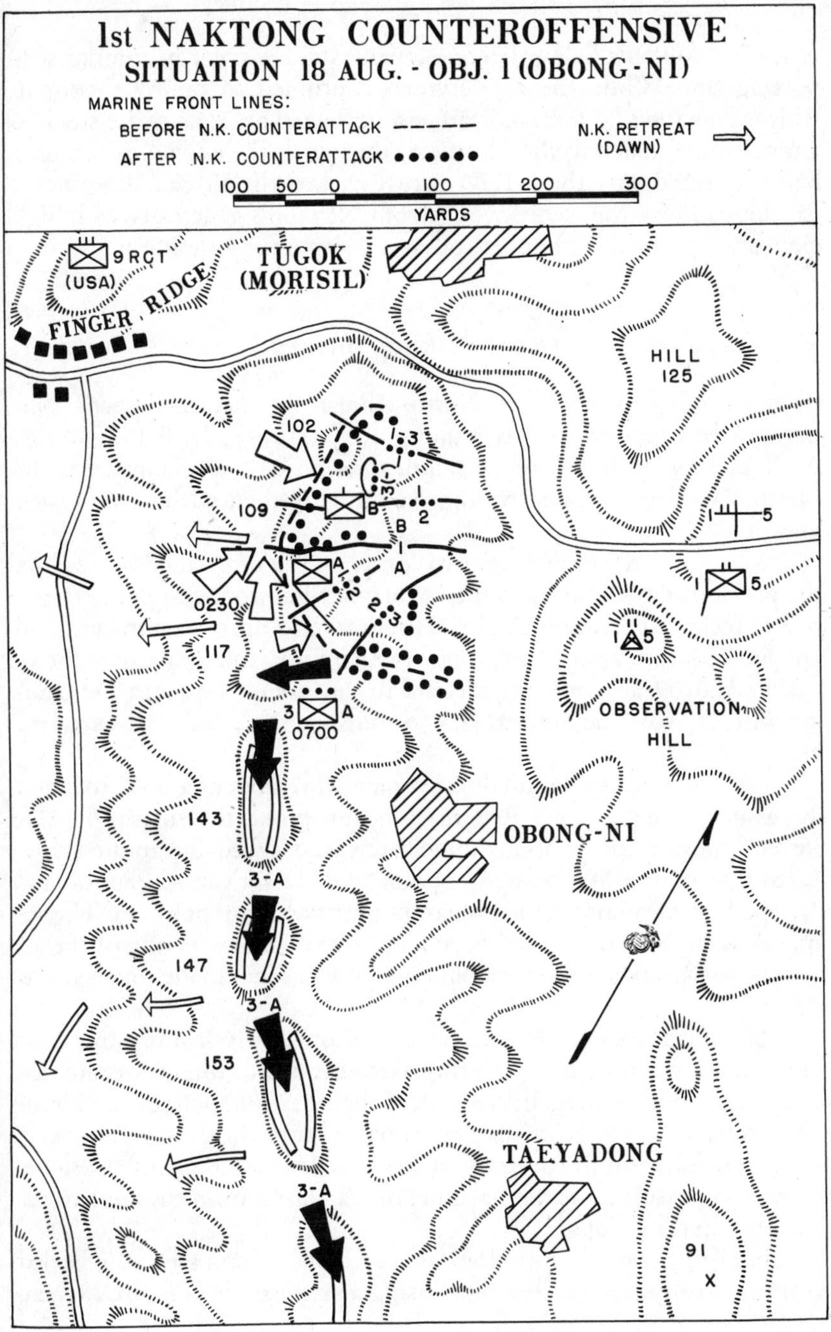
1st NAKTONG COUNTEROFFENSIVE
SITUATION 18 AUG. - OBJ. 1 (OBONG-NI)
MARINE FRONT LINES:
BEFORE N.K. COUNTERATTACK
AFTER N.K. COUNTERATTACK
N.K. RETREAT (DAWN)
100 50 0 100 200 300
YARDS
9 RCT (USA)
TUGOK (MORISIL)
FINGER RIDGE
HILL 125
102
109
117
0230
0700
143
147
153
3-A
OBSERVATION HILL
OBONG-NI
TAEYADONG
91

One at 0700 if his beleaguered companies did not get maximum supporting fire. While the artillerymen continued to pound Obong-ni Ridge, Newton's 81-mm. mortars, strengthened by 2/5's entire stock of ammunition, added to the hot metal thrown at the enemy. It can only be conjectured why the NKPA thrust against the Brigade lines never developed above the company level, but Newton's generosity with high explosives probably did not encourage Communist aspirations.

Obong-ni Ridge Secured

By dawn of 18 August, the North Korean attackers had spent their strength, leaving Company B in undisputed control of Hills 102 and 109. As if in frustration, enemy machineguns on 117 spat angrily at the Marines while the few surviving Red infantrymen withdrew to their lines.

Stevens prepared at first light to complete the unfinished business of the previous day. Thanks to the heroism of his wounded gunnery sergeant, Technical Sergeant Paul A. Hodge, the company commander had regained contact with Fox before dawn and was able to prepare for an attack. At 0700, after moving forward to the 3d Platoon's area and clearing with Newton, he ordered Fox to continue the attack and seize Hill 117.

The platoon leader shouted to his men who arose as a body to begin the ascent. When a lone Red machinegun broke the silence on 117, Stevens spotted the weapon immediately and called for an air strike. Within seconds a Marine fighter plane glided over the 3d Platoon and dropped a 500-pound bomb squarely on the enemy position. The response from Marine air had been so prompt that every one of the attackers was knocked off his feet and one of Fox's automatic riflemen was killed.

While the echoes of the shattering explosion were still reverberating through the morning haze, the thin skirmish line of Marines scrambled up the slope and carried Hill 117. McMullen's 1st Platoon drove in from 109, and the North Koreans fled in panic from the crest and reverse slope positions. A full company of Reds raced down the western slope, with Stevens' riflemen and machinegunners firing from the crest to rip into the enemy groups.

Capitalizing on a psychological advantage, Company A wheeled southward to sweep the crest. Fox, using a skirmish line of only 20 men, assaulted Hill 143 and took the peak against light resistance. A quick call to Newton brought Stevens immediate permission for maximum exploitation.

The 3d Platoon attacked Hill 147 vigorously, and though a few Red soldiers fought to the bitter end, the majority again chose to flee. The high ground was taken easily.

As the Marines moved over the crest of 147, they saw 150 enemy troops in formation halfway down the western slope. The withdrawal commenced in an orderly column of fours but the formation broke down quickly under Marine fire and turned into a routed mob.

Fox turned his attention to Hill 153, Obong-ni's crowning peak, reasoning that it would be the logical place for the enemy's last-ditch stand. But it was the same old story when the 3d Platoon rushed to the summit—abandoned weapons and equipment, a few scattered dead, and blasted foxholes. There was a variation, however, when a supposed clump of scrub pines arose from the reverse slope and rushed downward in headlong flight. The Leathernecks were reminded of Birnham Wood in Shakespeare's *Macbeth* as the camouflaged North Koreans disappeared with the agility of mountain goats before Marine marksmen could score more than a few hits.

While the 1st and 2d Platoons consolidated the central peaks, the 3d combed the southern reaches below Hill 153 without incident. The 1st Platoon, Able Company Engineers, patrolled the swampland south of the ridge and secured Fox's left flank with a minefield extending from the southern crest to the valley below and eastward across the swamp. By midafternoon all of Obong-ni Ridge belonged to the Brigade.

Supporting Arms Clear the Bulge

At midnight, 17 August, Lieutenant Colonel Murray had issued 3/5 a warning order for continuing the attack on the 18th. Shortly after dawn, Taplett and his two company commanders, Fegan and Bohn, visually reconnoitered Hill 207—Objective Two—from vantage points north and south of the MSR. Then, while the battalion commander set up his OP on the northern part of Obong-ni Ridge, Companies G and H advanced to an assembly area at the base of the Ridge.[14]

Taplett called down heavy artillery, air, and mortar preparations on

---

[14] This section is derived from: Annexes Easy and How to Brig SAR; Taplett, 20 Apr 54; and Fegan and Bohn, 17 Apr 54.

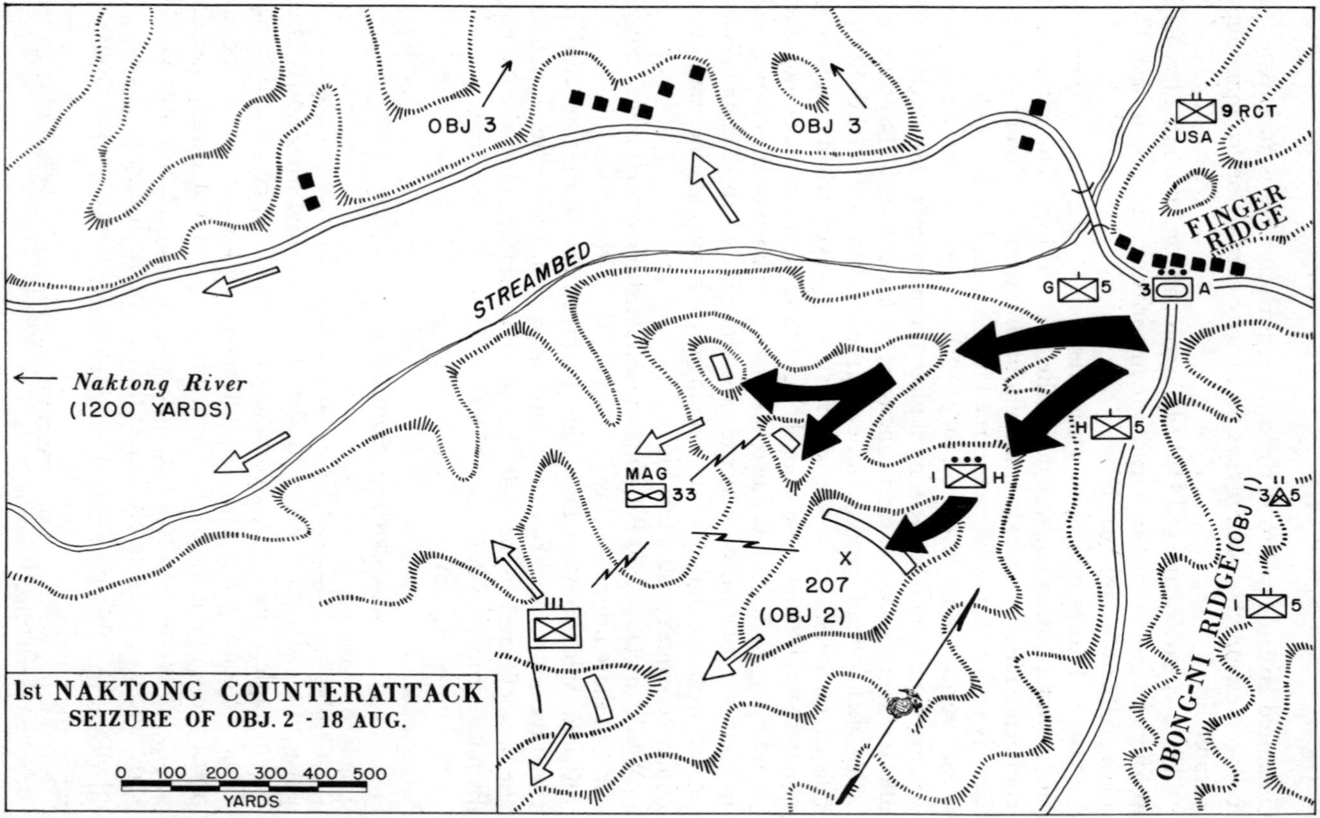

1st NAKTONG COUNTERATTACK
SEIZURE OF OBJ. 2 - 18 AUG.

Objective Two. Occasionally he shifted fires to blast large groups of enemy fleeing to Hill 207 from Company A's advance on Obong-ni Ridge.

Directly south of Finger Ridge, two large spurs form the northern approach to Hill 207. Company H emerged into the open at 1000 from the MSR between Obong-ni and Finger Ridges and attacked up the eastern spur. Following Fegan's unit was Company G, which veered to the right and advanced up the western spur. The two infantry units slowly ascended, separated by a deep gully, while the 3d Platoon of Able Company tanks fired overhead and to the flanks from its positions in the valley.

When Fegan's unit was halfway up the eastern spur, the Marine tankmen saw a platoon of North Koreans attempting to flank the attackers. Machinegun and 90-mm. fire from the M-26's killed or dispersed the Reds at a range of 300 yards.

As Lieutenant Williams worked How Company's 1st Platoon close enough for an assault of the summit, several NKPA soldiers rose from their holes and threw down hand grenades. The Marines hit the deck until the missiles exploded, then bounded up and rushed the crest. Unnerved by Williams' perfect timing, most of the North Koreans fled southward along the ridge. The remainder died in their positions during a brief but bitter fight.

Moving up on Fegan's right, Bohn's men pushed over the western half of the objective, finding only a handful of enemy who were quickly destroyed. Company G's assault completed the seizure of Objective Two at 1237.

During the last minutes of the fight on Hill 207, the entire Naktong Bulge suddenly swarmed with panic-stricken remnants of the 4th NKPA Division. What had been a retreat of small forces now became a widespread rout. Enemy troops poured down from Objective Two, some scurrying up the slopes of Hill 311 across the MSR, others making for the Naktong River.

Air, artillery, and mortars were now offered a profusion of targets by an enemy who ordinarily did not reveal himself during daylight hours. MAG-33 plastered the suspected CP of the 18th NKPA Regiment on a peak south of 207, shattering communications equipment and weapons. Other Marine planes alternated strafing runs with 1/11's continual artillery barrages along the river banks, where enemy troops were gathering by the hundreds.

Victory turned into slaughter when the Brigade supporting arms concentrated on the masses of Communists plunging into the river. All artillery having been turned loose on the river crossings, Taplett used his mortars, machineguns, and the supporting tanks to cut down targets in the valley and on Hills 207 and 311. He requested permission to attack the latter immediately, but was told to remain on Objective Two while the Brigade gave all of its attention to the astounding situation at the river.

At 1530 Companies G and H descended Hill 207. They were met at the bottom by First Lieutenant Pomeroy's 1st Platoon of tanks and escorted across the valley to the base of Hill 311—Objective Three. In advance of the infantrymen, MAG–33 scorched the high ground with napalm while artillery, mortars, and 75-mm. recoilless rifles worked over the slopes.

Again Fegan and Bohn moved up companion spurs which converged on their target, the 1,000-foot height. Progress was good until Company H came within 200 yards of the crest. Then a volley of rifle fire from the summit and forward slopes forced the Marines to the ground. Although confronted by only a platoon, Fegan was at a disadvantage. Scrub growth not only concealed the Communist riflemen, but also prevented the use of Company H's machineguns. Maneuver to the right or left was impossible, since the steep draws on either side were well covered by camouflaged enemy positions. Several Marines who tried to advance frontally were cut down by rifle fire.

The enemy platoon's defense was not based on the usual machinegun fire and grenade throwing. With calm, business-like efficiency, NKPA riflemen kept Company H pinned to the ground, finally wounding Fegan himself as the officer attempted to regain the initiative. After his evacuation, the attack bogged down completely.

At 1730, Company G had reached the southern portion of the long, narrow crest by brushing aside light resistance. Turning its attention northward, the company entered into a small-arms duel with the Communist force opposing Fegan's unit. When supporting arms failed to dislodge the enemy rifleman, Bohn enveloped the troublesome pocket by sending Cahill's 1st Platoon around to the left (west).

The young platoon leader completed the maneuver just before nightfall and overran the Reds on the northern half of the summit. But the enemy on the forward slopes facing Company H suddenly showed fight. The 1st Platoon, pushed rearward a short distance by the surprise resistance, slugged it out at close quarters.

With darkness closing in and the platoon so far beyond Marines lines,

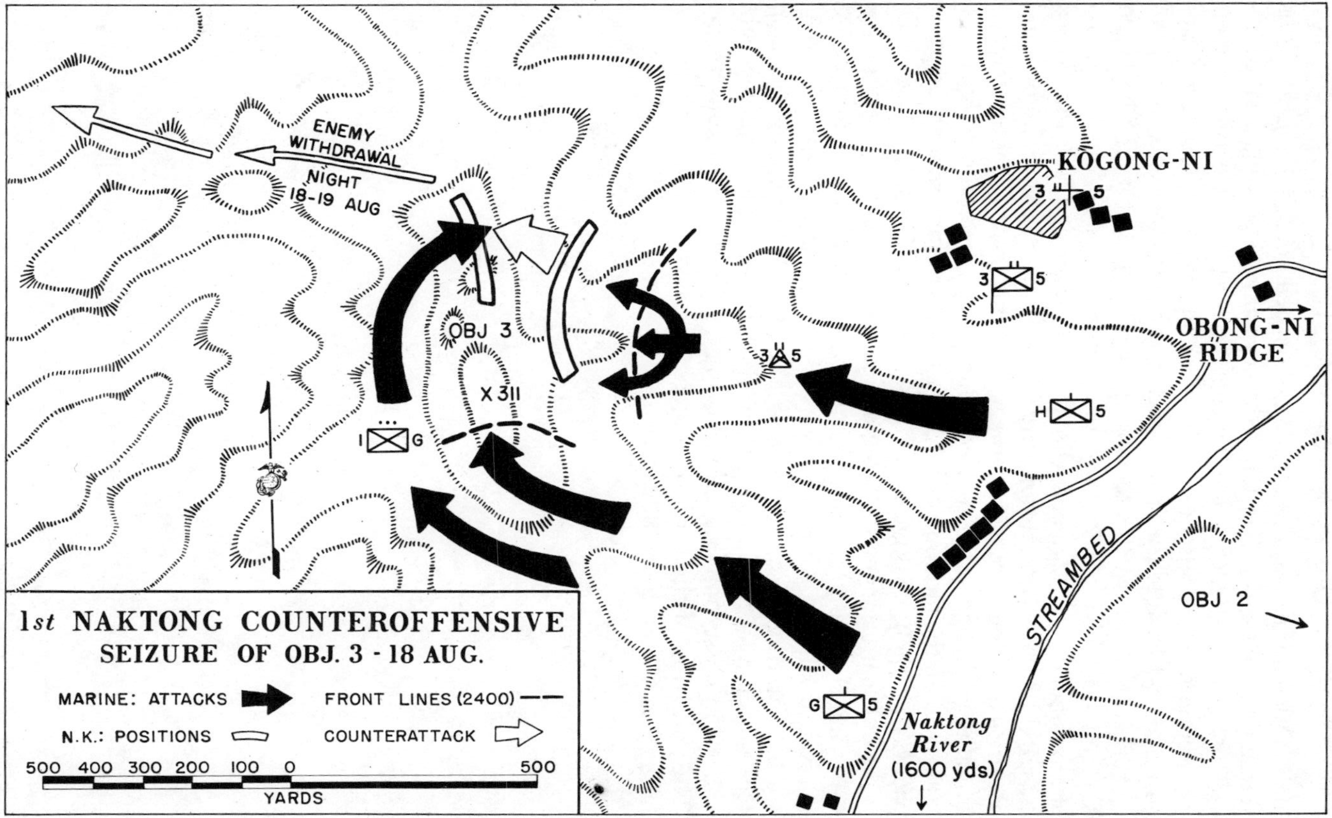

ENEMY
WITHDRAWAL
NIGHT
18-19 AUG
KOGONG-NI
OBONG-NI
RIDGE
OBJ 3
X 311
OBJ 2
STREAMBED
Naktong
River
(1600 yds)
1st NAKTONG COUNTEROFFENSIVE
SEIZURE OF OBJ. 3 - 18 AUG.
MARINE: ATTACKS
FRONT LINES (2400)
N.K.: POSITIONS
COUNTERATTACK
500 400 300 200 100 0 500
YARDS

Bohn ordered it to withdraw. Cahill, wounded himself, reported on his return that the platoon had suffered 10 casualties, including 2 killed.

Taplett ordered the two companies to deploy defensively in their present positions. Thus, during the quiet night of 18–19 August, Companies G and H faced the enemy pocket at right angles to each other.

Earlier on the 18th Lieutenant (jg) Robert J. Harvey, 3d Battalion surgeon, had the unpleasant task of examining an abandoned Army aid station under the bridge near the tip of Finger Ridge. The improvised hospital had been overrun during Army reverses a week before; and about 30 dead found by the Marines bore mute evidence of the enemy's brutality in dealing with captured wounded and medical personnel.

At 0610 on the morning of 19 August, 3/5's 81-mm. mortars prepared the way for the final drive on Objective Three. Following close in the wake of the mortar bursts, Second Lieutenant Thomas P. Lennon led Company H through evacuated enemy positions. He reached the northern part of Hill 311 without meeting any opposition.

This last Brigade objective was secured at 0645, leaving 1/5 atop Obong-ni Ridge, 2/5 on Hill 207 to which it had displaced on the 18th, and 3/5 in possession of the dominating height of the Naktong Bulge. The reduction of the enemy bridgehead cost the Marines 66 dead, 1 missing in action, and 278 wounded.

CHAPTER XI

Second Naktong

The Famous Bean Patch—Planning for Inchon Landing—Return to the Naktong Bulge—All-Out NKPA Offensive—The Marines Jump Off—Progress of Brigade Attack—Assault on Hill 117

IT WAS ALL over but the mopping-up operations. Battalion areas were carefully patrolled on 19 August to clear them of NKPA snipers or stragglers. During this process a patrol ranging along the Naktong river discovered three enemy 122-mm. howitzers hidden in a strip of woods on a hill. The pieces had not been touched by Marine air or artillery. What was more surprising, they were emplaced in a column to fire over one another—something new and wonderful that the Marines had never seen before.[1] General Craig concluded that these howitzers had fired the shells which landed on Marine positions to the bitter end.

The next day the Brigade commander took a helicopter to 24th Division Headquarters to confer with General Church. There he was informed that the Marines had been detached from 24th Division operational control to Eighth Army reserve. Church complimented the Brigade warmly on its performance, and letters of commendation were later received both from him and CG EUSAK.

At 1300 on the 21st Craig arrived by helicopter at a new Brigade bivouac area near Masan that was to be recorded in capital letters as the Bean Patch. It was just that—a bean patch large enough to accommodate a brigade: But from this historic spot the Marines were to fight their way around the peninsula during the next 5 months and complete the circuit to their identical starting point.

General Craig arrived along with the Brigade advance elements. After setting up his CP, he reported to General Kean, of the 25th Division,

[1] This section is derived from: LtGen Edward A. Craig (Ret), ltr to author, 23 May 54 (Craig, 23 May 54).

who was in control of the bivouac area. Kean divulged that the situation in his sector had deteriorated. The enemy had made several penetrations, and Brigade assistance might be required in the event of further breakthroughs. As it was, Kean had been authorized by Eighth Army to employ Brigade artillery along with his own; and 1/11 proceeded the next day to the familiar Chindong-ni area in support of 25th Division Infantry.

Orders were received from Eighth Army for the Brigade infantry to be prepared to counterattack in the 25th Division sector as part of its reserve mission. General Craig and Lieutenant Colonel Stewart made a helicopter reconnaissance of the areas of greatest activity, but events proved that the Marine rifle battalions were not needed.

The Famous Bean Patch

Unit training, including the checking and firing of all weapons, was conducted at the Bean Patch; and Marine patrols were sent out to the rear of the 25th Division to watch for infiltrating forces. Patrols in rugged country were fed hot meals delivered in special containers by the versatile helicopters of VMO-6.

Truckloads of supplies rolled in daily from Pusan, including some of the equipment left behind at the docks when the Brigade landed. But no tentage was available, and the exhausting marches of combat had forced the men to discard everything except fighting tools. In the lack of shelter tents, therefore, the Marines lived in the open at the Bean Patch.

General Craig conferred on 23 August with General Kean and a distinguished visitor, General J. Lawton Collins, Chief of Staff, USA. Collins was keenly interested in Marine methods of knocking out NKPA tanks and requested Craig to prepare a memorandum on the subject.

That evening the entire Brigade attended an outdoor entertainment given on an improvised stage by South Korean girls, who sang and played native instruments which sounded out of tune to Western ears. Translations of the songs were forthcoming, since some of the girls were English-speaking refugees from Seoul University. Afterwards, General Craig addressed the Brigade, paying a high tribute to his Marines for their conduct in battle. NKPA prisoners, he said, had told G-2 interviewers that they earnestly wished to steer clear of "the Americans in yellow leggings."

Letters from home and beer from Pusan [2] contributed to good Marine morale, even though no liberty was granted to nearby towns. On the 29th an honor guard of 87 Marines received Purple Heart medals at a ceremony attended by President Syngman Rhee, who arrived in a helicopter provided by VMO-6. General Craig had paid an official call on him the day before at Chinhae, being most courteously received. And after the presentation of medals, President Rhee gave a talk to the Marines.

He confided to Craig afterwards that he would like to confer some sort of an award on every man in the Brigade for heroic service in Korea. This was undoubtedly the inception of the Korean Presidential Unit Citation which the Brigade later received from the ROK executive.

Planning for Inchon Landing

General Craig, it may be recalled, had insisted that replacements be sent to the Brigade. Thanks to his determination, a long column of trucks arrived at the Bean Patch with more than 800 Marines just landed at Pusan.

Some of the 5th Marines outfits had been so thinned by combat that an appeal was made for volunteers from supporting units to serve temporarily in rifle companies, with the privilege of returning to their former status after the emergency. The hearty response was a tribute to Marine morale as well as Marine basic training which made every man a potential rifleman. Engineers, shore party troops and headquarters personnel came forward in such numbers that some could not be accepted after the arrival of replacements eased the situation.

No attempt was made at the Bean Patch to form the newcomers into third rifle companies. They were simply used to build up the strength of the present companies and given intensive unit training.

Rumors of an impending Marine amphibious operation had already filtered down to every PFC, and there were wild speculations as to when and where. At least, it could hardly be denied that the Brigade would

[2] The offer of Stateside breweries to send free beer to Korea precipitated a controversy in civilian circles. Opponents protested on the grounds that some of the troops were as young as 18. Proponents argued that if a man was old enough to fight, he was mature enough to drink a can of beer without harm. The issue was never definitely settled, though it resulted in a temporary drought.

soon be taking another voyage; for convoys of trucks left the Bean Patch every day laden with heavy supplies and equipment to be unloaded at Pusan.[3]

This was once that lower-echelon "scuttlebutt" came close to the. mark. In fact, planning for the Inchon landing had already gone so far that General Craig sent his chief of staff, G-3 and G-4 to Tokyo to confer with staff officers of the 1st Marine Division about the projected operation.[4]

Major General Oliver P. Smith, CG of the 1st Marine Division, had relieved General Erskine early in July when the latter was sent on a secret State Department mission. As the ADC of the Division during the fight for Peleliu in 1944, Smith knew how tough an amphibious operation can become when it encounters unexpected obstacles. He was determined to keep his Division intact with its three infantry regiments, the 1st, 5th, and 7th Marines. And after his arrival in Japan with the advance party, he returned a firm negative to proposals that the 5th Marines and other Brigade troops remain with the Eighth Army.

It would be putting the case mildly to say that this was the eleventh hour. The 1st Marine Division (less the 7th Marines) had landed at Kobe from 28 August to 3 September. And though a typhoon caused a good deal of damage, little time was lost at the gigantic task of unloading mixed-type shipping and combat-loading it into assault-type shipping. The LST's had to be ready to sail for the target area by 10 September, and the transports by the 12th.

The Marines at the Bean Patch would have been flattered to know that they were the objects of an official tug of war at Tokyo. It was maintained by the EUSAK command and staff that Army morale would be hurt by taking the Brigade away from the Pusan Perimeter at a critical moment. On the other hand, General Smith contended that he needed the Brigade all the more urgently because the 7th Marines,[5] sailing belatedly from San Diego, would not be able to reach Inchon until a week after the proposed D-day of 15 September 1950.

The Marine general was informed that the decision would depend upon the tactical situation in Korea. On 30 August he sent a dispatch to X Corps—the new Army tactical organization activated by CINCFE especially for the Inchon operation—requesting that the Brigade be re-

---

[3] Brig SAR.

[4] Craig, 23 May 54.

[5] Less a battalion making the voyage from the Mediterranean, where it had been afloat with the Sixth Fleet.

leased from its Army commitments on 1 September. In response, General MacArthur issued an order restoring the unit to the 1st Marine Division on the 4th.[6]

At this point the enemy rudely interrupted by launching an all-out offensive against the Pusan Perimeter on 1 September, and General MacArthur's order was rescinded. Even though most of the Brigade's heavy equipment was at the Pusan docks, waiting for shipping, GHQFEC decided that General Craig's troops should again be used as "firemen" to extinguish an NKPA conflagration.

Colonel Edward H. Forney, the Marine officer recently named deputy chief of staff of X Corps, suggested to General Smith the possibility of substituting an Army unit, the 32d Infantry of the 7th Infantry Division, for the 5th Marines. Smith demurred on the grounds that these troops had not been trained for amphibious warfare.

On 3 September, with D-day less than 2 weeks away, a conference was held in Tokyo to decide the question once and for all. X Corps was represented by General Wright, the G-3, and General Edward S. Almond, the new commanding general and former chief of staff, GHQFEC. COMNAVFE (Admiral Joy), COMSEVENTHFLT (Admiral Struble) and COMPHIBGRUONE (Admiral Doyle) were the Navy officers present. General Almond opened the discussion by reiterating that the 32d Infantry would be substituted for the 5th Marines. In reply, General Smith mentioned the complications of an amphibious assault landing and urged that the operations plan be amended if the untrained Army regiment were to be employed.

Another solution, offered by Admiral Struble, was baited with reciprocal concessions. He suggested that the Brigade be employed briefly for counterattacks in the Pusan Perimeter, but that meanwhile the 32d or some other 7th Infantry Division regiment be moved from Japan to Korea. There it would become a floating reserve for EUSAK, thus releasing the Brigade units to take their former places in the 1st Marine Division for the Inchon operation. This compromise was finally accepted, and orders were issued for the Brigade to be withdrawn from Eighth Army control at midnight on 5 September.

The first intimations to reach the troops at the Bean Patch were received on the 1st, at 0810, when the Brigade was alerted for a possible move by CG EUSAK to an unknown destination. At 1109 came the warning order for a road lift to the Miryang assembly area. The

[6] MCBS, I–II–B–4–6.

confirmation followed at 1215, with all units being scheduled to move out at 1330.[7]

The Marines had another date with destiny.

Return to the Naktong Bulge

General Craig set up his CP in the Miryang area at 1800 on 1 September. Billeting officers, having gone ahead by helicopter, were prepared to take care of Brigade units as they arrived. Among them was the 1st Battalion of the 11th Marines, which had been returned from 25th Division control to the Brigade.

The news from the front was depressing. Heavy attacks had been received all day along the 2d and 25th Infantry Division fronts. An enemy penetration of 4,000 yards was made at the expense of the 2d Division, with the old familiar Naktong Bulge being occupied again by Red Koreans who had gained a firm foothold on the east bank of the river.

This meant that General Craig's men, now under operational control of the 2d Division, were likely to revisit some scarred parcels of Korean real estate they had hoped never to see again. Major General Lawrence B. Keiser, commanding the 2d Division, informed the Brigade commander that several of his companies had been cut off by enemy advances which pushed his lines back almost to Yongsan.[8] There was a good deal of NKPA infiltration, he added, in his rear.

It had been a full day, and at 2230 that night Craig received orders from the Eighth Army to move the Brigade at first light to a reserve position south of Yongsan and in the rear of the 9th Infantry of the 2d Division.

At 0630, on 2 September, the 2d Battalion of the 5th Marines arrived at its assigned covering position on the road leading to Yongsan. The remainder of the Brigade moved out to assembly positions during the day.[9]

Craig proceeded by helicopter at 0830 to the 2d Infantry Division headquarters for a conference with Keiser to plan the move of the Brigade into his lines. Afterwards, the Marine general devoted the rest of the morning to reconnaissance of the terrain by helicopter. On the way

---

[7] Brig SAR.
[8] Craig, 23 May 54.
[9] Brig SAR.

he stopped at Lieutenant Colonel Murray's CP and learned that the 5th Marines units were well established along the road leading to the front.

The planning conference for the projected counterattack began at 1430 in the 2d Infantry Division CP. General Craig was accompanied by his assistant G-3, Major Frank R. Stewart, Jr., since his regular G-3 had not yet returned from the 1st Marine Division briefing at Tokyo. General Keiser and his staff officers emphasized the gravity of the situation in the 2d Division sector. They wanted General Craig to counterattack that very afternoon on a widely extended front, but he objected on both counts.

As for the time element, he pointed out that the hour was late. Some of his units were not even in their assembly positions, and others were still detraining or in trucks. Smoke and haze had resulted in such low visibility that planes could not operate effectively. Finally, Craig's TACRON had not arrived and he was out of touch with the aircraft carriers. He did not wish to commit his force piecemeal without air support; and in the end the Army staff officers agreed with him on the advisability of the Marines attacking in the morning.[10]

Next came a discussion as to the nature of the Marine counterattack. Craig cited the risks and disadvantages of advancing on too wide a front. He suggested that the 2d Infantry Division specify the Marine objectives and allow him to attack in such formations as he deemed most effective. Keiser and his staff assented, and the Marine officers hurried back to the Brigade CP.

All-Out NKPA Offensive

Glancing at the big picture, there could be no doubt that the enemy was making an all-out effort to smash through the Pusan Perimeter. Late in August it became evident that he was massing troops. The blow fell in the early morning hours of 1 September. The direction of the main attack remained in doubt until that afternoon, when it was revealed as a bid for a breakthrough in the Naktong Bulge which would expose the Pusan-Taegu lifeline.

Despite heavy casualties of the past 2 months, NKPA overall strength was estimated as high as 133,000 men as the result of filling the ranks

[10] Craig, 23 May 54.

305713 O-F-55--15

with hastily trained replacements. Thirteen infantry regiments, 3 security regiments and the remnants of the original 3 armored regiments were believed to be participating in the offensive.[11]

For 2 months the Eighth Army had been purchasing time with space, and the enemy realized that time was now fighting on the side of the United Nations. The first ground force unit sent by a member nation to reinforce United States and ROK troops was the British 27th Infantry Brigade, which landed and took over a sector early in September. But the enemy knew that other UN contingents had been promised.

The reorganized ROK army, moreover, had recovered from its early disasters and was giving a good account of itself in the northern sectors of the Pusan Perimeter. There the 1st, 3d, 6th, 8th, and Capital Divisions had not only maintained their tactical integrity throughout August but even delivered several counterattacks.[12]

The NKPA numerical superiority, in short, could not last much longer. It was now or never if the invaders hoped to batter their way to Pusan, and Pyongyang staked everything on a final offensive.

The brunt fell upon the United States 2d Infantry Division. Troops from four enemy divisions were identified on this sensitive front, well supported by armor and artillery. Within a few hours pressure became so great that EUSAK decided to send the Marine mobile reserve to the aid of the Army troops.

Not only was the terrain familiar to Marines who had fought their way up Obong-ni Ridge, but they were renewing acquaintance with the same enemy outfit. For G-2 reports confirmed that the NKPA 4th Infantry Division was back again at the old stand—or at least such survivors as had emerged with a whole skin from their defeat of 17–18 August in this area.

Perhaps because of the large numbers of new recruits filling the ranks, the retreaded outfit followed in reserve just behind the NKPA 9th Infantry Division as it crossed the Naktong and drove eastward. The 9th was one of the enemy units hastily raised from constabulary forces for purposes of the invasion. Assigned to guard duty at Seoul throughout July and half of August, the troops devoted themselves wholeheartedly to the pleasant mission of forcing South Koreans to "volunteer" as soldiers or laborers against their own people. Thus the division could be

---

[11] Maj H. D. Stewart, "Rise and Fall of an Army," *Military Review,* 30, no. 11:32–35 (Feb 51).

[12] U. S. Dept of State, "Fifth Report to the Security Council, October 5, 1950," *United Nations Action in Korea under Unified Command* (Washington: GPO, 1950).

considered a fresh and rested outfit, though deficient in training and combat discipline as compared to the older NKPA units.

Troops from the enemy's 2d and 10th Divisions were also identified on the front of the United States 2d Infantry Division, but the Marines had no contacts with these units.[13]

The Marines Jump Off

General Keiser's operational directive for the 3 September counterattack was half a page in length. As in the case of the first Naktong counterstroke, the Marine brigade was placed opposite the center of the Bulge, with the mission of driving westward "to restore former 9th Infantry positions." This time, however, Craig's force was scheduled to jump off 4 miles east of Observation Hill; for the North Koreans were knocking at the gates of Yongsan.

The Brigade's line of departure was a long north-south ridgeline about a thousand yards west of Yongsan and directly south of Myong-ni. This high ground was occupied on 2 September by the 9th Infantry. When the Marines passed through the next morning, the Army unit was to swing northward to attack on the Brigade right. Still farther north, the 23d Infantry had orders to hold positions on the right of the 9th and maintain contact with friendly units by patrolling.[14]

On the Brigade's left, a special task force of the Army's 72d Tank Battalion and 2d Engineer Battalion was to attack southward from Il-li to the Naktong River line below the Bulge. There it would link with the 25th Division's right.

The fact that the Communists upset the plan by smashing through the 9th Infantry lines on the night of 2–3 September was both bad and good news from the standpoint of the Marines. It was bad because an overextended friendly unit had been shattered by many times its numbers and forced into a disorganized withdrawal. It was good because the enemy was plowing ahead at full steam, obviously unaware that he was shortly due for a blow that would find him off balance and send him reeling.

Low hanging clouds and smoke made for poor visibility on the morning of the 3d when General Craig set out on his customary prebattle

---

[13] *Ibid.*

[14] 2d InfDiv Op Dir, 2 Sep 50; and Brig Op Order 19–50.

reconnaissance by helicopter. He was accompanied by Lieutenant Colonel Stewart, who had just returned from the 1st Marine Division planning conferences at Tokyo.

"We couldn't see anything but an occasional mountain peak," Craig recalled at a later date. "After flying around for some time, we had almost decided to return to the CP and complete the tour by jeep. Then Colonel Stewart noticed a hole in the clouds, and we dropped to an altitude where we had a good view of the front." [15]

What Craig and Stewart saw was a long column of Marines fighting their way toward the line of departure.

Lieutenant Colonel Murray's plan of attack for the 5th Marines called for the 1st and 2d Battalions to advance westward astride the Yongsan road, with 2/5 on the right. Taplett's 3d Battalion would initially be in reserve, blocking the southern approaches to Yongsan.[16]

At 0450, 3 September, 2/5 detrucked about 800 yards from Yongsan and marched forward in a route column. Moving into the town a short time later, the Marines received small arms fire from snipers hidden in buildings, ditches and culverts. Most of them were liquidated as the column pushed through to the road junction at the western end of Yongsan by 0630.[17]

At this fork a secondary route branches from the main road through the large village of Myong-ni, about 2,000 yards northwest of Yongsan.

Although still 1,000 yards from the designated line of departure, the 2d Battalion came under moderate fire from its right front. Moreover, dawn had brought indications of considerable activity and confusion ahead of the Marines. Ignoring the fire, Roise went forward about 500 yards to a low hill lying athwart the MSR. There he was jolted by the discovery that the 9th Infantry's lines had collapsed.[18]

On the right of the road there was no friendly situation worthy of the name. To the left of the MSR, an Army tank unit was parked behind the little hill which Roise had reached, and to the front were 4 of its tanks—2 destroyed and 2 abandoned. Included in the wreckage ahead were 2 burned-out NKPA T-34's.

Three hundred yards to the west, on the high ground south of the main road, Army troops were retreating from 1/5's line of departure. The soldiers had buckled under an onslaught by the NKPA 9th Divi-

[15] Craig, 23 May 54.
[16] Annex How.
[17] *Ibid.*
[18] *Ibid.*

sion, which had launched an all-out attack at first light.[19]

Having observed evidence of the confusing situation from their helicopter, Craig and Stewart landed some distance behind Yongsan and proceeded forward by jeep and foot. The Brigade commander located 1/5's CP south of Yongsan and discovered that the battalion was slightly out of position. During 2/5's delay in moving through the city, Murray had ordered Newton to swing westward and align his unit for the attack as best he could. Darkness, coupled with confusion caused by the Army's withdrawal and 2/5's fight, had caused the 1st Battalion to move south of Chukchon-ni instead of Yongsan, as planned. Craig instructed 1/5's commander to make a 500-yard correction northward during the actual attack.[20]

Roise was meanwhile taking the situation in hand north of the MSR. At 0645 he called Marine tanks forward to cover the withdrawal of 9th Infantry troops from the high ridge in 1/5's zone.

Second Lieutenant Robert M. Winter led his platoon of M-26's into hull defilade next to 2/5's OP on the low hill and unleashed overhead fire in support of the Army troops. The pursuit by the North Koreans began to lag.

Progress of Brigade Attack

Despite enemy artillery fire in the 2d Battalion zone, Companies D and E jumped off from the road junction at 0715 to clear the Yongsan-Myong-ni road and secure the 5th Marines' right flank.[21]

While this move was in progress, the last of the 9th Infantry troops vacated 1/5's line of departure to the left front. Roise immediately smothered that ridgeline with fire from Marine tanks, artillery, air, mortars, and machineguns.

Despite this blanket of steel, enemy guns from the high ground were able to fire across the MSR at Company E as it cleared a series of hills below Myong-ni. These hills had been designated 2/5's line of departure the previous day, but now were considered part of the first objective.

At 0800, when Captain Samuel Jaskilka reported that Easy Company had completed its mission, Roise ordered Company D to push through Myong-ni and take the hill just northwest of that village.

---

19 *Ibid.*

20 Craig, 23 May 54 (with comments by LtCol M. R. Olson, 17 Jun 54).

21 This section is derived from: Brig SAR; Muetzel, 5–6 Jan 50 (with comments by Col G. R. Newton, Maj J. R. Stevens, and Capt G. C. Fox); and Craig, 23 May 54.

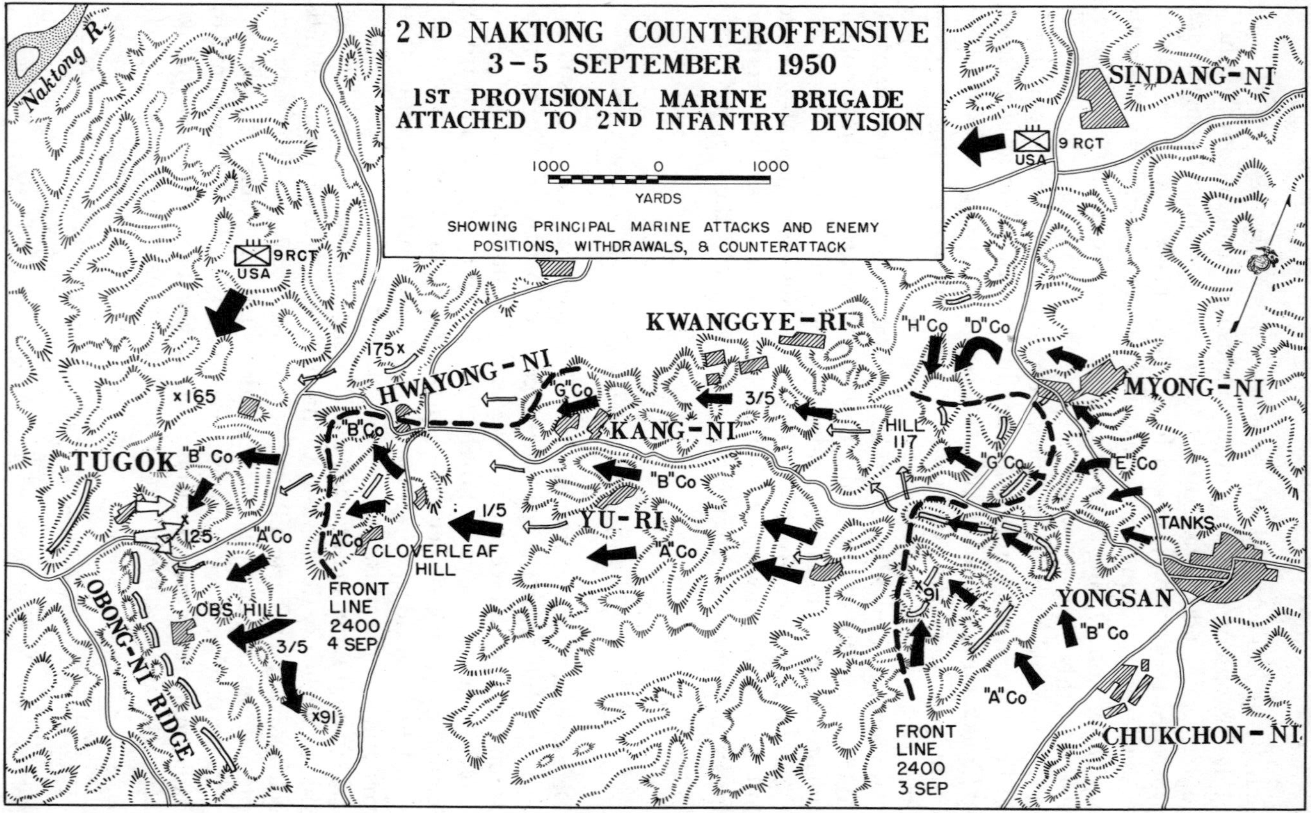

2ND NAKTONG COUNTEROFFENSIVE
3 – 5 SEPTEMBER 1950
1ST PROVISIONAL MARINE BRIGADE
ATTACHED TO 2ND INFANTRY DIVISION
1000
0
1000
YARDS
SHOWING PRINCIPAL MARINE ATTACKS AND ENEMY
POSITIONS, WITHDRAWALS, & COUNTERATTACK
Naktong R.
SINDANG-NI
9 RCT
USA
MYONG-NI
KWANGGYE-RI
"H" Co
"D" Co
HWAYONG-NI
"G" Co
KANG-NI
3/5
HILL
117
"G" Co
"E" Co
TANKS
YONGSAN
"B" Co
"A" Co
CHUKCHON-NI
FRONT
LINE
2400
3 SEP
x91
"B" Co
YU-RI
"A" Co
1/5
CLOVERLEAF
HILL
"B" Co
"A" Co
FRONT
LINE
2400
4 SEP
175x
x165
TUGOK
"B" Co
125
"A" Co
OBS. HILL
3/5
x91
OBONG-NI RIDGE

By this time the entire Brigade was shifting into high gear. Winter's tanks on the little hill straddling the MSR were joined by the 1st Platoon, Able Company Engineers. The Army armored unit behind the southern portion of the hill suddenly went into hull defilade and added its firepower to that of the Marine M–26's. Craig, Snedeker and Stewart crawled to the crest of the hill on the right side of the MSR and studied the front from positions between the Marine tanks and Roise's OP.

The NKPA 9th Division had been stopped in its tracks when the Brigade's supporting arms connected. Then the Reds concentrated their fire on the little hill where Craig's OP was located. Lieutenant Winter was shot through the neck and one of his men wounded while aiding him. Before being evacuated, the painfully wounded tank officer offered General Craig a bottle of whiskey left in his M–26.

Chaplains Sporrer and Hickey were taken under machinegun fire as they walked forward on the MSR toward the hill. "It's lucky they're poor shots," said Sporrer as a second and third burst cracked over his head. The two chaplains arrived just in time to administer to the wounded being carried off the hill by the engineers.

At 0855, the 1st Battalion jumped off from below Chukchon-ni. The attack having been launched too far to the south, Companies A and B had to veer northwest as they advanced toward the enemy-held ridge 1,000 yards away. Fenton's unit was on the right, gradually closing on the MSR as it moved forward.

To the south, Stevens deployed his 1st, 2d, and 3d Platoons from right to left in that order, the latter being slightly withheld to protect the open left flank.

As the men of 1/5 waded into the knee-deep muck of the rice paddy, they came under long-range small-arms fire from their objective. Newton countered immediately by plastering the ridge with artillery and mortar fire. The advance continued and only a few casualties were taken by the time the companies reached a drainage ditch midway across the rice paddy. Here the long skirmish line paused to check its direction and place the wounded on dikes where they would be seen by corpsmen.

During the advance from the drainage ditch to the base of the ridge, 1/5's commander frequently called on air, artillery and mortars to blast enemy automatic weapons on the crest and forward slopes of the objective. Company A had the added support of an Army tank destroyer which gave overhead fire from the hill south of Chukchon-ni. On one occasion Marine 75's joined with the Army weapon to silence Communist guns in a small village at the base of the ridge.

Throughout the rice-paddy crossing, the Marines were constantly meeting Army stragglers, some of whom had been isolated in enemy territory for as long as three days. Most of the soldiers were wounded, and all were weaponless and near exhaustion.

At 1100 Fenton and Stevens radioed Newton that they were ready for the assault, and the battalion commander immediately showered the objective with 81-mm. mortar fire to smother North Korean machine-guns.

Beyond the edge of the rice paddy in Company A's zone, a sharp step led to the gentle incline at the base of the ridge. After a few yards, the gradual slope gave way to a steep rise which shot up abruptly to the crest of the high hill.

Lieutenant Muetzel's 2d Platoon held up at the step, using its protection against enemy fire while 1/5's mortar barrage was falling. During the pause Technical Sergeant McMullen brought the 1st Platoon into position on Muetzel's right and Lieutenant Fox aligned his 3d Platoon on the left.

As soon as the supporting fire lifted, Muetzel jumped to his feet and shouted the command to assault. Every man in Company A's skirmish line responded by scrambling up the hillside. The Marines made such a fearful racket that a whole company of alarmed North Koreans suddenly jumped up from concealed foxholes on the forward slope and fled toward the summit.

The panic-stricken Reds were easy targets for Company A's riflemen and BAR men. Halting on the gentle incline, the Marines carefully took aim and killed most of the enemy soldiers. When the Communist survivors disappeared over the crest, Company A again surged upward and within minutes carried the summit.

Assault on Hill 117

The 1st Battalion secured its initial objective about noon on 3 September. Company B's next target was a continuation of the ridge running parallel to the MSR for 1,000 yards and topped by 4 conspicuous peaks. Able Company's second objective was a hill stretching across its front beyond a 200-yard valley. This hill was connected to Stevens' first objective by a narrow razorback ridge on the right which offered a poor route of approach.[22]

---

[22] *Ibid.*

The two companies paused on their newly won positions to reorganize, evacuate wounded, and wait for a resupply of ammunition. There they came under heavy fire from the reverse slopes of their first objective and the high ground to the west. Several casualties were taken before Corsairs, requested by Newton, appeared for an air strike. As the Marine fighter planes unloaded their ordnance, large groups of enemy broke. Most of the Reds fled down the northern slopes, crossed the MSR and ascended Hill 117 in 2/5's zone.

Newton reacted to reports of the rout by throwing heavy artillery fire across the enemy's avenues of retreat. The hillsides and road were soon littered with bodies and equipment.

While 1/5's attack on its first objective was in progress, Company D had secured the 5th Marines' right flank by clearing Myong-ni of moderate resistance and seizing the hill to the northwest of the large village. The new company commander, First Lieutenant H. J. Smith, reported to Roise that he was receiving considerable machinegun and mortar fire from Hill 117. This high ground lay directly across 2/5's front, stretching northward from the MSR to a point about 500 yards west of Myong-ni.

Smith's reports, together with the news of the enemy's withdrawal to Hill 117 from 1/5's zone, led Roise to order Company D to attack the high ground from the north and cut off the North Korean retreat. Shortly after 1200, Smith's company jumped off to the southwest from its positions above Myong-ni and fought across the rice paddies circling the objective.

Company E could not advance from the chain of hills won earlier in the day because of enemy troops along the high ridge in Baker Company's zone south of the MSR. But Jaskilka's men supported the attack on 117 by fire.

A platoon of 75's from First Lieutenant Almarion S. Bailey's Anti-Tank Company, taking positions on Jaskilka's right, quickly knocked out an enemy gun on the objective. The Communists answered with 85-mm. fire from a concealed T-34 tank, killing 2 and wounding 7 of the recoilless rifle crews.

Company D gained a foothold on one of Hill 117's spurs against light resistance. As the unit advanced south toward the crest, however, enemy troops pouring across the MSR from 1/5's zone had boosted the ranks of the defenders to approximately two battalions. Smith's company was caught in its isolated position 500 yards from the rest of 2/5 and blasted by North Korean artillery, mortars, and automatic weapons. Casualties mounted at such a staggering rate that the Marines were hard put to retain their foothold on the northern tip of the hill.

While the 2d Battalion was maneuvering and fighting on the right of the road, the 2d Platoon of tanks pushed westward along the MSR from its early morning position 500 yards west of Yongsan. The Brigade armor became heavily engaged with enemy antitank weapons, and several casualties were taken as Marines exposed themselves from unbuttoned M–26's to spot Communist emplacements. Second Lieutenant John S. Carson, who had taken over the platoon after Winter was wounded, fell before enemy machinegun fire and died instantly.

Going into hull defilade on another low hill overlooking the MSR, the 2d Platoon surprised three T–34 tanks on the road ahead and quickly destroyed them with 90-mm. fire. The tankmen then turned their guns on a wealth of targets spread across the front: Red antitank weapons, machinegun positions, troop concentrations, and groups either retreating or attempting to reinforce.

About noon, Second Lieutenant Sweet's 3d Platoon joined the 2d and added its firepower to the fusillade. Another T–34 was knocked out when Sweet's men blasted a thicket suspected of concealing an antitank gun. A fifth North Korean tank went out of action when it was abandoned by its crew on the left side of the road.

In the afternoon of 3 September, enemy resistance across 1/5's front weakened proportionately as it grew stronger in the 2d Battalion zone. Newton launched his attack on Objective Two at 1510, after MAG–33 and 1/11 had softened up the North Korean positions.[23]

Company B drove down the ridgeline paralleling the MSR and in little more than an hour had seized its part of the objective, a peak directly across the road from Hill 117. During the 1,000-yard advance, Fenton reported another large group of enemy fleeing to 2/5's zone. The information was quickly relayed to Roise, who had ample reason by this time to curse the fortunes of war.

In Company A's zone, Stevens and his platoon leaders worked out a classic scheme of maneuver for seizing Hill 91, their part of the battalion objective. McMullen's 1st Platoon and the company machineguns were to remain in position as the base of fire, while Muetzel's 2d Platoon feinted across the 200-yard valley to the front. Fox's 3d Platoon, earmarked for the main effort, would then circle to the south and flank the enemy's right.

Muetzel's unit jumped off with Company B at 1510, crossed the low

[23] *Ibid.*

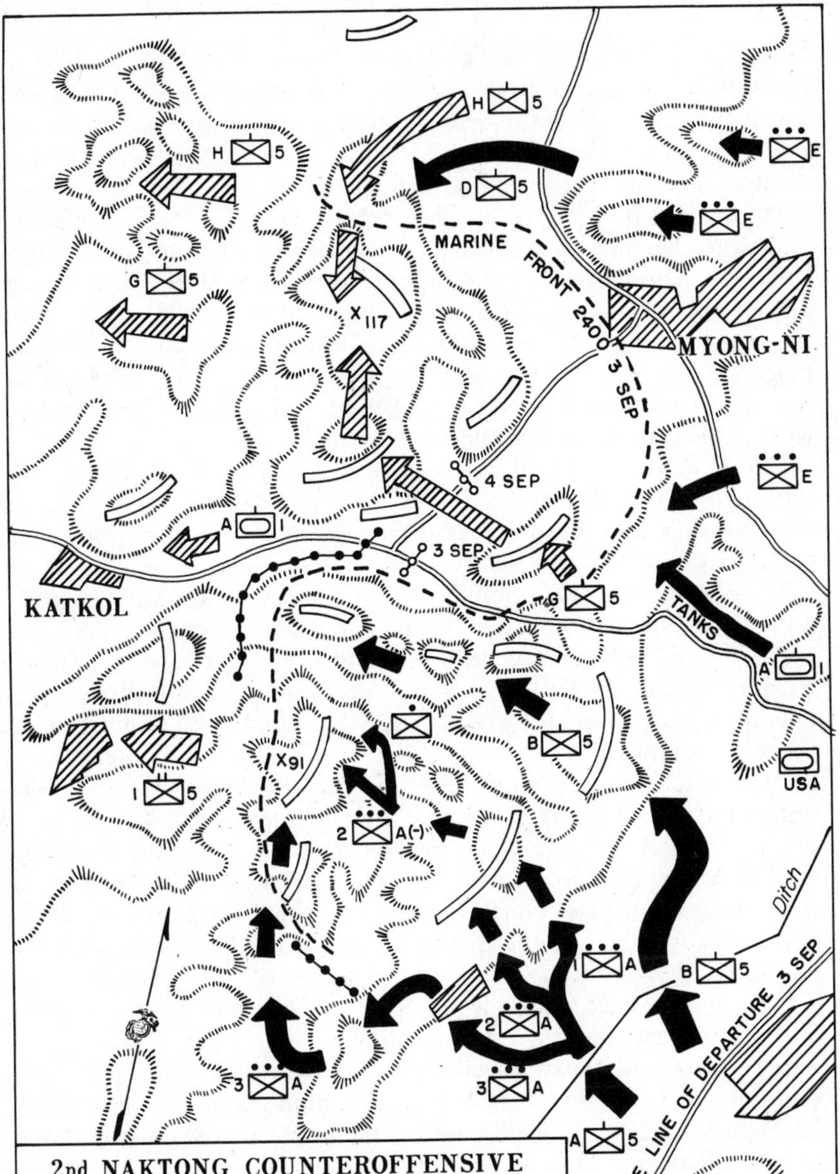
2nd NAKTONG COUNTEROFFENSIVE
MARINE ATTACKS: (3 SEP) (4 SEP)
MINES: FRIENDLY ENEMY
500 0 500 1000
YARDS
MYONG-NI
KATKOL
MARINE FRONT 2400 3 SEP
4 SEP
3 SEP
X 117
X 91
TANKS
Ditch
SUBSTITUTE LINE OF DEPARTURE 3 SEP
ARMY AT GUN
USA
USA
H 5
H 5
D 5
G 5
G 5
A 1
A 1
B 5
B 5
I 5
A 5
2 A(-)
1 A
2 A
3 A
3 A
E
E
E

ground, and ascended a draw leading to Hill 91. The Marines miscalculated, however, and climbed too far up the slope, so that they came within grenade range of the crest and were pinned down by machinegun fire. The platoon was split, with Muetzel and two squads on the left of the draw and Corporal Raymond E. Stephens and his squad on the right.

During the preparatory artillery barrage, Fox had led his platoon around to the enemy's right flank, concealed en route by a rice-paddy bank. Not knowing when the supporting fire would lift, he withheld his squads from an assault line by a wide safety margin. Thus when the artillery ceased, the North Koreans had time to come out of their holes and hit the envelopment with small arms fire. Fox was wounded, and command passed to Technical Sergeant George W. Bolkow who worked the platoon up into the enemy positions.

The 3d Platoon's assault was sparked by Corporal Virgil W. Henderson and his 3d Squad, who worked to the rear of a troublesome machinegun position and destroyed it. During the attack Henderson was painfully wounded in the jaw by a Communist bullet.

Since both forward platoons had SCR 300 radios, Muetzel heard the report that Fox was wounded. Concluding that the envelopment had failed, the 2d Platoon leader requested and received permission to make a frontal assault on Hill 91 from his position on the forward slopes. Enemy mortar fire had added to the woes of Muetzel's diversionary thrust. And though an OY-2 of VMO-6 had given information leading to the destruction of the mortar position, the beleaguered platoon leader sought the relative safety of a frontal assault.

Corporal Stephens, acting on his own initiative across the draw, had worked his squad up to the razorback ridge and around the enemy's left flank. Thus the hapless North Koreans on Hill 91 were hit by a "triple envelopment" when Stephens struck from the north, Muetzel from the east and Bolkow from the south.

Company A reported its objective seized at 1630, and Newton ordered Stevens and Fenton to dig in for the night.

Both Roise and Newton were confronted by serious space factors on the night of 3–4 September. The 2d Battalion's front was more than 2,000 yards long and formed a right angle. A gap of 500 yards stretched between Company D's precarious position on the northern tip of Hill 117 and Easy Company's lines below Myong-ni. This left Smith's depleted unit isolated and Jaskilka's right dangling.

The 1st Battalion's right flank was exposed more than 1,000 yards along the MSR; and its front was almost a mile in length, with a 200-

yard valley separating the two rifle companies. The Brigade Reconnaissance Company was deployed on high ground far out on Newton's left flank, but this was hardly ample protection for the many avenues of approach in the south.

Exhibiting his characteristic faith in high explosives, Newton called on the 1st Platoon, Able Company Engineers, to contribute their sundry lethal devices to 1/5's infantry defense. Beginning at 1800, 3 September, one group of engineers fanned out to the front and right flank of Company B's lines. Despite fire from Hill 117 and enemy positions to the west, the demolitions men strung out dozens of antipersonnel mines, hand grenades, and blocks of TNT wrapped with 60-penny spikes. Before darkness set in, Baker Company's forward slopes had the potential of an active volcano.

In Company A's zone, Technical Sergeant David N. Duncan and Sergeant Bryan K. White led the other half of the engineer platoon in laying a similar field of obstacles. Duncan crowned his handiwork with a 40-pound shaped charge hooked up in a gully with a trip wire.

Staff Sergeant Saweren J. Dennis and his 2d Squad of engineers crept forward at midnight 1,000 yards on the MSR and laid an antitank minefield across the road near the southern tip of Hill 117. On the way Dennis discovered an enemy antitank minefield embedded in the road. Although the engineers had never seen a Russian wooden-box mine before, knowledge gained from the study of intelligence manuals during the Brigade's sea voyage enabled them to detect, remove, and disarm every mine in the field during darkness. The work was delayed a few minutes when Dennis traced a clanking sound to the roadside ditch and killed a Communist soldier frantically trying to insert a loaded magazine into his submachinegun.

Before the engineers completed their work and retired to 1/5's lines, Nature added an obstacle of her own to any enemy plans for a counterattack. A rainstorm broke, and the heavy downpour, accompanied by unseasonably icy winds, wrought misery on friend and foe alike for the rest of the night.

CHAPTER XII

Mission Completed

Collapse of the 9th NKPA Division—Attacks of 5 September—Two Marine Tanks Killed—The Brigade's Final Action—Brigade Embarkation at Pusan—Results of Brigade Operations—Summaries and Conclusions

THE CASUALTIES OF 2/5 for 3 September totaled 18 dead and 77 wounded, most of them being taken by Company D. Lieutenant Colonel Murray ordered the 3d Battalion to pass through the 2d, therefore, and continue the attack on the right of the MSR at 0800 the next morning. The 1st Battalion was to resume its advance south of the MSR, while the Reconnaissance Company far out on the left would move forward to a new blocking position.[1]

Shortly after dawn on the 4th, the 1st Platoon of engineers went forward and removed the mines ahead of 1/5's positions. Preparatory fires by 1/11 at 0750 routed a group of enemy on the peak on Baker Company's front, and the Marine riflemen had a field day as the Reds threw away their weapons and pelted westward.

Companies A and B jumped off at 0800 and advanced rapidly over the high ground south of the MSR against negligible resistance. The attackers frequently observed small groups of enemy fleeing in all directions, and many of the Communists were cut down by Brigade air, artillery, and armor. Twelve prisoners were captured before 1/5 reached its half of Brigade Objective One at 1505. This was the high ground south of the MSR at Kang-ni, over 3,000 yards from the line of departure.

Shortly after 0800, 3/5 had launched a two-pronged assault against Hill 117, core of the NKPA 9th Division's resistance the previous day. Company G advanced through Easy Company's lines just above the MSR and pushed across the intervening rice paddies. The Marines

[1] This section is derived from: Brig SAR 3d Bn, 5th Marines (3/5) SAR, 1–6 Sep 50; Craig, 23 May 54; and Taplett, 20 Apr 54.

charged over a small knoll in their path but found the enemy positions unoccupied except for several dead. Bohn quickly led the company to the southern slopes of Hill 117, which was strangely quiet by comparison with the tumult of the previous day. In capturing the southern half of the hill, Company G killed only 15 North Koreans.

Simultaneously with Bohn's advance, Company H swung wide to the right and passed through the thin ranks of Dog Company on the northern tip of Hill 117. The attackers drove south against negligible resistance and quickly linked with Company G, securing the objective at 0840.

A connecting road runs from Myong-ni to the MSR, tracing the eastern base of Hill 117. Since engineers on the previous night had located the enemy minefield east of the junction on the main road, Taplett moved his headquarters to the MSR via the connecting road. The lead vehicle, a personnel carrier loaded with communications men, struck a Communist mine on the secondary route east of the newly captured objective. The resulting explosion caused 10 casualties.

By noon the engineers had cleared the road of several Russian-type mines identical to those found during the night. The two anti-vehicular minefields were among the first such obstacles encountered by the UN forces in the Korean conflict.

After seizing Hill 117, Companies G and H continued the attack westward by advancing abreast on the high ground north of the MSR. Contact with 1/5 on the left was maintained, but the 9th Infantry on the right soon fell behind and disappeared from sight.

At 1045 Company G ran into machinegun fire coming from the 3/5 area of the Brigade objective, the hill north of Kang-ni. Taplett blasted the hill with Marine air and artillery, and the North Koreans were in full retreat within an hour. MAG-33 and 1/11 rained death on the retreating Reds and continued to pound the hill preparatory to an assault by Company G. Bohn led his troops forward and secured the objective at 1515.

Looking across the stream bed to the north of their new positions, the Marines of George Company spotted enemy infantry escorting a T-34 tank and withdrawing into the 9th Infantry zone. The Communist column was quickly dispersed by machinegun fire.

Collapse of NKPA 9th Division

Marines following up the 3,000-yard advance along the MSR saw a picture of devastation unequalled even by the earlier defeat of the NKPA

4th Division. Hundreds of enemy dead were strewn along the road, hillsides and ridgelines. On the MSR between Hill 117 and Kang-ni lay a long column of North Koreans who had been caught by Marine air and artillery while attempting to reinforce Red lines. The dead leader was a lieutenant colonel whose briefcase contained a lengthy artillery treatise among other less scholarly documents.[2]

In addition to knocked-out and abandoned Communist tanks, vehicles, mortars, and antitank guns, the countryside was littered with enough small arms, ammunition, and gear to equip several hundred men. Even the North Korean paymaster had been caught in the sweeping tide of Brigade arms, and Marines distributed a huge quantity of worthless currency among themselves.

Not only did the Marines reap a harvest of enemy materiel; they also recaptured a great quantity of United States Army equipment lost during the Communist drive. American tanks, artillery pieces, mortars, vehicles, small arms, and ammunition and supply dumps were turned over to the 2d Division by the Brigade.

The destruction of the enemy camp left Army and Marine intelligence officers inundated by captured enemy documents. Muster rolls, ledgers, maps, orders, textbooks, and propaganda material were heaped into separate piles.

Late in the afternoon of 4 September, the 9th Infantry moved into positions on the high ground northeast of 3/5. This completed the advance to Phase Line One of the 2d Division's counterattack plan. The second phase line on G-3 maps was drawn through Hill 125 and Observation Hill, 3,000 yards west of Kang-ni.

When informed that the Brigade had completed the first part of its mission, General Keiser authorized General Craig to advance toward Phase Line Two.

Beyond Kang-ni, the Brigade's right boundary became the MSR, so that 3/5 could not advance westward from its half of Objective One. Major Charles H. Brush, Murray's S-3, radioed Newton and passed on orders for the battalion commander to take the next piece of high ground, Cloverleaf Hill, just south of the MSR at Hwayong-ni, about a thousand yards away.

The 1st Battalion struck out through the intervening rice paddy, Company A on the left and Baker Company just below the MSR. Fenton's unit had hardly begun the advance when it was stopped by

---

[2] *Ibid.*

305713 O-F-55--16

heavy machinegun fire coming from the high ground north of Hwa-yong-ni. Newton then called for an air strike on the ridge and also requested 3/5 to keep it covered with supporting fire during Company B's attack.

Enemy resistance evaporated with accustomed rapidity, and the Marines reported Cloverleaf Hill secure at 1800. Murray then ordered both front line battalions to establish night defenses and be prepared to continue the attack at 0800, 5 September.

The extent and trace of the Brigade front line on the night of 4–5 September was almost identical to that of 24 hours before. Again Newton's battalion was in front on the left by a good 1,000 yards, and Companies A and B were stretched across a line almost a mile long, with the left flank wide open.

Separated from both 1/5 on the left and the 9th Infantry on the right, the 3d Battalion established a perimeter defense, even though it was in the center of the counterattack zone.

There was considerable tension and excitement after darkness on 4 September, although the Brigade lines were never seriously threatened. The engineers were busy in 1/5's zone until after midnight, creeping to the front and flanks to lay mines. The 3d Battalion was shelled heavily throughout the night, and 1/5's CP took direct hits killing 1 Marine and wounding 2 others. One of the wounded was Second Lieutenant James R. Young, Newton's Assistant S–3. The artillery liaison officer, First Lieutenant Joris J. Snyder, was knocked unconscious for several hours, though he received not a scratch from the 120-mm. explosion a few yards away.

At 0230 night-fighter planes of Major Joseph H. Reinburg's VMF(N)–513 bombed the North Korean mortar position causing most of the damage, and the shelling slackened appreciably. Completing this mission, the Marine pilots dumped general purpose and fragmentation bombs on enemy vehicles and troops in the area.[3]

Companies G and H reported movement forward of their lines before dawn, and 3/5's 81-mm. mortars quickly illuminated the front, disclosing several small groups of enemy. There was a flurry of fire, but the Reds gave no indication of organizing for an assault. One of the groups, either by error or suicidal folly, stumbled into the area of Taplett's CP. A listening post of Weapons Company took the intruders under fire, killing an NKPA officer and routing the others.

---

[3] VMF(N)–513 SAR, Appendix 6, 16.

Attacks of 5 September

Marines of the 3d Battalion were startled at daybreak, 5 September, when a company of North Koreans attacked the 9th Infantry's left flank in full view of 3/5's positions on the adjacent high ground. George, How, and H & S Companies poured machinegun fire into the mass of Reds at ranges of 600–1,000 yards. Most of the Red attackers were cut down before they could flee into the hills west of the Army lines.[4]

Company B, on its high ground south of Hwayong-ni, heard the firing in 3/5's area at daybreak and steeled itself for a possible counterattack from the right flank. When Newton received word of the abortive attack on the 9th Infantry, he ordered his two rifle companies to prepare to move out at 0800 as planned.

The Marines of Companies A and B were organizing their attack formation on Cloverleaf Hill when two Air Force P–51's came in for an uncontrolled air strike on the high ground north of Hwayong-ni. Strafing the ridge from north to south, the planes riddled Cloverleaf Hill as they pulled out of their dives. The 2 exposed companies were showered with bullets, and it seemed miraculous that only 1 Marine was wounded.

At 0820, 1/5 jumped off to the west to seize the Brigade's portion of Phase Line Two—Hill 125 and Observation Hill. Beyond these hills lay Obong-ni Ridge, blocking the path to the Naktong River, third and final phase line of the 2d Division counterattack. Because of its tactical importance and great significance, battle-scarred Obong-ni was designated a special objective, apart from the phase lines.

Half a mile west of Hwayong-ni the MSR makes a right-angle turn to the south, proceeds in that direction for 1,000 yards, then resumes its westward course through the cut between Hill 125 and Observation Hill.

Companies A and B, with the latter on the right, moved rapidly through the rice paddy below the MSR after leaving their line of departure on Cloverleaf Hill. At the road bend mentioned above, the MSR turned across Baker Company's front. When Fenton's unit crossed over to the base of the high ground leading to Hill 125, Companies A and B were separated by the MSR as it resumed its westward course. Stevens' unit started up the long eastern slopes of Observation Hill, while Fenton's men secured the eastern extension of Hill 125.

Obong-ni Ridge rumbled its first greeting to 1/5 at 0935 when

---

[4] This section is derived from: Annex How; 3/5 SAR, 1–6 Sep 50; Taplett, 20 Apr 54; and Fenton, 8 May 54.

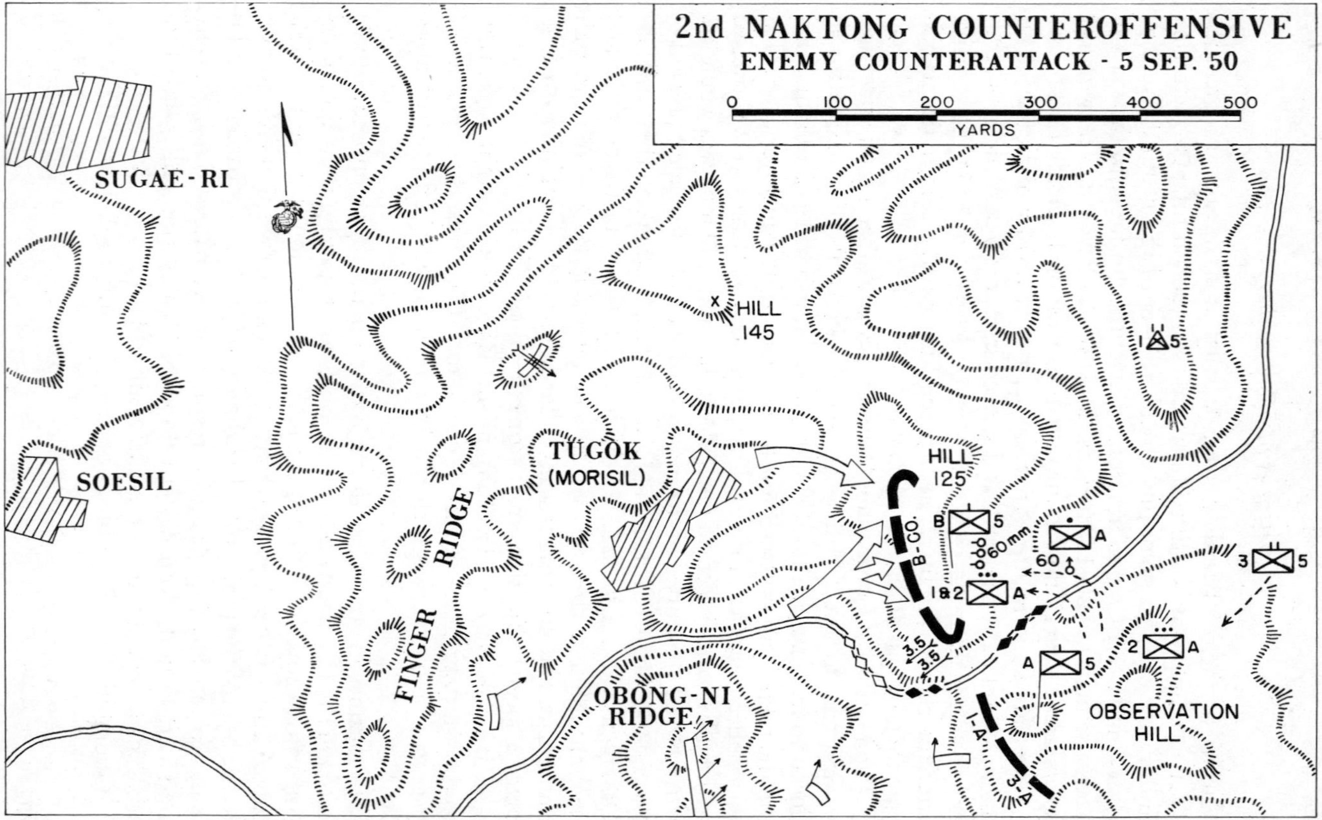

2nd NAKTONG COUNTEROFFENSIVE
ENEMY COUNTERATTACK - 5 SEP. '50
0
100
200
300
400
500
YARDS
SUGAE-RI
SOESIL
HILL
145
TUGOK
(MORISIL)
FINGER
RIDGE
OBONG-NI
RIDGE
HILL
125
B-CO.
60mm
60
1&2
3.5
3.5
1-A
3-A
OBSERVATION
HILL

mortars and artillery fired at the Marine attackers from emplacements around the hill. The Reds were answered immediately by 1/11 and Newton's 81-mm. mortar platoon; and the rifle companies continued the advance to Phase Line Two, securing their objectives at 1100.

Murray ordered 1/5 to hold up until the 9th Infantry tied in on Fenton's right. Communist automatic weapons on Obong-ni Ridge fired on the Marines sporadically during this interlude.

At 1000, while 1/5 was attacking to the west, the 3d Battalion had swung southward behind Cloverleaf Hill to take positions on the 5th Marines' left. This was in preparation for Murray's contemplated assault on Obong-ni Ridge by two battalions. It was planned that Newton's unit would take the northern half of the long hill and 3/5 the southern portion.

Company G led the 3d Battalion advance through the rice paddy south of Cloverleaf Hill. Artillery and 75-mm. recoilless guns paved the way by raking possible enemy hiding places, enabling the infantrymen to proceed rapidly. Bohn's destination was Hill 91, a shoe-like projection jutting out from the southern reaches of Obong-ni Ridge. Reaching the base of the high ground, Bohn requested that supporting fires be lifted. Attached tanks, 75's, and 1/11 immediately shifted their destruction to Obong-ni Ridge.

Company G started up the slopes of Hill 91, while an attached 75-mm. recoilless gun obliterated a wheel-mounted machinegun and its crew going into position on the crest. The Marines had climbed only a few yards when Bohn was ordered by Taplett at 1230 to withdraw the company to Observation Hill.

Company H, then passing between Hill 91 and Observation Hill on its way to Obong-ni's eastern approaches, received the same order from the Battalion commander. The assault on the ridge had been canceled, and Murray was concentrating his regiment along the MSR.

Two Marine Tanks Killed

Throughout the Brigade advance on 5 September, the Marines were hampered by heavy rain and fog which prevented MAG–33 and VMO–6 from operating effectively. Thus the enemy was offered a rare opportunity to mount a daylight attack.[5]

---

[5] This section is derived from: Annex How; LtCol M. R. Olson, interv with author, 15 Jun 54; Taplett, 20 Apr 54; Muetzel, 5–6 Jan 54 (with comments by Maj J. R. Stevens); and Fenton, 8 May 54.

After Company B received orders to hold up on Hill 125, Fenton ordered his men to dig foxholes along the rain-soaked crest facing Tugok village and Finger Ridge to the west and Obong-ni Ridge to the southwest. The company commander directed the attached 1st Platoon of tanks to remain in the road cut, just to the rear of the famous bend around the forward slopes of Hill 125. Peering through the rain and fog, the Marine tankmen could see the dead, black hulls of the three T-34's knocked out by the Brigade 2 weeks earlier.

At 1420 the sporadic sniping from the front suddenly increased to the intensity of preparatory fire, and Baker Company was pinned down on its ridgeline positions. The northern tip of Obong-ni Ridge blazed with NKPA machineguns, whose chatter was soon joined by that of automatic weapons concealed in Tugok and at the northern base of Observation Hill. A Communist antitank gun on Finger Ridge added its voice intermittently to the chorus.

Fenton's radio went dead just as he reported the situation to Newton at his OP on the high ground to the east. As luck would have it, every other radio in the company area was inoperative because of the mud and rain; and Fenton was unable to warn the Marine tanks in the road cut that enemy armor and troops were advancing toward the road bend from the west.

As the Communist vehicles swung into the turn, a company of Red soldiers left the road and assaulted Company B's positions by advancing up the draw on the Marines' left front. The intense overhead fire supporting the Red Infantry enabled them to get well up the forward slopes. Meanwhile, a squad of North Koreans advanced up the draw leading from Tugok and harassed Fenton's right front.

To stop the attack, the Marines were forced to man the crest of Hill 125. Thus exposed to the enemy's supporting fire, Company B had to pay a heavy price in casualties.

During the advance of the Communist armor, it was determined that the first 2 of the 3 vehicles were T-34 tanks and the last a tracked armored personnel carrier. Fenton immediately deployed his assault squad on the slopes below his left flank to meet the threat on the MSR.

Lieutenant Pomeroy, unaware of the enemy tanks around the bend, advanced his M-26's so that the machineguns on Obong-ni Ridge could be taken under massed fire. Thus, as the first Marine tank reached the bend, its 90-mm. gun was pointing to the left front, a quarter turn away from the enemy armor.

The lead T-34 fired on the Marine vehicle as soon as it came into view. Before the turret of the M–26 could be turned to take aim, several more 85-mm. projectiles struck; and the Brigade lost its first tank to enemy action. The second M–26 in column tried to squeeze by the first to render assistance, and it too was knocked out by 85-mm. fire in the restricted passageway.

The crews of both Marine tanks managed to get out of their vehicles through the escape hatches. Some of the wounded were aided by the engineer mine-clearance team accompanying the tank column.

Since the road bend was now blocked, the remainder of Pomeroy's tanks could do nothing but park in the road cut. It was Marine infantrymen who stepped in at this point and blunted the NKPA victory on the MSR.

Company B's assault squad plastered the lead T–34 with 3.5″ rocket fire and stopped it cold. Shortly afterwards, the 1st Battalion's assault platoon reached the fight scene and went into action with its 3.5's. In short order the infantrymen had completed the destruction of the first tank, knocked out the second, and destroyed the enemy personnel carrier.

The historic road bend, as seen through the rain and mist, had become a graveyard of armor. A total of 8 steel monsters were sprawled there in death: 5 T–34's and 1 armored carrier of the NKPA, and 2 Pershing tanks of the 1st Provisional Marine Brigade.

The Brigade's Final Action

On Hill 125 the fight reached a climax as Marines exchanged grenades and small-arms fire with the North Koreans slithering up the slopes in the driving rain. Company B had used all of its 60-mm. mortar shells and was running low on grenades and small arms ammunition. Enemy automatic weapons on the ridges to the front were still cutting down the Marine defenders at 1500 when Fenton sent a runner to Newton requesting more ammunition.[6]

The endurance contest was still in progress half an hour later, as the 9th Infantry moved into positions on the high ground north of Hill 125. Having no communications with his own supporting arms, Fenton sent a messenger to the Army unit commander, asking that he place artillery fire on the Marine front.

When Army shells began falling in answer to the request, 1/5's 81-mm. mortars belatedly got into the fight and worked over the forward

---

[6] *Ibid.*

slopes of Hill 125 to within 50 yards of Company B's positions. The heavy supporting fire turned the tide, and enemy pressure slackened considerably.

During the final stage of the enemy's attack, Company A was being relieved on Observation Hill by 3/5. Stevens told his platoon leaders to leave their grenades and extra ammunition on the hill, since his orders were to withdraw to the rear. While the relief was taking place, however, Company A was ordered to reinforce Fenton's unit against the enemy's attack on Hill 125. Muetzel's 2d Platoon, after recovering its ammunition, was augmented by a machinegun section, mortar squad, and two SCR-300 radios, before the young officer led the unit across the MSR to lend a hand.

When Stevens' relief by 3/5 was completed, he added the 1st Platoon to Company B's reinforcements, and himself withdrew to Cloverleaf Hill with the 3d Platoon as ordered.

The reinforcements were fed into Fenton's line as fast as they reached the summit of Hill 125. By this time every man in Company B had been committed to the forward wall— mortarmen, clerks, signalmen, and all. Lieutenant Howard Blank combined his Able Company mortars with those of the defenders and immediately followed up the artillery and 81-mm. fire which had blunted the attack. These final concentrations of 60-mm. mortar fire on Obong-ni and Finger Ridges and the forward slopes of Hill 125 ended the enemy attack. The surviving Reds withdrew to Tugok.

At 1600, during the dying minutes of the Brigade's final action in the Pusan Perimeter, Newton was ordered back to the regimental CP for a conference. The executive officer, Major Merlin R. Olson, took over 1/5 from the battalion OP on the ridge east of Hill 125.

The 5th Marines commander had called the leaders of his battalions to brief them on General Craig's last field directive, which began with the long awaited words:

> "THIS MY OPN ORDER 22–50 X COMMENCING AT 2400 5 SEPT BRIG MOVES BY RAIL AND MOTOR TO STAGING AREA PUSAN FOR FURTHER OPERATION AGAINST THE ENEMY X PRIOR TO COMMENCEMENT OF MOVEMENT 5TH MARS WILL STAND RELIEVED BY ELMS OF 2ND INF DIV COMMENCING AT DARKNESS . . . CONCEAL FROM THE ENEMY ACTIVITIES CONNECTED WITH YOUR WITHDRAWAL . . ."

Taplett's 3d Battalion had sustained 24 casualties from artillery and mortar fire between its occupation of Observation Hill and the time it was relieved by a company of the 23d Infantry shortly after midnight.

Plodding rearward through mud and driving rain, 3/5's long column began its three-and-a-half-mile march to an entrucking point 2,000 yards west of Yongsan.

Following 3/5 were the weary, mud-soaked troops of the 1st Battalion. Having successfully defended Hill 125 at a cost of 2 killed and 23 wounded, Baker Company had filed down to the road after being relieved by another company of the 23d Infantry. Muetzel brought up the rear with Company A's contingent, and a battalion column was formed at Olson's check point east of Hill 125.

By dawn of 6 September, the two battalions were loading aboard trucks to follow the rest of the Brigade. Numbed by fatigue and icy rain, the bent forms huddled together in the cargo vehicles had no regrets as they bade good-bye to the Pusan perimeter.

Brigade Embarkation at Pusan

The movement to Pusan was completed by the morning of 7 September, and the Brigade troops found themselves back at the docks where they had landed a little more than a month before. In fact, the docks were to be their bivouac area during the next 6 days; the men slept in the open and took their meals on board the transports in which they would soon be sailing around the peninsula.

The survivors of the Naktong fights—even the latecomers who had joined the Brigade at the Bean Patch—felt old and worn when they saw the large draft of shiny new Marines just landed as third rifle companies organized with their own NCO's and platoons. The veterans had forgotten how young and untroubled a Marine could look; how neat and clean he could appear in a recently issued utility jacket.

The new companies were immediately assigned to their battalions. It was another job for officers and NCO's who had the responsibility of replacing equipment lost in action as well as servicing ordnance, motor transport and other heavy equipment which had been sent from the Bean Patch to Pusan late in August.[7]

General Craig and his staff had their headquarters in one of the Pusan University buildings. There was no opportunity for planning, let alone rehearsals, for the forthcoming amphibious assault at Inchon. Craig and his officers had all they could do to get the Brigade ready for embarkation.

---

[7] Col J. L. Stewart, interv with author, 10 Jun 54.

Among the tasks to be accomplished in less than a week, it remained to give some weapons training to the 3,000 troops of the 1st Korean Marine Regiment. This newly raised unit, attached to the Brigade for embarkation, was to make a name for itself within the next year and become the fourth rifle regiment of the 1st Marine Division. But in September 1950 there were great gaps in the training of the KMC's. The men kept their rifles scrupulously clean, and they could strip an M-1 expertly, but few of them had ever fired a shot.

Marine NCO's had the hazardous duty of giving the eager and excited KMC's their first target practice after eight rounds of ammunition for each man had been acquired. No Marine casualties resulted, fortunately, but puffed and bruised cheeks were the rule among Koreans having their first experience with an M-1's recoil.

There was, of course, no end of "scuttlebutt" going the rounds of the Marines as to their destination. One day the troops were lined up in formation and read a long lecture on the hydrographic aspects of the west coast port of Kunsan. It is to be hoped that this red herring made some impression upon the Koreans who were listening, since Pusan was a headquarters of enemy spies. As for the Marines, most of them concluded that at least Kunsan could be eliminated from the list of possible objectives.

The secret was well kept by Brigade officers in the higher echelons. Two engineer officers, First Lieutenant Ernest P. Skelt and Commissioned Warrant Officer Willard C. Downs, were given the secret mission of constructing wooden scaling ladders for the next operation. This project gave rise to more rumors, but it is safe to say that few men in the ranks knew the answer when the Brigade was deactivated at 0001 on 13 September 1950. The components immediately resumed their old unit designations in the 1st Marine Division and sailed to take part in the amphibious assault on Inchon scheduled for the 15th.[8]

Results of Brigade Operations

As the mountains behind Pusan faded from sight, General Craig and his men could reflect that the Brigade's 67 days of existence had been productive. Altogether, the Marine air-ground team had fought three difficult offensive operations in a month while traveling 380 miles with

[8] The Inchon-Seoul operation of the 1st Marine Division and 1st Marine Air Wing from 15 September to 7 October 1950 is to be the subject of Volume II of this historical series devoted to Marine operations in Korea.

a third of its organic transportation plus Army vehicles.

Total casualties for the Brigade included 148 KIA, 15 DOW, 9 MIA (seven of whom were later reclassified as KIA after recovery of the bodies) and 730 WIA.[9] It was estimated that the Marines inflicted total casualties of 9,900 killed and wounded on opposing NKPA units. Enemy losses of arms and equipment were on such a scale as to impair the effectiveness of the forces concerned.

In its initial operation, as a component of Task Force Kean, the Brigade had the major part in the first sustained Eighth Army counterattack—the military equivalent of a hard left jab which rocks an opponent back on his heels. General MacArthur, when reporting to the United Nations, asserted that "this attack not only secured the southern approaches to the beachhead, but also showed that the North Korean forces will not hold under attack." [10]

The Communist drive in this sensitive area came closest of all NKPA thrusts to the vital UN supply port of Pusan. Up to that time the NKPA units spearheading the advance—the 6th Infantry Division and the 83d Motorcycle Regiment—had never suffered a reverse worth mentioning since the outset of the invasion. Then the counterattack by the 1st Provisional Marine Brigade hurled the enemy back 26 miles in 4 days from the Chindong-ni area to Sachon.

It was estimated that the Marine air-ground team killed and wounded 1,900 of the enemy while destroying nearly all the vehicles of an NKPA motorized battalion in addition to infantry armament and equipment. The enemy threat in this critical area was nullified for the time being, and never again became so serious. Marine efforts assisted Army units of Task Force Kean in taking new defensive positions and defending them with fewer troops, thus freeing some elements for employment on other fronts. Finally, the Marines earned more time and space for the building up of Eighth Army forces in preparation for a decisive UN counteroffensive.

The next Brigade operation, the first battle of the Naktong, ranks with the hardest fights of Marine Corps history. The enemy, after showing skill and aggressiveness in breaching the last natural barrier of the Pusan Perimeter, widened his Naktong bridgehead and took strong defensive positions in preparation for an all-out offensive while still maintaining his material superiority.

---

[9] Brig SAR, basic report.

[10] MCBS, I-II-A-18-19. This valuable operational study by Marine senior officers has been the guide for the summaries and analyses of Brigade results in these pages.

Only two Eighth Army units were available for a counterattack—the 27th Infantry and the 1st Provisional Marine Brigade. The Army regiment being needed in reserve on the southern front, the "firemen of the Pusan Perimeter" were placed under the operational control of the 24th Infantry Division on the central front. There the Marines had the mission of clearing the enemy from Obong-ni Ridge and two other large hill masses of the Naktong Bulge.

The NKPA 4th Infantry Division had taken maximum advantage of strong defensive terrain in accordance with the precepts taught by Soviet and Chinese Communist military instructors. This enlarged bridgehead was credited by CINCFE with giving the enemy the capability of mounting a serious threat to the main railroad from Pusan to Taegu.

It took a bitter and costly effort on the part of the Brigade, but the result was the most smashing defeat ever given an NKPA major unit up to this time. This reverse turned into a rout and slaughter toward the end as Marine air, artillery, armor, and mortars inflicted terrible losses. Broken NKPA forces were cut down in flight or while trying to swim the Naktong.

If the Brigade's first operation may be likened to a hard left jab, the fight in the Naktong Bulge is comparable to a solid right dealing a knockdown blow. The enemy lurched back to his feet, it is true, but the three rifle regiments of the NKPA 4th Infantry Division had to be filled up with hastily trained recruits.

Arms ranging from rifles to howitzers were abandoned as impediments by the routed Communists, so that the rebuilt NKPA 4th Infantry Division needed new armament and equipment of all sorts. General MacArthur's summary of the action, reported to the UN Security Council on 18 September 1950, stated that "attacks by the United States 24th Division and the Marines eliminated a major penetration of the Naktong defense line on 18 August. Here, the enemy 4th Division was decisively defeated, lost its bridgehead, and was thrown westward across the Naktong River, suffering very heavy losses in both personnel and equipment."

Never before had a major NKPA unit taken such a staggering defeat. As evidence of recent victories won over United States troops, the 4th Infantry Division had brought captured American machineguns and 105-mm. howitzers into the Naktong Bulge. Among the most important results achieved by the Brigade, therefore, was the hurt done to Red Korean morale.

Not only was the enemy's Naktong bridgehead liquidated; he also lost heavily in time, which was becoming more valuable to him than space if he hoped to profit from his rapidly dwindling advantage in numbers. Not until 10 days later did the Communists establish another bridgehead in the Naktong Bulge area, and then it was their misfortune to encounter the 1st Provisional Marine Brigade again.

During the early morning hours of 1 September 1950, the enemy made his final effort to smash through to Pusan. Again the 27th Infantry was needed on another front, so that the Marines, as the only other mobile reserve unit, were committed under the operational control of the 2d Infantry Division. The seriousness of the situation in the Naktong Bulge is indicated by the fact that the enemy had enlarged his new bridgehead with a penetration of about 4,000 yards in the sector of the 2d Division. Elements of four enemy divisions had been identified on the central front when the Marines jumped off on the morning of 3 September.

The Brigade's 3-day fight did not end as decisively as the first battle of the Naktong. That is because it was an unfinished fight. The Marines were pulled out on the night of 5 September, after gains of 2,500 to 3,000 yards that day, and it can only be conjectured what General Craig and his men might have accomplished during the next 48 hours.

As it was, the Brigade had a prominent part in disrupting the enemy's effort to sever the Pusan-Taegu lifeline. Heavy losses both in personnel and equipment were inflicted on NKPA forces, and the Marines helped to reduce the enemy's new bridgehead by 8,000 to 10,000 yards.

Not only had the enemy lost the battle; he had lost the war, as it proved, for EUSAK staff officers were even then planning a great UN counterstroke in the Pusan Perimeter. This drive was to be in conjunction with the amphibious assault on Inchon.

The turning point in the UN fortunes of war owed in no small measure to the three counterattacks by the Marines in the Pusan Perimeter. As for the overall effects, it would be hard to improve upon the analysis and evaluation in the Marine Corps Board Study:

> "A careful examination of any of these operations in which Marines engaged discloses that a single failure would have a profound effect upon the entire UN effort. . . . On 3 separate occasions the Brigade was attached to the defending UN forces at points of dangerous enemy penetrations and 3 times Marine units spearheaded the counterattacking elements and effectively stopped the enemy's efforts, seizing the initiative from him, inflicting serious losses upon him, and forcing the abandonment of immediate attempts at decisive penetration." [11]

---

[11] MCBS, I–II–A–36.

Summaries and Conclusions

No Marine tactical organization of history ever did more than the Brigade to uphold the tradition of the Corps as a force-in-readiness. The transition from activation to embarkation took only 6 days, and it may be recalled that the Brigade became the first United States unit to get into the fight after crossing the Pacific from the American mainland.

Although the components had been hastily thrown together without opportunity for training or rehearsals, there were singularly few instances of tactical fumbling during the early actions. Some of the men had their only weapons familiarization instruction in actual battle, when they fired new arms for the first time. But thanks to the steadying influence of combat-wise company officers and NCO's, the Marines of the Brigade soon gained competence.

The Brigade command and staff faced unusual problems arising from such factors as emergency situations, hurried planning, oral orders, incomplete intelligence, and lack of adequate maps. There were decisions now and then which officers would not have made if they had been endowed with the wisdom of knowledge after the event. But on the basis of information at the time, the Brigade command and staff need no whitewashing from history. Marine victories, on the other hand, may be attributed in large degree to a high order of leadership and professional ability in the upper echelons as well as on the company and platoon level.

It might have been argued that it was a waste to commit amphibious specialists to the operations of mountain warfare. But Marines were also trained as infantry, and gravel-crunching fighting men were needed to correct an illusion held by many of their countrymen. Atomic bombs, guided missiles, jet planes, and other marvelous new weapons had convinced a large section of the public that the day of push-button warfare was at hand. These Americans sincerely believed that wars could be waged at long distance, and the Marines of the Brigade served their country well by demonstrating that even in the tactical millenium it was necessary to seek out the enemy and close with him. For if there was any outstanding figure of the conflict in Korea, it was some second lieutenant making split-second decisions which meant life or death for a platoon holding a hill position against enemy attack in the darkness.

The three squadrons of MAG–33 provided support which the Brigade reported as "the best close air support in the history of the Marine Corps . . . outstanding in its effectiveness." Army infantry officers were frankly envious on occasion; and Colonel Paul L. Freeman, USA, commanding the 23d Infantry, commented that "the Marines on our left were a sight to behold. Not only was their equipment superior or equal to ours, but they had squadrons of air in direct support. They used it like artillery. It was 'Hey, Joe—This is Smitty—Knock the left of that ridge in front of Item Company.' They had it *day and night.* It came off nearby carriers, and not from Japan with only 15 minutes of fuel to accomplish mission." [12]

The UN forces, of course, had complete supremacy in the air. On two occasions the Marines of the Brigade were briefly strafed by NKPA night hecklers making a "scalded-cat" raid. During the interlude at the Bean Patch an enemy plane winged its way under cover of darkness to cut loose with a brief burst of machinegun bullets before disappearing into the night. But United States Air Force planes had virtually destroyed the little NKPA air force during the first few weeks of the war, so that the men of the Brigade were virtually unopposed in the air.

The time interval between a request for Marine air support and the actual delivery varied according to local conditions, but the ground forces seldom had cause for complaint. All-weather Squadron VMF(N)-513, based at Itazuke, Japan, was prevented by reason of faulty communications and liaison from responding to every request for dawn, dusk or night support during early Brigade operations, but such missions were flown effectively in the Naktong Bulge. Meanwhile, the Corsairs of VMF-214 and VMF-323, orbiting on station and always available for short notice employment, gave fresh proof that the Navy-Marine concept of carrier-based tactical aircraft was sound in practice. Following are the statistics of MAG-33 operations in Korea from 3 August to 14 September 1950:

			Missions in close support			
Squadron	*Total sorties*	*Miscellaneous sorties*	*USMC*	*Army*	*ROK*	*Total*
VMF-214	670	162	337	111	60	508
VMF-323	498	90	304	83	21	408
VMF(N)-513 . . .	343	264	21	50	8	79
Totals	1511	516	662	244	89	[13] 995

Demands on the time of the original 4 helicopters of VMO-6 made it necessary to fly 2 more machines in from Japan. The rotary-wing aircraft

[12] Quoted in MCBS, I-II-A-35; and I-IV-B-9.

[13] MCBS, II, Appendix 64.

had so many "firsts" to their credit in the Pusan Perimeter that a major tactical innovation was obviously in the making. The flights of General Craig, Colonel Snedeker and Lieutenant Colonel Stewart alone were enough to indicate that the helicopter was capable of working a revolution in command and staff procedures.

Altogether, the participation of the 1st Provisional Marine Brigade was an important factor in stopping the NKPA invasion in August 1950 and punishing the invaders so severely that they were ripe for a crushing defeat the following month. The Marines, moreover, did a great deal to restore the national pride of countrymen who had been hurt and bewildered by the outcome of the first month's operations.

It was humiliating to read on the front page that only 5 years after reaching our greatest military strength of history, United States troops were being pushed around by Asiatic peasants of a Soviet-trained organization calling itself the North Korean People's Army. Perhaps these Americans did not remember that the decline in our Armed Forces was due to overwhelming popular demands for the disbanding of our victorious armies of 1945. At any rate, the United States paid the penalty of unpreparedness in 1950 when its first ground-force units were beaten by better trained and equipped NKPA troops. Worse yet, correspondents at the front intimated that these defeats were due to the softness of our youth. It was charged that United States troops had been so pampered by motor transport that they could no longer march, let alone fight.

The Marines helped to change all that. The Marines and the better Army units proved that they were more than a match for the enemy when it came to marching as well as fighting. The Marines did their best to restore the pride of Americans who read about the advance to Kosong or the fight on Obong-ni Ridge. The Marines, in short, deserved the pat on the back conveyed in a dispatch to the Brigade on 23 August 1950 from their Commandant, General Clifton B. Cates:

> "I AM VERY PROUD OF THE PERFORMANCE OF YOUR AIR-GROUND TEAM. KEEP ON HITTING THEM, FRONT, FLANKS, REAR, AND TOPSIDE! WELL DONE!"

APPENDIX A

Glossary of Military and Aeronautical Terms

AKA—Attack cargo ship.
APA—Attack transport ship.
ADC—Assistant Division Commander.
BAR—Browning automatic rifle.
BLT—Battalion landing team.
CCF—Chinese Communist Forces (refers to entire Chinese force employed in Korea).
CG—Commanding general.
CINCFE—Commander in Chief, Far East.
CincPacFlt—Commander in Chief, Pacific Fleet.
CINCUNC—Commander in Chief, United Nations Command.
CNO—Chief of Naval Operations.
CO—Commanding officer.
COMNAGFE—Commander Naval Air Group Far East.
COMNAVFE—Commander Navy Far East.
COMPHIBGRUONE—Commander Amphibious Group One.
COMSEVENTHFLT — Commander Seventh Fleet.
COS—Combined Operations Section.
CP—Command Post.
CSG—Combat Service Group.
CTF—Commander Task Force.
CVG—Carrier Air Group.
DOW—Died of wounds.
EUSAK—Eighth United States Army in Korea.
FAC—Forward Air Controller.
FEAF—Far East Air Force.
FECOM—Far East Command.
FL—Flight leader.
FMF—Fleet Marine Force (Pac=Pacific; Lant=Atlantic).
GHQFEC—General Headquarters, Far East Command.
HF—High frequency (radio).
InfDiv—Infantry Division.
JCS—Joint Chiefs of Staff.
JOC—Joint Operations Center.
KIA—Killed in action.
KMC—Korean Marine Corps.
KVA—Korean Volunteer Army.
LST—Landing ship, tank.
MAG—Marine Aircraft Group.
MCBS—Marine Corps Board Study.
MGCIS—Marine Ground Control Intercept Squadron.
MIA—Missing in action.
MSR—Main supply route.
MTACS—Marine Tactical Air Control Squadron.
NCO—Noncommissioned officer.
NK—North Korea(n).
NKPA—North Korean Peoples Army.
OP—Observation post.
OY—Light observation plane.

POL—Petroleum oil lubricants.
POW—Prisoner of war.
ProvCasCo—Provisional Casual Company.
RCT—Regimental Combat Team.
ROK—Republic of Korea.
SAC—Supporting Arms Center.
SAR—Special Action Report.
SecNav—Secretary of the Navy.
TAC—Tactical Air Coordinator.
TAC X Corps—Tactical Air Command, X Corps.
TACC—Tactical Air Control Center.
TACP—Tactical Air Control Party.
TACRON—Tactical Air Control Squadron.
TAD—Tactical Air Direction.
TADC—Tactical Air Direction Center.
TAO—Tactical Air Observer.
TAR—Tactical air request.
T/E—Table of equipment.
T/O—Table of organization.
UN—United Nations.
VHF—Very high frequency (radio).
VMF—Marine fighter type aircraft (squadron).
VMF(N)—Marine night fighter type aircraft, all-weather (squadron).
VMO—Marine observation type aircraft (squadron).
VMR—Marine transport type aircraft (squadron).
WIA—Wounded in action.

APPENDIX B

Command and Staff List of the First Provisional Marine Brigade

7 July—13 September 1950

Commanding General	BrigGen Edward A. Craig
Deputy Commander	BrigGen Thomas J. Cushman
Chief of Staff	Col Edward W. Snedeker
G–1	Maj Donald W. Sherman
G–2	LtCol Ellsworth G. Van Orman
G–3	LtCol Joseph L. Stewart
G–4	LtCol Arthur A. Chidester

Special Staff Section

Adjutant	Capt Harold G. Schrier
Supply Officer	Maj James K. Eagan
Air Officer	Maj James N. Cupp
Signal Officer	Maj Elwin M. Stimpson
Air Observer	Capt Edwin L. Rives
Signal Supply Officer	1stLt Joseph E. Conners
Engineer Supply Officer	Capt William R. Gould
Liaison Officer	LtCol Edward R. Hagenah
Brigade Surgeon	Capt Eugene R. Hering, Jr., USN
Brigade Dental Officer	LtComdr Jack J. Kelly, USN

Headquarters and Service Battalion

(32 officers—183 enlisted men)

Commanding Officer	Maj Richard E. Sullivan
Executive Officer	Capt Samuel Jaskilka (to 18 Aug 50)
CoComdr, Hq Co	1stLt Nathaniel F. Mann, Jr.

Detachment, 1st Signal Battalion

(4 officers—99 enlisted men)

DetComdr.................. Capt Earl F. Stanley

Company A, 1st Motor Transport Battalion

(6 officers—112 enlisted men)

Commanding Officer......... Capt Arthur W Ecklund

Company C, 1st Medical Battalion

(5 officers—94 enlisted men)

Commanding Officer......... Comdr Robert A. Freyling, USN

Company A, 1st Shore Party Battalion

(12 officers—213 enlisted men)

Commanding Officer......... Maj William L. Batchelor

Company A, 1st Engineer Battalion

(9 officers—209 enlisted men)

Commanding Officer......... Capt George W. King

Detachment, 1st Ordnance Battalion

(5 officers—119 enlisted men)

DetComdr.................. 1stLt Meyer La Bellman

Company A, 1st Tank Battalion

(9 officers—173 enlisted men)

Commanding Officer......... Capt Gearl M. English
PlatComdr, 1st Plat......... 1stLt William D. Pomeroy
PlatComdr, 2d Plat.......... 2dLt Robert M. Winter (to 3 Sep 50, WIA)
2dLt John S. Carson (3 Sep 50, KIA)
PlatComdr, 3d Plat.......... 2dLt Granville G. Sweet

1st Battalion, 11th Marines

(44 officers—474 enlisted men)

Commanding Officer . . . . LtCol Ransom M. Wood
Executive Officer . . . . Maj Francis R. Schlesinger

Headquarters Battery:
Commanding Officer . . . . Capt James W. Brayshay

Service Battery:
Commanding Officer . . . . 1stLt Kenneth H. Quelch

Battery A:
Commanding Officer . . . . Capt James D. Jordan

Battery B:
Commanding Officer . . . . Capt Arnold C. Hofstetter

Battery C:
Commanding Officer . . . . Capt William J. Nichols, Jr.

Detachment, 1st Service Battalion

(11 officers—161 enlisted men)

DetComdr . . . . Capt Thomas M. Sagar

Detachment, 1st Combat Service Group

(5 officers—104 enlisted men)

DetComdr . . . . Maj Thomas J. O'Mahoney

Detachment, Reconnaissance Company

(2 officers—37 enlisted men)

DetComdr . . . . Capt Kenneth J. Houghton

Detachment, Military Police Company

(2 officers—36 enlisted men)

DetComdr . . . . 1stLt Nye G. Rodes

1st Amphibian Tractor Company

(10 officers—244 enlisted men)

Commanding Officer . . . . Maj James P. Treadwell

1st Amphibian Truck Platoon

(1 officer—75 enlisted men)

Commanding Officer	1stLt James E. Condra

VMO–6

Commanding Officer	Maj Vincent J. Gottschalk

5th Marines

(132 officers—2452 enlisted men)

Commanding Officer	LtCol Raymond L. Murray
Executive Officer	LtCol Lawrence C. Hays, Jr.
S–1	1stLt Alton C. Weed
S–2	Maj William C. Esterline
S–3	LtCol George F. Waters, Jr. (to 29 Aug 50)
	Maj Charles H. Brush, Jr.
S–4	Maj Harold Wallace
Special Staff, 5th Marines:	
Chaplain	LtComdr Orlando Ingvolstad, Jr., USN
Medical Officer	Lt (jg) William E. Larsen, USN (to 11 Aug 50)
	LtComdr Byron D. Casteel
Supply Officer	Capt John V. Huff
Motor Transport Officer	Capt William F. A. Trax (to 15 Aug 50)
	1stLt James O. Alison
Ordnance Officer	CWO Bill E. Parrish
Disbursing Officer	Capt Kenneth L. Shaw
Communications Officer	Maj Kenneth B. Boyd
Naval Gunfire Officer	Lt Jerry C. Ragon, USN
Air Officer	1stLt Leo R. Jillisky
1st Battalion, 5th Marines:	
Commanding Officer	LtCol George R. Newton
Executive Officer	Maj Merlin R. Olson
CO, H & S Company	Capt Walter E. Godenius
CO, Company A	Capt John R. Stevens
CO, Company B	Capt John L. Tobin (to 17 Aug 50, WIA)
	Capt Francis I. Fenton, Jr.
CO, Weapons Company	Maj John W. Russell

2d Battalion, 5th Marines:

Commanding Officer	LtCol Harold S. Roise
Executive Officer	LtCol John W. Stevens, II
CO, H & S Company	1stLt David W. Walsh
CO, Company D	Capt John Finn, Jr. (to 8 Aug 50, WIA)
	Capt Andrew M. Zimmer (to 17 Aug 50, WIA)
	1stLt Robert T. Hanifin, Jr. (to 22 Aug 50)
	1stLt H. J. Smith
CO, Company E	Capt George E. Kittredge (to 7 Aug 50, WIA)
	1stLt William E. Sweeney (to 18 Aug 50)
	Capt Samuel Jaskilka
CO, Weapons Company	Maj Walter Gall (to 10 Aug 50)
	Maj Theodore F. Spiker

3d Battalion, 5th Marines:

Commanding Officer	LtCol Robert D. Taplett
Executive Officer	Maj John J. Canney
CO, H & S Company	1stLt Arthur E. House, Jr. (to 22 Aug 50)
	1stLt Harold D. Fredericks
CO, Company G	1stLt Robert D. Bohn
CO, Company H	Capt Joseph C. Fegan, Jr. (to 18 Aug 50, WIA)
	Capt Patrick E. Wildman
CO, Weapons Company	Capt Patrick E. Wildman (to 19 Aug 50)
	Maj Murray Ehrlich

Forward Echelon, 1st Marine Air Wing

Commanding General	BrigGen Thomas J. Cushman
Chief of Staff	Col Kenneth H. Weir

Marine Air Group 33:

Commanding Officer	Col Allen C. Koonce (to 20 Aug 50)
	Col Frank G. Dailey
Deputy Commander	LtCol Norman J. Anderson
Executive Officer	LtCol Radford C. West
CO, VMF–214	LtCol Walter E. Lischeid
CO, VMF–323	Maj Arnold A. Lund
CO, VMF(N)–513	Maj Joseph H. Reinburg
CO, Hq Squadron	Capt Norman D. Glenn
CO, Service Squadron	LtCol James C. Lindsay
CO, MTACS-2	Maj Christian C. Lee

APPENDIX C

Citations and Commendations

September 29, 1950

PRESIDENTIAL UNIT CITATION

The President of the Republic of Korea takes profound pleasure in citing for outstanding and heroic performance of duty on the field of battle during the period 2 August 1950–6 September 1950.

THE FIRST UNITED STATES PROVISIONAL MARINE BRIGADE

for the Award of

THE PRESIDENTIAL UNIT CITATION

The First United States Provisional Marine Brigade was a vital element in the first major counterattack against the enemy.

In late July and early August 1950, the enemy had swept through the Chulla Provinces and had rapidly approached along the south Korean coast to a point only 35 miles from the vital port of Pusan. Together with the 25th Infantry Division, the First United States Provisional Marine Brigade, from 7 August to 12 August 1950, played a major role in attacking and driving back the enemy.

During the period 17 August to 20 August 1950 in conjunction with the 24th Infantry Division and units of the 2d Infantry Division, the First United States Provisional Marine Brigade attacked a great pocket of enemy forces who had successfully crossed the Naktong River and established a firm beachhead on the eastern bank. The Brigade attacked with such determination and skill as to earn the admiration of all who saw or knew of its battle conduct.

Later, on the night of 31 August–1 September, the enemy again launched an all-out offensive against the United Nations Forces. The First United States Provisional Marine Brigade was in Army reserve at that time. With the 2d Infantry Division, the Brigade again was committed in almost the same area of its earlier action against the Naktong pocket in the neighborhood of Yongsan. Again the gallant Marine forces were instrumental in preventing the enemy from capturing their objective and cutting the north-south lines of communication of the United Nations Forces.

The brilliant performance of duty in combat in Korea of each individual of the First United States Provisional Marine Brigade is in accord with the highest traditions of the military service.

This citation carries with it the right to wear the Presidential Unit Citation Ribbon by each individual of the First United States Provisional Marine Brigade which served in Korea in the stated period.

(Signed) SYNGMAN RHEE

THE SECRETARY OF THE NAVY
WASHINGTON

The President of the United States takes pleasure in presenting the PRESIDENTIAL UNIT CITATION to the

FIRST PROVISIONAL MARINE BRIGADE, REINFORCED

for service as set forth in the following CITATION:

"For extraordinary heroism in action against enemy aggressor forces in Korea from 7 August to 7 September 1950. Functioning as a mobile, self-contained, air-ground team, the First Provisional Marine Brigade, Reinforced, rendered invaluable service during the fierce struggle to maintain the foothold established by friendly forces in the Pusan area during the early stages of the Korean conflict. Quickly moving into action as numerically superior enemy forces neared the Naktong River on the central front and penetrated to within 35 miles of Pusan in the southern sector, threatening the integrity of the entire defensive perimeter, this hard-hitting, indomitable team counterattacked serious enemy penetrations at three different points in rapid succession. Undeterred by roadblocks, heavy hostile automatic weapons and highly effective artillery fire, extremely difficult terrain and intense heat, the Brigade met the invaders with relentless determination and, on each crucial occasion, hurled them back in disorderly retreat. By combining sheer resolution and esprit de corps with sound infantry tactics and splendid close air support, the Brigade was largely instrumental in restoring the line of defense, in inflicting thousands of casualties upon the enemy and in seizing large amounts of ammunition, equipment and other supplies. The brilliant record achieved by the unit during the critical early days of the Korean conflict attests to the individual valor and competence of the officers and men and reflects the highest credit upon the First Provisional Marine Brigade, Reinforced, and the United States Naval Service."

All of the First Provisional Marine Brigade except the First Amphibian Tractor Company participated in operations against enemy aggressor forces in Korea from 7 August to 7 September 1950.

The following reinforcing units of the First Provisional Marine Brigade participated in operations against enemy aggressor forces in Korea from 7 August to 7 September 1950:

Forward Echelon, First Marine Aircraft Wing (less ground personnel)
Marine Air Group Thirty-Three, Reinforced (less ground personnel)
Marine Observation Squadron Six plus Helicopter Section, Headquarters Squadron
Air Support Section of Marine Tactical Air Control Squadron Two
United States Army: Counter Intelligence Corps and Military Intelligence Special Detachment personnel attached to the Headquarters Company, Headquarters and Service Battalion, First Provisional Marine Brigade.

For the President,

(Signed) R. A. ANDERSON
Secretary of the Navy

HEADQUARTERS

EIGHTH UNITED STATES ARMY KOREA (EUSAK)

Office of the Commanding General

APO 301

Subject: Commendation 22 August 1950

Thru: Commanding General, 24th Infantry Division

To: Commanding General, 1st Provisional Marine Brigade

1. It gives me great pleasure to commend you, your officers and men, for the part your organization played in the successful attack which began 17 August 50 against a determined enemy occupying a bridgehead east of the NAKTONG RIVER in the vicinity of KUJIN-SAN and ended only when the bridgehead had been eliminated with great loss of men and equipment to the enemy.

2. Through excellence in leadership and grit and determination in all ranks, your organization helped materially in preventing the enemy from penetrating our lines at a critical time. In so doing it has upheld the fine tradition of the Marines in a glorious manner and by close cooperation has proved unification of the services a success.

3. Please accept my sincere thanks and congratulations. I ask that you convey to your splendid command, the traditional "Well Done."

WALTON H. WALKER
Lieutenant General, United States Army
Commanding

HEADQUARTERS

24TH INFANTRY DIVISION

APO 24, 28 August 1950

To: Commanding General, 1st Provisional Marine Brigade, APO 25

1. I am pleased and privileged to add my personal commendation to that of the Army Commander. And, on behalf of all officers and enlisted personnel of my command, I desire to express our sincere appreciation for the decisive and valiant offensive actions conducted by your command which predominately contributed to the total destruction of the Naktong pocket.

2. The esprit, aggressiveness and sheer determination continuously displayed by all personnel of the 1st Provisional Marine Brigade in the face of fierce enemy resistance and counteraction has aroused the highest admiration of every member of my command.

JOHN E. CHURCH
Maj Gen, USA
Commanding

HEADQUARTERS

1ST PROVISIONAL MARINE BRIGADE, FMF (REINFORCED)

% Fleet Post Office, San Francisco, Calif.

1355
1:DWS/1dp
Ser 596
9 Sep 1950

From: The Commanding General

To: All officers and men of the 1st Provisional Marine Brigade, FMF (Reinforced)

Subj: Letter of commendation from the Commanding General, Eighth United States Army in Korea, of 22 August 1950 with first endorsement by the Commanding General, 24th Infantry Division

Encl: (1) Copy of subj ltr and endorsement

1. It is with extreme pride in your accomplishments that I publish to all officers and men of the 1st Provisional Marine Brigade the enclosed copy of a letter from the Commanding General, Eighth United States Army in Korea, and endorsement by the Commanding General, 24th Infantry Division, United States Army, commending the Brigade.

2. The realization that your professional skill, esprit de corps, outstanding bravery, and determination to succeed in all missions has been specifically commended by the Army and Division Commanders under whom the Brigade was serving at the time is indeed a source of gratification to me as it will also be to you.

(Signed) E. A. Craig
E. A. CRAIG

Bibliography

Primary Sources

U. S. Marine Corps. Headquarters, Marine Corps (HQMC) incoming and outgoing dispatches, 1949–50. HQMC Secret and Classified Files, Naval Records Management Center, Alexandria, Va.

U. S. Marine Corps. Interviews with participants in the Korean War, 1951–54. Interviews (Korea) File, HQMC, Historical Branch, Records and Research Section (Historical).

U. S. Marine Corps. Letters to Historical Branch concerning Korean operations. Monograph and Comments File, HQMC Historical.

Headquarters, Eighth U. S. Army in Korea. War diaries and supporting documents, July–September 1950. Army Record Group (RG) 207–0.3, Code 208, Departmental Records Branch, The Adjutant General's Office, Alexandria, Va. (DRB, TAGO).

2d Infantry Division. War diaries, supporting documents, histories, and General and Special Staff activities reports, July–September 1950. RG 207–0.3, Code 302, DRB, TAGO.

24th Infantry Division. War Diaries supporting documents, histories, and General and Special Staff activities reports, July–September 1950. RG 207–0.3, Code 324, DRB, TAGO.

25th Infantry Division. War diaries supporting documents, histories, and General and Special Staff activities reports, July–September 1950. RG 207–0.3, Code 325, DRB, TAGO.

1st Provisional Marine Brigade. Messages, plans, and reports. Classified Correspondence File, HQMC Historical.

——. G–2 Journal, 5 August–5 September 1950. Classified Correspondence File, HQMC Historical.

——. G–3 Journal, 2–14 August 1950. Classified Correspondence File, HQMC Historical.

——. G–4 Journal, 3 August–9 September 1950. Classified Correspondence File, HQMC Historical.

——. Special Action Report, 2 August–6 September 1950: Operations with Eighth U.S. Army Korea, dtd 11 September 1950. 3 Folders.
- Basic Report
- Annex Able, G–1 Report
- Annex Baker, G–2 Report
- Annex Charlie, G–3 Report
- Annex Dog, Logistics
- Annex Easy, Air Section Report
- Annex Fox, Signal Section Report
- Annex George, Motor Transport Section
- Annex How, Special Action Report (SAR) 5th Marines
  - SAR 1st Bn, 5th Marines
  - SAR 2d Bn, 5th Marines
  - SAR 3d Bn, 5th Marines
  - SAR 4.2″ Mtr Co, 5th Marines
  - SAR Anti-Tk Co, 5th Marines
  - SAR, Co. A, 1st Tk Bn, 5th Marines
- Annex Item, 1st Bn, 11th Marines
- Annex Jig, Co A, 1st Engr Bn
- Annex King, Co A, 1st MT Bn
- Annex Love, Co C, 1st Med Bn
- Annex Mike, 1st Shore Party Bn
- Annex Nan, Reconn Co
- Annex Oboe, VMO–6
- Annex Peter, Military Police Det
- Annex Queen, Combat Serv Grp
- Annex Roger, 1st Ord Bn
- Annex Sugar, 1st Serv Bn
- Annex Tare, Med Sec
- "SAR" File (Korea), HQMC Historical.

5th Marines. Periodic reports, 4–31 August 1950, Classified Correspondence File, HQMC Historical.

MAG–33. Special Action Report, 5 July–6 September 1950. "SAR" File (Korea), HQMC Historical.

VMF–214. Special Action Report, 14 July–6 September 1950. "SAR" File (Korea), HQMC Historical.

VMF–323. Special Action Report, 3 August–6 September 1950. "SAR" File (Korea), HQMC Historical

VMF(N)–513. Special Action Report, July–6 September 1950. "SAR" File (Korea), HQMC Historical.

Secondary Sources

Appleman, Roy E., LtCol, USA. Ms history of UN operations in Korea, July–November, 1950. Copy in Office of the Chief of Military History, Washington, D. C. (OCMH).

Byrnes, James F. *Speaking Frankly.* New York: Harper and Brothers, 1947.

Dallin, David J. *Soviet Russia and the Far East.* New York: Yale University Press, 1948.

Geer, Andrew. *The New Breed: The Story of the U.S. Marines in Korea.* New York: Harper and Brothers, 1952.

General Headquarters, Far East Command, General Staff, Allied Translator and Interpreter Section.

Interrogation Reports Series.

Research Supplement No. 1, *North Korean Forces.*

Research Supplement No. 2, *Documentary Evidence of North Korean Aggression.*

Research Supplement No. 4, *Enemy Forces.*

Research Supplement No. 94, *North Korean Security Forces; North Korean Second Infantry Division; North Korean Fourth Infantry Division.*

Research Supplement No. 100, *North Korean Air Force; North Korean Sixth Infantry Division.*

Research Supplement No. 106, *North Korean Artillery.*

General Headquarters, Far East Command, Military Intelligence Section, General Staff, Theater Intelligence Division, Order of Battle Branch. *Supplement: Order of Battle Information, North Korean Army, General History of North Korean Units.* Processed; copy at OCMH.

Giusti, Ernest H. "Marine Air Over the Pusan Perimeter." *Marine Corps Gazette,* 36, No. 5:20–21 (May 1952).

——. *The Mobilization of the Marine Corps in the Korean Conflict.* Processed; copy at USMC Historical.

Green, A. Wigfall. *Epic of Korea.* Washington: Public Affairs Press, 1950.

Grew, Joseph C. *Turbulent Era: A Diplomatic Record of Forty Years.* Boston: Houghton Mifflin Company, 1952. 2 vols.

Karig, Walter, Capt, USN. *Battle Report: The War in Korea.* New York: Rinehart, 1952.

Montross, Lynn. *Cavalry of the Sky.* New York: Harper and Brothers, 1954.

——. *War Through the Ages.* New York: Harper and Brothers, 1946.

Oliver, Robert T. *Why War Came to Korea.* New York: Fordham University Press, 1950.

Opie, Redvers, *et al. The Search for Peace Settlements.* Washington: The Brookings Institution, 1951.

Stewart, H. D., Maj. "Rise and Fall of an Army." *Military Review,* 30, No. 11:32–35 (February 1951).

Tompkins, Pauline. *American-Russian Relations in the Far East.* New York: The Macmillan Company, 1949.

Gugeler, R. A., Capt. "Attack Along a Ridgeline." *Combat Actions in Korea.* Washington: Combat Forces Press, 1954. 20–30.

U. S. Department of the Army. *Russian Combat Methods in World War II.* Washington: Government Printing Office, 1950. (DA Pamphlet No. 20–230).

U. S. Department of State. "Fifth Report to the Security Council, Ocober 5, 1950." *United Nations Action in Korea under Unified Command.* Washington: Government Printing Office, 1950 (State Dept Publications 3986, International Organization and Conference Series III 6).

U. S. Department of State. *Guide to the UN in Korea.* Washington: Government Printing Office, 1951 (State Dept Publications 4229, Far Eastern Series 47).

U. S. Department of State. *United States Relations with China, with Special Reference to the Period 1944–49, Based on the Files of the Department of State.* Washington: Government Printing Office, 1949 (State Dept Publications 3573, Far Eastern Series 30).

U. S. Marine Corps Board. *An Evaluation of the Influence of Marine Corps Forces on the Course of the Korean War (4 Aug 50–15 Dec 50).* Processed; copy in USMC Historical. 2 vols.

U. S. Military Academy, Department of Military Art and Engineering. *Operations in Korea.* West Point, 1953.

Wood, Ransom M. "Artillery Support for the Brigade in Korea." *Marine Corps Gazette,* 35, No. 6:16–17 (June 1951).

Index

SET AND PRINTED FOR THE UNITED STATES MARINE CORPS BY THE UNITED STATES GOVERNMENT PRINTING OFFICE: 1955. TEXT SET BY PHOTO COMPOSITION IN 12-POINT GARAMOND AND PRINTED ON MAX-OPAQUE VELLUM STOCK BY DEEP-ETCH OFFSET.

For sale by the Superintendent of Documents, U. S. Government Printing Office
Washington 25, D. C. - Price $2

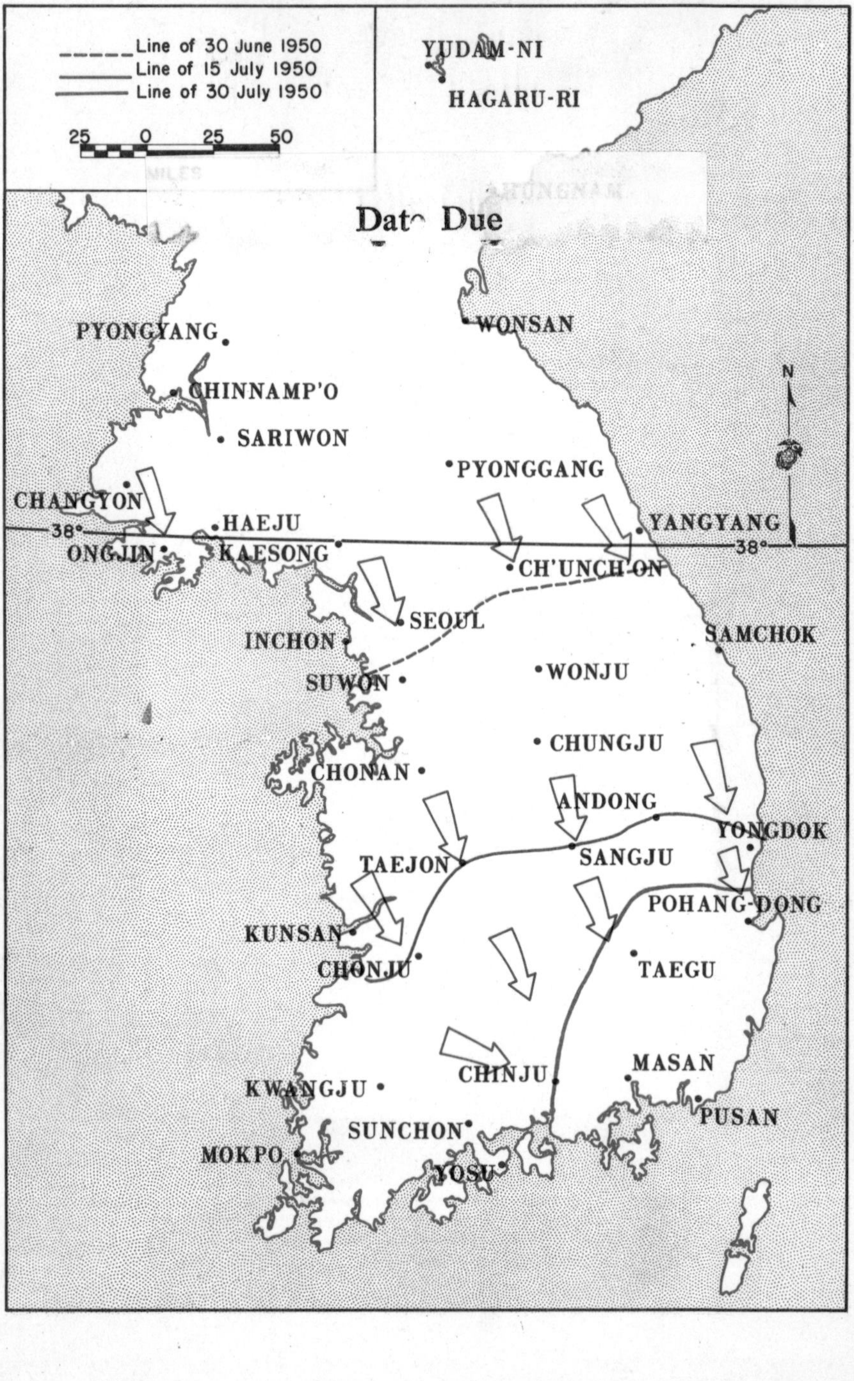
Line of 30 June 1950
Line of 15 July 1950
Line of 30 July 1950
25 0 25 50
YUDAM-NI
HAGARU-RI
WONSAN
PYONGYANG
CHINNAMP'O
SARIWON
PYONGGANG
CHANGYON
HAEJU
YANGYANG
38°
ONGJIN
KAESONG
CH'UNCH'ON
SEOUL
INCHON
SAMCHOK
SUWON
WONJU
CHUNGJU
CHONAN
ANDONG
YONGDOK
TAEJON
SANGJU
POHANG-DONG
KUNSAN
CHONJU
TAEGU
MASAN
CHINJU
KWANGJU
PUSAN
SUNCHON
MOKPO
YOSU
N